the
cook's
herb
garden

the cook's herb garden

MARY BROWNE
HELEN LEACH
NANCY TICHBORNE

GODWIT

DEDICATION

To the gardeners and cooks who kept faith with herbs even when they were unfashionable.

ACKNOWLEDGEMENTS

Individually we wish to acknowledge each other's support in putting together this book. Mary was responsible for the cooking and gardening advice, and took all the photographs; Helen contributed the Introduction and herb 'biographies'; Nancy provided the watercolour illustrations. The inspiration was shared, and the book was made possible with the help of our families.

We should also like to thank the following: Victoria and Jim Pike of The Superb Herb Company, Auckland; Mike Rockell, NZ Dairy Foods Ltd, Auckland; Gaylene Sloane of Yates New Zealand Ltd, Auckland; Gerard and Barbara Martin of Kings Seeds, Katikati; and Mary's neighbour Jeanette McAtamney for providing herbs for photographs.

To the Godwit team we should like to express our appreciation.

A GODWIT BOOK
published by
Random House New Zealand
18 Poland Road, Glenfield, Auckland, New Zealand
www.randomhouse.co.nz

First published 2001

© 2001 Mary Browne, Helen Leach, Nancy Tichborne

The moral rights of the authors have been asserted

ISBN 1 86962 041 0

Layout and production by Kate Greenaway
Cover photograph by Sue Linn
Back cover photographs by Mary Browne
Printed in Singapore

CONTENTS

INTRODUCTION 7
'What, no herb garden?'
'How do you decide what is or isn't a herb?'
'Are culinary herbs essential?'

GARDEN NOTES 11
*Propagation: raising herbs from seeds indoors, raising herbs
from seeds outdoors (in situ), planting out, dividing herb
plants, layering, cuttings
Garden design: what herbs to grow where?
Growing herbs in containers: containers, potting mix,
collections of herbs, care*

KITCHEN NOTES 16
*Ways to preserve herbs: preparing herbs, drying herbs,
storing dried herbs, freezing, herb vinegars, herb-flavoured
oils, herb butters
Herb teas
Storing fresh herbs in the kitchen
Notes on ingredients
Abbreviations and measurements*

BASIL 22

BAY 34

CHERVIL 42

CHIVES 48

CORIANDER 55

DILL 62

FENNEL 70

GARLIC CHIVES 76

LEMON BALM 80

LEMON VERBENA 86

MINT 92

OREGANO & SWEET MARJORAM 103

PARSLEY 114

PERILLA 123

RAU RAM (VIETNAMESE MINT) 129

ROSEMARY 135

SAGE 142

SAVORY 150
Summer savory and winter savory

TARRAGON 158

THYME 166

MORE HERBS 176
Borage, epazote, scented geraniums, lemon grass, lovage, Mexican tarragon, pineapple sage, salad burnet, tree onions, lavender, mitsuba, sorrel

MIXED HERB RECIPES 180

BOOKS WE HAVE FOUND USEFUL 186

USEFUL ADDRESSES 188

INDEX OF RECIPES & PLANT NAMES 189

INTRODUCTION

'WHAT, NO HERB GARDEN?'

Writers of cooking–gardening books are often asked by curious visitors for 'just a quick look at the garden'. While we were working on *The Cook's Salad Garden*, Mary's kitchen garden became a local attraction with garden clubs, who came to see the dozen or more varieties of lettuce, the edible flowers, the exotic Asian greens and the profusion of other salad plants that she grows and cooks. Recently, friends and visitors, hearing that we were writing a sequel, *The Cook's Herb Garden*, have been asking to see our herb gardens. 'We don't have one,' is our mischievous reply. 'How can you write about the cook's herb garden, then?' At this point we take our visitors on a tour of the entire garden.

For most of the 20th century, as herbs became fashionable, gardeners confined their cultivation to a single part of the garden, referred to as the 'herb garden' and often treated like an outdoor room. Such a focus has good historical precedents—but not if you are raising herbs for the kitchen. If you want to have a medicinal herb garden, like the *herbularius* in a mediaeval monastery or an apothecary's 'physick' garden of the 16th–17th centuries, then you are well advised to grow all your herbs together in one place, securely fenced, hedged or even walled. These old-fashioned herb gardens contained many poisonous herbs, such as nightshades and foxgloves. We can surmise that, if they were popular today, there would be laws requiring them to be fenced as securely as a swimming pool. But this is not a book about the growing or administering of herbs as medicines, and we claim no expert knowledge of this potentially dangerous field.

Alternatively, you may want to have an ornamental herb garden, a private haven from a busy life. This is an extremely popular 20th-century garden type, featured in great gardens such as Sissinghurst in England, and included in many botanic and public gardens. It usually has a formal symmetrical design, with graduated plantings. Lovage and bronze fennel provide height at the back of the beds, and creeping thymes carpet the paving in the centre, around the sundial or water feature. Such formal herb gardens can be very beautiful to look at. If your need for kitchen herbs is limited to an occasional sprig of rosemary, thyme, sage or oregano, such a garden will be a delight to spend time in, and useful too. There are already lots of books written about the design and planting of such formal ornamental herb gardens.

For the serious cook, however, a formal ornamental herb garden provides daily conflicts of interest. Take this scenario: it's mid-summer and the chive border is about to send up its attractive mauve-pink flowerheads, which will look superb against the silvery-leaved artemisias and purple sages planted behind. But leaf production needs to be kept up to supply the household's need for fresh chives in salads, sandwiches and omelettes. This means cutting off the flower buds and old leaves, and fertilising the plants. Will the cook or the flower gardener inside you win out? Compromise is unsatisfactory, for the cook will be frustrated by too few young leaves, and the garden artist needs as many open flowerheads as possible to achieve the right effect.

There are certain herbs that dedicated cooks use in large quantities, such as parsley and chervil, coriander and basil. They have to be grown quickly and replaced frequently. You will not find them occupying prominent positions in formal herb gardens, if they are included at all. They produce more tender leaves in the fertile, friable soil of a kitchen or vegetable garden than in the drier, less nourishing soils of a herb garden designed for the aromatic Mediterranean herbs like sage, thyme, rosemary and the oreganums. As well, this sort of formal ornamental herb garden seldom accommodates members of the mint genus, because of their unwelcome habit of spreading under and through other herbs. But these wanderers are no more welcome in the vegetable beds. We like to give them their own plot in a damp corner of the kitchen garden, and if necessary confine them closely.

It would be fair to conclude that, though we have no herb gardens, we grow numerous herbs in our gardens. The planting position for each herb is chosen according to the following criteria:
- whether it is sun loving or shade tolerant
- whether it is frost tender or perfectly hardy
- whether it likes dry gravelly soil or well-watered rich ground
- whether it is invasive and/or prone to self-sowing
- whether it is harvested in small quantities or large
- whether it may need to be accessed by the cook (wearing slippers) on a dark, wet winter's evening, or can be tucked away at the bottom of the garden.

Most herbs are attractive and often have interesting variegated or bronze forms, so there is no reason to banish them to the old-style 'back garden'. You can incorporate many herbs in borders containing flowers and shrubs, as long as they have the same preferences for soil type and sun exposure. Others, like basil and perilla, satisfy your needs as a cook only if they receive the same intensive care as you give to tomatoes, peppers or egg-plants— depending where you live, that may mean glasshouse or tunnel house cultivation. The herbs like parsley and chervil that you gather and use by the handful are most easily grown like spinach or salad greens, in rows in the vegetable garden. Like the leafy vegetables, they will need to be within reach of a hose or sprinkler in hot summers.

Not all gardeners have large enough sections to subdivide into 'front', 'back', 'kitchen' or 'herb' gardens. Their front path, courtyard or deck, comprising their outdoor living area, may be the only space available for gardening. But the same principles apply. Don't grow different herbs together in one pot, unless it is large and each occupant enjoys the same sort of potting mix and watering regime. A pot containing parsley, mint and sage is a recipe for an unhappy and brief co-existence. Considering the range of pot and trough shapes and sizes and the different types of potting mix now available, it is possible to meet the needs of most culinary herbs in their own individual container 'mini-garden'.

Treating your whole garden as a place for herbs allows you to provide the best possible conditions for each type, and that means the best possible quality for the kitchen.

'HOW DO YOU DECIDE WHAT IS OR ISN'T A HERB?'
Since certain herbs are to be found in rows in our vegetable gardens, it is reasonable to ask why we still describe them as herbs. And at the other end of the spectrum there is another grey area: what distinguishes a herb from a spice? To answer both questions we would need to isolate the properties of vegetables, herbs and spices that are distinct and non-overlapping. This is a fruitless exercise because many common words for grouping things can be interchangeable. You will find coriander mentioned just as frequently in books about spices as in books about herbs, while sorrel can be found in books on vegetable growing as well as herb manuals.

A further complication is the drift in the meanings of words from one generation to the next, involving both contraction and expansion in what they cover. When the Elizabethan herbalist John Gerard was writing about 'herbes' in the 1590s, the word meant 'all useful non-woody plants'. 'Sallet herbes' included lettuce, rocket, sorrel and endive, while 'sweet herbes' included lavender, marigold and the flavouring herbs, like thyme, dried for winter use. An alternative name for the kitchen garden was the 'garden of herbes'. 'Kitchen herbes' encompassed plants as diverse as melons, cabbages, leeks, carrots and parsley. The word 'vegetable' didn't acquire its modern meaning of 'plant cultivated in a garden for food' until the 1760s. Then it became the fashionable category name for many of the plants formerly classed as herbs. As 'vegetable' expanded its usage, the word 'herb' contracted to the point where it was retained only for 'flavouring herbs' and 'medicinal herbs'. Such a sharp separation wouldn't have been likely in Gerard's day because nearly all edible plants were believed to have medicinal properties, as well as being more or less good to taste. Though we retain elements of this approach when we classify certain items as 'healthy' or nutritious rather than 'junk' foods today, we seldom select foods on the basis that they will counteract specific medical conditions, as the Elizabethans did five centuries ago.

We believe that it is easiest to think in terms of a continuum of edible plants. At one end there is the exotic spice, such as the clove, which we import from a distant country in a dried form. To be worth the cost of transportation, a spice has to impart a very strong and desirable flavour to our food. At the opposite end is a vegetable like the lettuce, which has a high water content and short shelf-life, and which we enjoy in large servings for its crispness rather than any distinctive flavour. In the middle are the plants we call herbs. They can be arranged along the centre of the continuum according to their flavour intensity. Near the vegetable end we would place chervil, basil and parsley because of their moist leaves and mild flavour. Near the spice end we would place bay leaves and dried coriander 'seeds'. In fact, ground coriander fruits (as they are technically described) are an ingredient of curry powder, which we usually describe as a spice mixture. Like cloves, bay leaves are cooked in ways which allow their flavour to infuse into the surrounding food without actually being eaten themselves. The aromatic herbs like thyme, rosemary, sage and tarragon occupy the central section in this herb portion of the continuum. We eat their leaves, but only in small quantities.

When selecting the herbs to describe in this book, we applied various criteria. The herb had to be viable in gardens within the temperate or subtropical climatic zones, or able to be grown with the assistance of an unheated glasshouse. (In fact, we have raised most of them in a range of conditions.) It had to be used as a fresh ingredient in cooking, although it might also be dried for out-of-season use. Above all, it had to contribute to the flavour of the dish rather than providing the bulk or body. This is why we dealt with rocket in our 1997 book, *The Cook's Salad Garden*. Although it started its recent rise in popularity as a herb, added to salads made of milder-tasting leaves, it has graduated to being the foundation ingredient. Essentially, herbs are flavouring plants, supporting the cereals, other staple foods, vegetables or meats providing the body of the dish. They should be able to be harvested as fresh as vegetables, while contributing to flavour as distinctively as spices.

Because herb flavours are stronger than those of vegetables, we recommend that you use them in moderation. The essential oils in their leaves, which convey much of their complex and evocative aromas, can be very potent. Some, like thymol and carvacrol, are powerful antibacterial agents. Unlike vegetables, which can be enjoyed as second or even third helpings, herbs can spoil a recipe if quantities are doubled or trebled.

Writers on culinary herbs half a century ago made their selection from a much narrower range than is now available. Today, at the start of the 21st century, we not only have new introductions from Asian cuisines to explore, but also many new varieties of our traditional herbs. We could not include them all. Instead we assembled a 'pot pourri', consisting firstly of culinary herbs that have contributed to Western cuisines for two or even three thousand years, secondly of herbs that started off as medicinal or bee plants and found their way more slowly into the kitchen, thirdly of herbs that were brought to Europe only a few centuries ago, and lastly of herbs that have made a greater impact around the Pacific rim than they have so far in Europe. Having made the 'short list', these were then subjected to a final test for inclusion: they had to cope with the different conditions prevailing in our gardens, and we had to like eating them. A few that narrowly missed selection appear in a separate table. Of these, lovage could be described as an acquired taste, while borage contributes more to appearance than to flavour. Scented geraniums, though strong on flavour, are limited to just a few uses. But, as you will become aware once you have read the herb 'biographies' in this book, herbs that are insignificant in one century can become highly esteemed in another.

'ARE CULINARY HERBS ESSENTIAL?'
We have all seen recipes that have inserted the word 'optional' in brackets beside some herb ingredient. While this may encourage cooks to proceed with the recipe even

if they don't have the herb in question, it also sends the message that the overall flavour of the dish is not very important. The omission of a flavouring substance can transform the product more dramatically than leaving out one of the bulk ingredients.

In our opinion, culinary herbs should seldom be treated as optional extras. They provide the signature of the cook, the signing-off of the dish before it comes to the table. The recipe may be derived from an inspiring cookbook or a favourite magazine, but the herbs incorporated in it embody the flavours of a particular garden and the judgement of the cook who picked and prepared them.

Certain combinations of herbs and other flavouring substances have come to stand for particular regional cuisines. Thus dishes from the central Mediterranean often make abundant use of garlic, oregano, basil and thyme, while a cinnamon and lemon combination is more characteristic of the eastern Mediterranean. These 'flavour principles', as they were called by Elizabeth Rozin, are believed to serve as markers of group identity, branding the dishes to members of that group as 'ours' and 'safe to eat'. In an era when other people's cuisines are explored from the convenience of one's own kitchen, a sort of virtual culinary tourism, these combinations may be borrowed to brand a dish as exotic and adventurous, and to give an impression of authenticity. This carries the risk of borrowing the form but not the meaning, for a cuisine is much more than the sum of its dishes. We feel happier acknowledging the origin of a foreign herb while at the same time adapting it to suit our own culinary tradition and cultural tastes. In the long term we believe that this keeps our tradition vibrant and viable, like our language, without threatening regional cuisines with extinction from an internationalised cooking style that appears everywhere but is claimed by no-one as their own.

Besides playing this important role in issues of identity, flavouring herbs are a source of endless inspiration. International fast-food chains pride themselves on the uniformity of their product. Home cooks who use herbs can vary the flavour of their meals to suit the weather, the tastes of family members, the type of meat or vegetable being served, and the combination of dishes on the menu. In the home kitchen, herbs contribute to variety—aptly called the 'spice' of life—not to uniformity.

Home-grown herbs can be picked fresher, before their volatile oils start to disperse and their flavour deteriorates. They are on hand when commercial supplies have sold out, or are not even stocked because they wilt rapidly. Many herbs are good to look at, having coloured leaves with interesting textures and shapes, and bee-attracting flowers. Most are hardy and long-lived perennials. More than half of the herbs described in this book can be described as heritage plants, with pedigrees going back into prehistory. They are as significant as historic places and family heirlooms. Our ancestors grew many of them long before flower gardens became fashionable.

With all of these outstanding qualities, of course they are essential!

GARDEN NOTES

Detailed information on the construction of built-up beds, soil fertility, making compost, sources of organic matter, watering, weeds and pests is given in our 1997 book, *The Cook's Salad Garden*. As raising plants from seed is fundamental to herb cultivation, we have repeated this section here with some extra herb-specific advice. Check our sections on individual herbs for ideal germinating temperatures and light requirements.

PROPAGATION

RAISING HERBS FROM SEED INDOORS

1. Choose a plastic punnet that has drainage holes in the bottom. Fill to the brim with a seed-sowing mix to which horticultural grit, sharp sand or fine pumice has been added to improve the drainage. We use 5 parts of seed-raising mix to 1 part of grit, sand or pumice. Level and firm the surface gently.

2. Place in a bowl, tub or bucket containing sufficient water to come almost to the top of the punnet. Leave for a short time, until the water soaks right through to the surface. Stand on a bench to drain. The level of the seed-sowing mix will have dropped slightly.

3. Place the seeds evenly on the surface. Don't sow too thickly: if you want 10 plants, sow only 20 seeds. Except for herbs which require light to germinate, sprinkle very lightly with extra seed-sowing mix, and cover the punnet with a piece of black plastic, cut to fit. Alternatively, cover the box and pane of glass, used in step 4 below, with newspaper. If sowing more than one type of seed, add a label with the variety name.

4. Place the punnet in a loosely tied clear plastic bag, a propagator or a box with a pane of glass for a lid. (Mary uses a polystyrene mushroom box.) If you have a heated propagator or a separate heating pad, use this to speed germination when the weather is cold. Until you know the operating temperatures of your heating system, it is wise to check the range with a maximum–minimum thermometer. A temperature range of 15–23°C is satisfactory for most herbs, but check the ideal range for each.

5. Look for signs of germination each day and keep moist by spraying with a fine mister, if necessary. As soon as the first tiny seedling appears, remove the black plastic or newspaper. From now on, maximum light (but not direct sunlight) is required. Remove the plastic bag, propagator lid or pane of glass as soon as a few more seeds have germinated.

6. A few days after most of the seed has germinated, and before the true leaves grow, the tiny seedlings can be pricked out into other punnets or several small individual containers. Some writers suggest waiting until the first true leaves appear before pricking out. We have found that the root system is often too well established by this stage and damage is inevitable. Combine a commercial potting mix with horticultural grit, sharp sand or pumice (5:1) to improve the drainage. If necessary, add water to the mix to dampen but not saturate (it should still be crumbly). Lightly fill each container to within 1 cm of the top. Do not soak. Make a deep hole for each seedling.

7. Lower the punnet with the tiny seedlings up to its brim in a container of water, to ensure that the soil is wet. Carefully ease out the strongest seedlings with an old screwdriver, kitchen knife or blunt chisel. Hold each one by its seed leaves, never its stem and carefully lower it into a hole. Position it so that the seed leaves are just above the surface. Press the soil gently around the stem, and dribble in sufficient water to settle and thoroughly dampen the mix. If you have a mister, use it to cover the seedlings with a fine layer of moisture.

8. Place the seedlings in a bright place but not in direct sunlight for a day or two (a tunnel house, glasshouse, conservatory, cold frame or cloche is ideal). Adequate light is important to encourage the growth of strong, stocky plants. Low light levels result in leggy plants which are vulnerable to disease. Once the plants have recovered from their move, sunshine is needed, but don't place tender seedlings too close to glass or they may scorch.

9. After about 2 weeks, you can start the hardening-off process for herbs intended to be planted in the garden or, if the weather is not warm enough, you can delay it a little longer. Place the seedlings in a sheltered place outside, at first just on warm days, then every day, and finally overnight as well. This should take about 10 days. There is no need to harden off plants which are to be transplanted into a glasshouse or other protected environment. Herb plants waiting for soil conditions and/or weather to improve may need to be given a weak dose of liquid fertiliser to ensure that they don't run out of nutrients.

RAISING HERBS FROM SEED OUTDOORS (SOWING *IN SITU*)

Don't attempt to sow seeds outdoors until the soil is warm enough and not too wet.

1. Prepare the seedbed by forking over the ground, adding extra organic matter, forking or chopping it in with a hoe to mix thoroughly and then raking the surface level. Don't worry too much about any coarse composting material or the odd soil lump. If the soil is not moist, give a thorough watering a day or two before sowing the seed.

2. Mark the row with a gardener's line or, as Mary does, with a length of conduit pipe. Use a hand trowel to scoop out a drill about 5 cm deep. Place the soil from the drill in a garden sieve over a container approximately the same diameter as the sieve. Push and shake to encourage as many of the finer particles as possible to pass through the sieve. Lumps and coarse pieces can be tossed onto another area of the garden.

3. If the soil is dry, dribble water into the drill. Sprinkle about two-thirds of the sieved soil into the bottom of the drill to make a nice fine layer for the seeds to grow into.

4. Tip a small quantity of seed into the palm of your hand. Take a pinch of the seed and sow it thinly and evenly along the drill. Use a finger to gently press the seeds into the soil. Sprinkle the remaining sieved soil over the seed to the required depth (check sowing depth for individual herbs).

5. Cover your row with protective netting or cloches if required. Ensure that the soil does not dry out.

6. As soon as the seedlings are large enough to handle, and with the soil moist, make your initial thinning and weeding. Firm the soil back around the remaining seedlings. Keep the soil hoed between the rows. Provide liquid fertiliser if required (see requirements for individual herbs) and keep the soil moist.

7. Once the leaves are just touching, do the final thinning to the recommended spacing. Remember that thinnings make a delicate addition to the salad bowl.

PLANTING OUT

To avoid transplant shock, plant your seedlings out while they are still relatively small and before the roots are visible through the drainage holes. If outdoor conditions are not ready and your herb plants have outgrown their pots, shift them to larger containers.

1. Prepare the bed as you would for sowing seed outdoors. Choose a cool, calm day.

2. Work out the correct spacing, and dig holes slightly deeper than required. Add extra fertiliser if needed, and mix it into the bottom layer of soil. Return a small quantity of soil to the hole so that the depth will be right for the seedlings. Dribble some water into the bottom of the hole.

3. Place the punnets with the seedlings in a container of water, almost up to the brim, and allow the water to soak to the surface. For individual container-grown plants, place a finger either side of the seedling, palm side against the soil, and carefully tip upside down. Remove the container. When seedlings have been grown with others, you can either use an old chisel, kitchen knife or narrow planting trowel to scoop out each plant along with its share of the soil, or carefully tip all the seedlings out as a unit and then divide them by prising their roots apart as gently as possible. Hold the seedlings by their leaves, not their easily damaged stems. Place each plant gently in its hole, crumble the surrounding soil back into the hole, and firm lightly.

4. Give each plant a thorough watering and, simultaneously, a dose of weak liquid fertiliser. Position a protective cover over the plants, if required.

DIVIDING HERB PLANTS

To maintain or control the vigour of many herbs, they should be divided every few years. Replant vigorous outer sections in a new site. Division is also a reliable and simple method of propagation. Division of herb clumps is usually made in spring, just as the first new growth begins.

1. Use a large spade to dig as deeply as possible around the perimeter of the plant.
2. Lift the whole clump with most of its roots intact. If the clump is so large that it is likely to cause a back injury, use a sharp spade to cut it into smaller sections. Keep the roots moist and out of the sun.
3. Use a trowel, knife, axe or 2 garden forks positioned back to back and levered apart to divide the clump into smaller sections. Select healthy outer portions, ensuring that each has at least one shoot and one root. Use secateurs to trim off any damaged roots or old stalks. If the herb has developed long, leafy shoots, these should be pruned back by a third to half to prevent excessive wilting. Take the opportunity to remove any persistent weeds that have invaded the clump.
4. Replant larger portions as soon as possible. Smaller pieces are best potted up and allowed to grow on in a protected environment.

LAYERING

Many herbs spread by underground or surface stems, called stolons or runners. If you lift one of these, you will find parts with small roots and tiny shoots. These can be severed from the parent plant and potted up.

Some herbs may need encouragement to produce rooted stem sections. This can be achieved in spring/early summer by bending a young and flexible stem down to the ground and securing it with a wire hoop or small stakes. First prepare the soil in the area where the stem is to be pegged. Fork lightly, and if necessary incorporate horticultural grit and/or compost. Remove any foliage from the stem where it will touch the ground. Make a small nick in the stem through the bark to encourage roots to develop. When the stem is firmly pegged, mound the soil over the contact point and keep the area moist but not wet. Once a good set of roots has developed (this may take several months), separate the young plant from its parent. Plant out into a permanent position or pot up to grow on in a protected environment.

CUTTINGS

Many herbs can be propagated from either softwood or semi-hardwood (semi-ripe) cuttings. Softwood cuttings are taken in spring/early summer when the new shoots of the parent plant are almost fully developed and just beginning to harden. They are generally taken from the tips of the shoots. At this stage the cuttings wilt easily and need to be kept in a controlled environment. Semi-hardwood cuttings are usually taken from mid- to late summer, from slightly more mature wood as growth begins to slow. They are less likely to wilt, so a controlled environment is not as important. Check the individual herb sections for the recommended method and timing. For both methods, use very clean containers and tools.

SOFTWOOD

1. Fill a 15–20 cm diameter plastic pot to within 2 cm of the top with a specially formulated proprietary cutting mix, or a 1:1 mix of peat and horticultural grit, vermiculite or perlite. The mix should be evenly moist but not sodden.
2. Collect your cuttings early in the morning. Choose sturdy shoots with plenty of healthy leaves. Cut 12–15

cm shoots with secateurs. Place the stems in water and keep cool. If they have to be kept for any time, wrap the stems in damp paper towels and store in a plastic bag in a refrigerator or portable ice-chest (but not in direct contact with the ice brick).

3. Using a very sharp knife, scalpel or razor blade on a hard board, cut the base of each stem just below a leaf joint, to leave a cutting about 8–10 cm long. Use a knife to remove the leaves from the lower third of the cutting.

4. Make a hole in the cutting mix with a dibber or blunt pencil. Insert the cutting up to its leaves. Firm in lightly. Several cuttings can be positioned in the pot, though they should not be overcrowded. Water the cuttings lightly with a watering can fitted with a fine rose.

5. Cover the pot with a clear plastic bag supported by 2 wire hoops to prevent the bag from touching the leaves. Place the pot in a warm place or on a heated pad. Aim for a temperature of about 18°C. Good light is required but avoid direct sun.

6. Remove the plastic bag 2–3 times a week, and turn inside out to avoid excess condensation. Spray the cuttings with a fine mist of water every day for the first few days. After that, water only when necessary to keep the cutting mix damp but not saturated. If rot becomes a problem, you may need to spray future cuttings with a fungicide.

7. Once the tips of the cuttings begin to grow rapidly, you can be fairly certain that they have rooted. When roots appear in the drainage holes, you can be confident of success. After a thorough watering, carefully tip the cuttings from the pot and gently separate. Transfer to individual pots containing a standard proprietary potting mix, lightened with horticultural grit (5:1). Water well and provide a sheltered environment until well established. Gradually harden off before planting in the garden.

SEMI-HARDWOOD

These are prepared from the current year's shoots which are becoming firm or woody at the base while the tops are still soft. Use the same method as for softwood cuttings, except use individual pots. Position the cuttings in a cool, well-lit position (bottom heat is seldom required). The ideal situation is in a cold frame with a glass or clear plastic lid which can be propped open on hot days. Some cuttings, for example bay, are more difficult to root and may require an enclosed misting unit. Usually, however, it is sufficient to mist the cuttings frequently by hand for the first few days and then to keep the cutting mix moist but not sodden.

GARDEN DESIGN

As discussed in the introduction, we don't have separate areas dedicated to growing herbs in our gardens but instead position them throughout, wherever they grow best. To assist gardening cooks wanting to establish a supply of herbs in a garden, we have listed some possible locations. Specific site requirements are given with each individual herb. Remember the general rule for planting mixed borders or beds: group plants rather than position them singly. For example, grow 3 or 5 parsley plants together for a luscious green effect (the cook will need at least that many). Don't forget to provide easy access to the herbs at the back of the border by stepping stones or small paths.

HERBS TO GROW IN THE VEGETABLE GARDEN
basil (annual), chervil (annual), chives, coriander (annual), dill (annual), sweet marjoram (frost-tender annual), parsley (biennial), summer savory (annual), sorrel, tarragon, mitsuba (annual), perilla (annual)

HERBS TO GROW IN THE FRONT OF A SUNNY
MIXED BORDER
sweet marjoram (frost-tender annual), sage, winter savory, thyme, chives, salad burnet

HERBS TO GROW IN THE MIDDLE OF A SUNNY
MIXED BORDER
garlic chives, lemon balm, oregano, parsley, perilla (frost-tender annual), Mexican mint (frost-tender annual), lemon grass (frost tender), scented geraniums (frost tender), borage (annual)

HERBS TO GROW AT THE BACK OF A SUNNY
MIXED BORDER
bay, fennel, lemon verbena, pineapple sage (frost tender), lovage

HERBS TO GROW IN A MOIST (NOT WATER-LOGGED), PARTLY SHADED BORDER
lemon balm, rau răm, mint, mitsuba (annual), sorrel, salad burnet, epazote (annual)

HERBS TO GROW IN A SUNNY ROCKERY
rosemary, sage, thyme, oregano, winter savory

HERBS FOR EDGES
chives, garlic chives, lavender (compact forms of *Lavandula angustifolia*)

HERBS FOR HEDGES
lavender (taller cultivars of *Lavandula angustifolia*), rosemary (upright varieties), bay

GROWING HERBS IN CONTAINERS

Many herbs make easy-care, productive and attractive pot plants. Grown this way, they are the solution for cooks with a patio, balcony, sunny porch or conservatory, but no garden. Even a sunny window sill can be used to grow a few herbs. In each herb section we have included specific advice for container growing along with the general cultivation information. Read both to appreciate the habits and requirements for each herb.

CONTAINERS

All types of containers can be used, providing they have provision for good drainage and are large enough to allow the development of vigorous root systems. Unglazed terracotta pots provide the best drainage but allow the potting mix to dry out more quickly. We use them for herbs, such as thyme and rosemary, which are prone to root rot if too wet. Herbs that like moist conditions are best in plastic pots.

To avoid disease problems, wash containers well with soapy water and a scrubbing brush. Follow this by soaking them in a dilute bleach solution or scrubbing.

To ensure good drainage, fill the bottoms of the pots up to a quarter or a third of their depth with broken crockery or sharp, coarse gravel or small angular stones. To keep the weight of large pots manageable, use broken-up polystyrene packing instead.

POTTING MIX

Choose a good quality proprietary brand, preferably one which provides information on how old the product is and when additional fertiliser will be needed. We prefer mixes that contain plenty of coarse matter, as these are easier to wet initially and don't compact, allowing for good root development. To ensure a potting mix remains well aerated, we add horticultural grit (the sharp pieces of stone averaging 3–6 mm) to most brands, generally adding 1 part grit to 5 parts potting mix. Other products such as pumice, perlite or vermiculite can also be used.

COLLECTIONS OF HERBS

We prefer to grow herbs individually, either one or several of the same variety in their own container. If you want to group different herbs together, choose compatible ones. They should have similar horticultural requirements and similar growing habits.

CARE

Some potting mixes contain slow-release fertilisers which will maintain nutrient levels for a few months. Read the information on the bag. As soon as extra nutrients are required, apply a suitably diluted liquid fertiliser every 2–3 weeks. Herbs requiring a different feeding programme are covered under their individual sections.

Try to prevent herbs from drying out, as potting mixes are sometimes very difficult to wet again. If this happens, complete submersion in a bucket is often the only solution. During hot summer months, stand the pots in deep saucers to retain some water. Many will require daily watering. A surface mulch of horticultural grit, shells or pebble collections look attractive and will help to slow evaporation. During colder months, avoid over-watering, particularly those herbs that are not actively growing.

Most herbs should be repotted each year in spring. Submerge the plant in its pot in a bucket of water until air bubbles cease rising to the surface. Tip from the pot and carefully remove most of the potting mix. Untangle the roots and prune off any damaged sections. Preferably repot into a larger container. If this is not possible, prune the roots back to allow room for fresh potting mix. Trim the foliage by a similar amount. Water well and leave in a shady, sheltered place for a few days to recover.

KITCHEN NOTES

WAYS TO PRESERVE HERBS

'Fresh is best' applies to herbs but, where a cook is unable to access the fresh, a source of preserved herbs is far better than none at all. We used to dry a range of herbs to take with us when tramping to enliven the limited range of dehydrated foods available. The herbs were processed quickly and simply in a microwave oven.

Each year Mary dries a selection of aromatic herbs to combine in the classic herbes de Provence (see page 180). We enjoy making herb vinegars and save pretty bottles so that we can share our abundant harvests with friends. Pesto is the best way of preserving basil, if you have any to spare, and herb butters give great scope for experimenting with interesting combinations of flavours. Pesto and herb butters can both be successfully frozen.

PREPARING HERBS

To ensure maximum flavour, herbs should be harvested just prior to flowering. Pick the stems in the morning, before temperatures rise but after any dew has evaporated. Discard woody stems and damaged or diseased leaves, and brush gently to remove any dust. Herbs should be washed if they have been exposed to city air pollution or have been grown in soil enriched or mulched with animal manure. Pat dry with paper towels.

DRYING HERBS

The aim in drying herbs is to evaporate water as quickly as possible without loss of colour and the volatile oils which are so essential for flavour. However pretty bunches of herbs may look hanging in the kitchen to dry, this is not the ideal way. There are 4 reliable methods.

1. This uses no artificial heat, relying on warm air temperatures and low humidity. Choose a warm, dry, dark and well-ventilated place, such as an airing cupboard, attic space under the roof, a spare room with the curtains pulled and door open, or a dark shed or garage.

   For small-leaved herbs, group several stems together into small bunches, secure with string or rubber bands and suspend from hooks or a line by tying or with paper clips. In dusty places, such as a garage or roof space, the herb bunches should be hung inside paper bags. Punch several holes to allow ventilation. Paper bags should also be used when drying seedheads (e.g.dill, fennel or coriander) to catch the seeds as they fall.

   Herbs with larger leaves can be dried as above, or the leaves can be carefully stripped from their stems and dried flat on racks, spread in a single layer on muslin or netting. They should be turned several times during the first few days.

   The length of time taken to dry herbs by this method depends on air temperature and humidity, and on the types of herbs being dried. It may take a few days or a few weeks. The method is not suitable for damp climates, where moulds are likely to be a problem.

2. Domestic electric ovens can be used for drying herbs. During humid weather this method is more reliable than using only natural heat. Set the oven to a low

heat. In a conventional oven, the temperature should not be above 35°C. In a multifunction oven, select the defrost setting with fan-assisted heat circulation and set the thermostat to 50°C. Cover an oven rack with brown paper with lots of holes punched in it, or a piece of cotton muslin, and spread the herb sprigs, leaves or small stems in a single layer. Leave the door ajar and turn the herbs several times during the drying period.

3. Small home dehydrators are purpose built and dry herbs efficiently. Follow the manufacturer's instructions. The temperature should not exceed 35°C. Position sprigs, leaves or small stems in single layers on the racks. Dry for the recommended time but keep a close watch so as not to over-dry.

4. Small quantities of herbs can be quickly and efficiently dried in a microwave oven. This method results in the best colour and flavour retention.

Place 2 thicknesses of paper towels on the turntable and spread a single layer of sprigs or individual leaves on top. Cover with 2 more paper towels and dry on high for 1 minute. Turn the herbs and continue drying in 30-second bursts, checking and turning after each, until the herbs are nearly crisp. The paper towels may still be damp but, as soon as the herbs are removed onto a rack, the leaves quickly dry to a brittle consistency.

CAUTION: Over-dry herbs can ignite or scorch in a microwave oven, so watch carefully and never leave the room.

STORING DRIED HERBS

Properly dried herbs should crackle and crumble when rubbed between your fingers. If they just bend, still feel soft and not crisp, they need a longer drying time. As it can be difficult to assess the degree of dryness accurately, it is wise to check for signs of moisture in the storage containers a few days after packing. If necessary, dry again rather than risk losing your herbs to mould.

Dried herbs should be stored intact (whole unbroken leaves or sprigs are best). Carefully strip larger leaves from stems. Crumbling is best done just before using. The intact herbs will take up more space but retain their flavour better. Use glass jars with airtight screw tops or resealable plastic bags. Label with the name of the herb and date of harvest. Store in a cool, dark cupboard, not in pretty jars on a spice rack in a bright, hot kitchen. Dried herbs are at their best for up to 6 months, but quickly lose flavour after that. Discard after 12 months.

FREEZING

Unfortunately, you can't just put fresh herbs in bags and place them in the freezer, expecting them to retain their texture, colour and flavour. Freezing and thawing causes the cells to collapse, and so lose their fresh characteristics. Some herb writers advocate this method but we have found it is not worth the effort. The only way we preserve herbs in our freezers is as herb butters (see pages 18–19), pesto with basil (see page 29) and similar herb pastes made with chopped herbs and oil, but without nuts, cheese and garlic. Herb pastes are convenient, as they don't freeze hard and you can use a knife to scoop out a small portion and then reseal the remainder. We use these concentrated herb pastes in cooked foods: soups, sauces, casseroles and breads. We do not use them in uncooked dishes, because of the slight risk of food poisoning inherent in this method. Freezing does not kill some potentially harmful bacteria.

To make herb and oil pastes for the freezer, combine clean, dry herb leaves in a food processor with about 1/4 cup of mild-flavoured oil for each cup of lightly packed herbs. Process until smooth. Spoon into small, labelled, resealable plastic bags and freeze as quickly as possible. Use within 3 months.

HERB VINEGARS

In our opinion making herb vinegar is the most successful method of retaining the flavour of summer herbs for use in dressings for winter salads. The all-time favourite would have to be tarragon vinegar, which is so popular that it is now made commercially. Other types of herb vinegar are not widely available, so the cook with good supplies of fresh herbs has the advantage of being able to produce a home-made brand quickly and simply. Make varietal herb vinegars or experiment with blends. A recipe for tarragon vinegar follows (the same method can be used for other herbs and for herb-blend vinegars).

Choose a vinegar which will complement rather than

overpower your herbs. Malt and distilled white vinegars are too harsh in flavour. Instead, choose from red or white wine vinegar, champagne vinegar, cider vinegar or an unseasoned rice wine vinegar. Use an enamel or stainless steel pan when heating the vinegar. Sterilise both the initial infusing jar and the storage bottles by immersing them in boiling water for 10 minutes or by heating in an oven at 120°C for 15 minutes. Don't use metal caps for sealing, as these may react with the acid in the vinegar. Ensure that your herbs are clean and dry (see page 16).

Store herb vinegars in a cool, dark place and use within 6–8 months. Herb vinegars are often added to vinaigrettes and other dressings, and can also be used to flavour soups, sauces and casseroles.

TARRAGON VINEGAR
makes approximately 750 ml

sufficient clean, dry sprigs of tarragon to 2/3 fill a 1 litre preserving jar
750 ml white wine vinegar

Gently twist the tarragon sprigs with your hands to release their flavour oils and place them in a sterilised 1 litre preserving jar. Heat the vinegar gently until hot but well below boiling point. Pour over the herbs, stirring well. Ensure that the herbs are submerged. Cover with a sterilised plastic lid and store in a cool, dark place for 3–4 weeks. You will know that the vinegar is ready to be bottled if you can smell tarragon when the lid is lifted.

Use a paper coffee filter in a small funnel to strain the vinegar into a sterilised bottle or bottles. Take care not to disturb any sediment in the bottom of the jar. Add an extra sprig of tarragon to each bottle for decorative purposes, if desired. Seal with sterilised lids. Label with the herb name and date of bottling.

Variations
Other herbs which make flavoursome and worthwhile vinegars include: marjoram, spearmint, summer savory, dill or fennel (use unripe seeds, flowers and leaves), basil (especially the purple variety), purple perilla and chives (leaves and flowers).

HERB-BLEND VINEGARS
Lemon-flavoured vinegar
Combine a selection of lemon-flavoured herbs, such as lemon thyme, lemon balm, lemon basil, lemon verbena or crushed lemon grass, with a white wine or champagne vinegar.

Marinade vinegar
Combine parsley, bay, basil, oregano, thyme and 10 crushed garlic cloves in red wine vinegar.

Rice vinegar with flavours of Asia
Combine rau răm, purple perilla, garlic chives (leaves and flowers), 3 slices of crushed fresh ginger root and a sliced shallot with unseasoned rice vinegar.

HERB-FLAVOURED OILS
Home-made herb oils may not be safe, as they could contain harmful bacteria. Unlike vinegar, oils do not inhibit the growth of bacteria. The risk can be reduced if dried herbs are used, as these generally do not contain enough water to foster bacterial growth. They should be stored in a refrigerator and consumed within 3 weeks. Commercially made infused oils have added acidifiers and/ or microbial inhibitors, or the added herb flavour is obtained from the extracted essential oil rather than fresh leaves. Read labels when purchasing these products and be wary of unlabelled ones from market stalls.

We infuse oils with herbs for immediate use: for example, when making foccacia bread (see page 184) or for basting food on a barbecue.

HERB BUTTERS
Herb butters look attractive with their specks of green scattered through the yellow butter. They also taste fresh and, even after freezing, provide a special touch to baked potatoes, cooked vegetables, toast, sandwiches, scones, muffins, grilled fish and meats, or simply as part of a tray of freshly baked assorted breads with the herb butter as the centre-piece. Herb butters freeze well for up to 12 months, so are an ideal way of preserving summer herbs for winter use. Once thawed, they should be stored in a refrigerator and used within a few days, so are best frozen in small quantities.

Use fresh salted or unsalted butter (we prefer the sweeter taste of unsalted) and ensure that your herbs are clean and dry (see page 16). Choose the herbs to complement the foods your butter is to accompany. For example, try lemon balm and a little grated orange rind for breakfast toast or muffins; dill and chives to adorn grilled fish or spread in cucumber sandwiches; or basil with oregano and garlic for tomato-topped *crostini*. There are endless possibilities! Here is our basic recipe for a savoury herb butter: vary the herbs according to what you have available and its intended use.

150 g softened butter
2 tablespoons finely chopped parsley
1 tablespoon finely sliced chives
1 tablespoon finely chopped tarragon or summer savory or basil or mint
1 clove garlic, very finely chopped
1 teaspoon grated lemon rind

Blend the herbs, garlic and lemon rind into the butter. This can be done in a food processor. Form into a long roll on a piece of plastic food film or grease-proof paper. Alternatively, pack into small pottery crocks. Wrap in freezer bags. Store in a refrigerator and use within a few days or freeze for up to 12 months.

HERB TEAS

So popular have herb teas become that whole books are devoted to the subject. Guests used to be asked at the end of a dinner party whether they would like 'tea or coffee'; now they are more likely to be asked, 'tea, coffee or herb tea?' and several choices of the latter are offered.

We make herb teas in several ways: as tisanes brewed from fresh or dried herb leaves; as blended tisanes, where fresh or dried herbs are brewed together; as herb-flavoured Indian or Chinese teas; or as iced tisanes and flavoured teas. We also make an extra-quick tisane in our microwave ovens designed as a 'pick me up' for tired gardeners.

TISANES
Here are our general instructions for making tisanes or infusions, using either fresh or dried herbs.

We prefer to use fresh herbs, but admit that on a cold winter's night it is much nicer to scoop up some dried herb leaves from a tea caddy than to venture out into the dark. Well-dried garden-fresh herbs, less than 6 months old, are far superior to purchased herb teas. It is well worth drying some of your own (see pages 16–17).

Use a non-metal teapot reserved for tisanes. Glass ones look pretty but heavy pottery ones retain heat well. Tea cosies have a function. Alternatively, make individual cups of herb tea with a dedicated tea infuser.

Water quality is worth considering, as the more delicately-flavoured tisanes may be tainted by chlorine or pollutants. If you use a filter for your drinking water, use it for herb teas too.

Method
1. Gather fresh herbs and wash if necessary. Dried herbs are best kept whole until required: crumble just before measuring.
2. Heat fresh cold water (filtered if preferred) in a kettle until boiling. Use a little to pre-heat a non-metal teapot.
3. Chop fresh herbs and measure 2 tablespoons for each cup. Crumble dried herbs and measure 1 tablespoon for each cup. Add to the hot teapot. To make an individual cup, measure the fresh or dried herbs into a tea infuser and place in a mug or cup.
4. Pour the freshly boiling water over the herbs. Stir and replace the lid.
5. Infuse for about 3–5 minutes. It is important not to over-brew tisanes as they may become bitter. We prefer to use the more concentrated proportions suggested above and a shorter infusing time, rather than using the more commonly suggested amounts and longer brewing times. As tisanes do not darken perceptibly, their strength has to be judged by taste rather than sight. Experiment until you get your own formula.
6. As soon as the flavour is right, strain the tisane into cups or mugs.
7. Offer lemon slices, honey or raw sugar. Thyme honey blends well, adding an additional complexity to the herbs.

We enjoy both single herb tisanes and blends of 2 or 3. A

popular blend combines roughly equal quantities of spearmint, rosemary and lemon verbena. Another combines lemon balm and winter mint. Armed with a pair of scissors, make an excursion into your garden or onto the patio, sniff various herbs and make a selection which appeals. Try lots of combinations—you will soon develop some firm favourites.

HERB-FLAVOURED TEAS

A good way of introducing tisanes to suspicious family or guests is to make herb-flavoured Indian or Chinese teas. Follow the method given for tisanes, but use 1/2 teaspoon of tea, 1 tablespoon of chopped fresh herbs or 1/2 teaspoon of dried herbs for each cup.

We enjoy lemon balm with Indian tea, spearmint with Chinese tea, tarragon with Earl Grey tea, and rosemary with smoky-tasting Lapsang Souchong. A recipe for Moroccan mint tea is given on page 102.

ICED TISANES OR HERB-FLAVOURED TEAS

Both tisanes and herb-flavoured teas can be served iced. To counter the diluting effect of the ice, double the concentration of the brew. Use the amounts specified for fresh chopped herbs, dried herbs or blends of Indian/Chinese tea plus herbs with 1/2 cup of water rather than a full cup. Prepare as for a tisane, strain into a jug, add sweetening if desired, and allow to cool. Chill in a refrigerator until required. Half fill tall glasses with ice, fill with the chilled herb tea, and decorate with sprigs or flowers of the appropriate herbs.

MICROWAVED TISANES

A quick and easy method for making a reviving tisane for a tired gardener is to gather a few sprigs of selected fresh herbs before coming inside—for example, 2 leaves of lemon verbena, a 4 cm sprig of sage and a 6 cm sprig of peppermint or eau de Cologne mint. Put these in a pyrex jug and add a cup of cold filtered water or tap water. Microwave on high until the water boils. Leave to stand for a minute or two before straining into a cup or mug. Sweeten if desired, and relax.

STORING FRESH HERBS IN THE KITCHEN

If you have fresh herbs in the garden, it is preferable to delay picking them until just before they are needed. If, however, your mint is in the next paddock or your rosemary climbs down a wall remote from the kitchen, you may wish to store herbs for short periods in the kitchen. Cooks with a herb shortage will have to purchase supplies from a supermarket, and these will need to be stored as well.

Cut herbs sold in plastic bags have a very short shelf-life, so check their condition before purchasing. The leaves should be fresh-looking, with no signs of yellowing, wilting, mould or rot. Even if there is a 'use by' date, it pays to examine them carefully in case they have not been stored correctly. Once you have them home, unwrap and remove any wilted or damaged leaves. Except for basil, place them in a fresh plastic bag and store in the vegetable compartment of a refrigerator. Use as soon as possible. Wash the leaves just before using—they are best stored dry. Basil leaves are susceptible to cold and turn black in a refrigerator. Instead, store with the stems in a container of water on the kitchen window sill. Garden-harvested herbs should be stored in a similar way. Wash the leaves, if necessary, just before using.

By far the best way to purchase herbs is as living plants growing in small pots. With care, these will last on a kitchen window sill for many weeks and can even be potted on or planted in the garden in the appropriate seasons. An impressive number is now available: all the usual ones plus some surprises, such as sweet marjoram, Thai and lemon basil, dill and garlic chives. Remove the protective plastic sleeve and place the pots in saucers on a well-lit window sill. Keep watered but don't allow the pots to stand in more than 1 cm of water. If not used up within a few weeks, the herbs will benefit from a feed of liquid fertiliser at pot plant strength plus a pinch of lime sprinkled on the surface of the potting mix. If the stems need supporting, insert a plastic pot plant stake and make a loose tie around the plant.

NOTES ON INGREDIENTS

BLACK PEPPER
Use freshly ground black pepper.

FRESHLY ROASTED NUTS OR SEEDS
Dry roasting nuts and seeds enhances their flavour by removing any raw taste. There are 3 methods:

1. Use a heavy-based frying pan over a low heat. Stir frequently to avoid scorching.
2. Use a slow oven (150°C).
3. Use a microwave on full power. Stir every 2 minutes.

Over-roasting or burning will quickly spoil the flavour. With all methods, spread the nuts or seeds out in a single layer. Shake the pan or stir frequently to ensure even roasting. They will be done when their colour has darkened slightly.

OILS
In recipes where we specify extra virgin olive oil, we mean one with a fresh and pleasant flavour. Unfortunately, many extra virgin olive oils on supermarket shelves or tucked in the back of hot kitchen cupboards develop a strong, unpleasant, rancid taste which can detract from the delicate flavour of some herbs. As extra virgin olive oils are unstable and have a short shelf-life, care is needed with purchasing and storage. Look for brands in cans or dark glass bottles rather than clear glass. Extra virgin olive oil should be used within a year of pressing, so 'use by' dates would be helpful to consumers but are seldom seen.

Specialist food shops and some bigger supermarkets may stock single-estate extra virgin olive oils which are grown, harvested, pressed and bottled by the producer. They are expensive, but providing they are fresh their flavour is unique and special. Again, look for dark bottles or cans with a 'use by' date. Keep a watch out for any locally produced olive oils, as these are likely to be the freshest. All oils should be kept in a cool, dark place and used within 3 months of opening.

A newcomer to the market is avocado oil. Its fresh and delicate flavour complements herbs to perfection. It is sold in dark bottles and has a 'use by' date.

ABBREVIATIONS AND MEASUREMENTS

ABBREVIATIONS

ml	millilitre
g	gram
kg	kilogram
cm	centimetre
mm	millimetre
°C	degrees Celsius

MEASUREMENTS
New Zealand standard metric kitchen measures have been used for all the recipes. All measures should be level.

1 cup holds 250 ml
1 tablespoon holds 15 ml
1 dessertspoon holds 10 ml
1 teaspoon holds 5 ml

(In New Zealand, South Africa, Canada, the USA and Britain, 1 tablespoon equals 15 ml. In Australia 1 tablespoon equals 20 ml or 4 teaspoons.)

basil

Most of our generation first tasted basil (*Ocimum* species) in the 1950s and 60s as a packaged dried herb. We thought it was wonderful and quickly became addicted. Then we attempted to grow it, not always successfully, in our kitchen gardens.

Basil has since become known as the 'Italian herb' and, as Rosalind Creasy puts it in her book, *Cooking from the Garden*, it is used in such large quantities in dishes originating from Italy that you might call it an Italian vegetable. It has become synonymous with pizzas, pasta sauces and the famous pesto from Genoa.

We should not overlook the very long history of basil in Eastern cuisines, where it has been used probably a lot longer than in the West. It appears in Thai and Vietnamese salads, soups, curries and stir-fries, to give just a few examples.

Basil is grown as a tender annual in temperate climates. Sadly, it is so sensitive to low temperatures that it grows very poorly when day and night temperatures average below 15°C and it is killed by even the lightest frost. This makes it one of the most difficult herbs to grow in colder regions. Despite the problems, many keen cooks battle on to produce, most years anyway, worthwhile harvests of freshly picked leaves. If you grow your own basil you will appreciate the superior flavour of fresh leaves compared with dried basil or the commercially grown and packaged store-bought fresh version. Basil leaves are damaged easily, resulting in bruising, loss of flavour and

discolouration. Commercial growers who are producing several varieties of living basil in pots for supermarket sales are to be commended for their superior product.

Cooks in colder areas may have to grow their basils in containers on window sills, in conservatories, glasshouses or tunnel houses, or on sheltered patios. Fortunately, this is relatively easy to do and extremely rewarding. Growers in more favourable climates can use similar methods to extend the harvesting season of their basil plants when temperatures begin to drop in autumn.

The trouble with basil is that you never seem to have enough. However much you plant, you always want more.

VARIETIES

So many culinary basils are available that it is hard to know where to start. There are some with a sweet flavour, some spicy, some with overlying flavours such as lemon, cinnamon or cloves. Some are purple, some have smooth leaves, some have ruffles, some have tiny leaves, and there is even one called 'Elephant' because of its huge leaves. Many names, both botanical and common, are confusing. We have grown only a small number of these varieties and so we will describe our favourites, so far. But each year, as new varieties appear in the seed catalogues, we are tempted to try more. We suspect that many keen cooks are just as addicted to collecting basil varieties as they are to eating them.

The two main culinary species of basil are *Ocimum*

basilicum, to which the well-known common basil (also called sweet basil) belongs, and *O. minimum*, which includes most of the smaller bush basils. Many of the varieties listed in catalogues are selections of these or they are cultivars bred by crossing various basil species.

When a recipe calls for 'basil' it is likely that common basil is intended. It is the one most often available in supermarkets and the one most likely to be seen growing in kitchen gardens or window sill pots. Its popularity is due to its delightful sweet flavour with none of the strong aftertastes present in some other basils. It is high yielding and is probably the best basil to start with, in both the garden and the kitchen.

The Genovese basils are selections of common basil originating in Genoa, in northern Italy. They are the traditional basils for making pesto. Their flavour is reportedly stronger than common basil, even when cooked. Mary has grown two varieties, called by the seed

Bush basil, 'Green Bouquet'

Purple basil, 'Osmin'

Basil, 'Genovese Special Select'

Basil, 'Compatto'

companies 'Genovese Special Select' and 'Compatto', a compact form. Genovese basil can be used in place of common basil.

The advantage of bush basils with their low-growing compact forms is their small leaves, which can be added to salads whole without having to be chopped. This way they look more attractive and retain their full flavour. Some bush basils have a very similar taste to common basil while others taste more of cloves or aniseed. We have grown one called 'Spicy Globe' which does very well in containers and tastes like common basil but with a hint of spice.

The delightful lemon basil has distinctly lemon-flavoured pale green leaves. It is reportedly less hardy than common basil so we have grown it only in containers.

Purple basil or dark opal basil has gorgeous dark purple leaves and a very similar flavour to common basil. Its colour makes it attractive in salads and in the garden. We like to use it for making basil vinegar as it will give a lovely pink colour to wine vinegars.

According to most authorities, one authentic Thai basil for Thai cooking is *O. sanctum* (syn. *O. tenuiflorum*). It is said to have a strong aniseed flavour with a hint of cloves. There are others but we have been unable to ascertain their correct names.

If you want to try the many varieties available, we suggest that you order directly from seed catalogues or purchase plants from specialist herb nurseries. Very few types are sold as seedlings from garden centres.

CULTIVATION

Warmth is basil's greatest need. It is a tropical plant which survives in temperate regions. Those gardening cooks who live in cooler climates must be patient and not plant basil too early in the season, as it will not grow when night temperatures are below 10°C and it succumbs at 1–4°C, so even the lightest frost will be fatal. To hasten soil warming, cover the bed with black plastic for several days before sowing basil seed or planting out.

In some areas it is possible to obtain good harvests only if basil is grown under cover—in a glasshouse or tunnel house or on a sunny window sill or sheltered patio.

Moisture is the second-greatest need. Our experience has shown that basil requires much more water than the other herbs, such as thyme, marjoram and rosemary, that we associate with Mediterranean countries. We have found that container-grown basil thrives when its pot sits in a shallow dish kept topped up with water—rather like a waterbath for baking custards in. The roots of large basil plants quickly grow out of the drainage holes and appear happy submerged in the water. Garden-grown basil also requires adequate moisture. Keep the soil constantly moist but not waterlogged—a mulch will help achieve this. Avoid watering the leaves in the evening and when the temperatures are low.

Good drainage around the base of the stem is another requirement, in both containers and garden beds. If necessary, build up beds with plenty of well-rotted manure or compost and, if clay is a problem, lighten the soil with horticultural grit. A moderately rich, light soil is preferred and by adding organic matter both texture and fertility are improved.

Full sun is essential in cooler climates and at least half a day of sun in warmer areas. A little shade at midday and early in the afternoon is reported to be beneficial in places where temperatures exceed 30°C and where wilting of the leaves can be a problem.

Shelter is another requirement, as wind may bruise leaves—the large-leaved varieties are particularly vulnerable.

Basil is easy to raise from seed and, if you are interested in trying the many varieties now available, you will be able to choose from a much greater selection. Well-grown seedlings can also be obtained from specialist nurseries and garden centres. We recommend buying plants in individual pots as these are less likely to be damaged when transplanting.

In cooler areas it is quickest to raise seedlings indoors, ready to plant outside once night temperatures are regularly above 10°C, or to plant in containers if outdoor crops are impossible. Basil seed remains viable for several years if it is stored in a cool dry place. Plan to start seed 4–5 weeks before the likely date to plant out. Sow a few seeds per small pot filled with a damp proprietary seed-sowing mix lightened with horticultural grit, about 5:1 (see page 11). Don't use unsterilised home-made mix as basil is very prone to damping-off diseases. Sow the seed on the surface and barely cover with fine mix. Cover the pots with clear plastic or place in a propagator. They should then be put in a warm place—a constant room temperature of 18–21°C is ideal. Better still, use a heating pad under a propagator—the soil temperature should be about 21°C. In ideal conditions the seed can germinate in just a few days. Watch closely as it is necessary to provide maximum light and plenty of ventilation once the leaves appear. If necessary, thin the seedlings to either just one healthy plant or allow 3–4 to develop and treat them as one plant. Commercial growers producing living plants rather than cut leaves for supermarkets appear to use this method. Keep young seedlings moist but avoid overwatering at this vulnerable stage. Water well early in the day.

If the seedlings are intended for planting in the garden, they may need to be potted on into larger containers if garden soil conditions are not ready. Do this carefully to avoid damaging the delicate roots. Basil destined to be raised in boxes or pots should be planted into these as soon as the seedlings are large enough to be handled.

Outdoor basil should be planted only when soil and air temperatures are warm, about the same time as tomatoes are planted. Space them 25–30 cm apart. Plant deeply, like tomatoes, up to their first leaves. This encourages maximum root development and ensures a stable plant. Six to eight plants are usually sufficient for a small family, though twice that many would be needed to make pesto for freezing.

In warmer climates, many gardeners prefer to wait for soils to warm and then to sow their basil direct in well-prepared beds. Some writers maintain that they get better crops this way, as transplant shock does not slow growth. Sow the seeds thinly in damp shallow drills and barely cover with a little sieved soil or proprietary seed-raising mix. Keep well moistened, though not saturated, until germination occurs. Thin the seedlings early to prevent overcrowding. This can be done progressively to achieve a final spacing of 25–30 cm apart. Eat or transplant the thinnings.

In ideal climates, successive crops of basil can be sown to ensure optimum harvests of the best quality leaves. Follow-up crops are also possible and desirable for container-grown basil plants.

Outdoor crops should be kept moist but not waterlogged at all times. A mulch of compost or straw will help to retain moisture in the soil. Don't apply a mulch until after the soil has warmed up, as the roots need heat to grow. In a dry area and for large crops, drip irrigation is worth considering. Watering should be done early in the day and avoid wetting the leaves, especially if temperatures are marginal.

Occasional feeding with a fish emulsion or other liquid fertiliser will be beneficial if you are harvesting heavily.

In order to encourage basil plants to make leaves, it is important to continually keep them well picked. Start while still quite small, by pinching out the growing tips to the next pair of leaves. The bonus is some early basil for the kitchen. The more you prune by harvesting early, the bushier your basil will become. Never allow flowers to develop, as once this happens the basil plant directs its energies there and leaf production ceases. Also, we have found that the older leaves on basil bushes with flowers are too tough to use uncooked and they seem to lose flavour intensity.

Whitefly and aphids are occasionally a nuisance, especially with indoor basil plants. These are best washed off. Watch for slug damage on outdoor plants. Catching the culprits at night with a torch is effective.

GROWING IN CONTAINERS

As growing basil in containers is the only option for gardeners in cooler areas, we have covered the main aspects in the previous section. Here are a few specific pointers.

- Bush basil is ideal for pots because of its compact growth habit.
- Common basil (sweet basil) and other larger varieties need to be grown in 20 cm diameter pots. These varieties may need staking.
- Once summer temperatures warm sufficiently, pots of bush basil arranged formally make attractive borders and focal points around flower and vegetable beds. Regular harvesting of the growing tips keeps these compact basil plants looking neat and round, almost like topiaries—much more valuable to the cook than the trimmed box hedge of a potager.
- Bring container-grown basil indoors before the first frost. Cut stems well back to just above lower pairs of leaves. Apply a suitably diluted liquid fertiliser and place

BASIL

(*Ocimum* spp.)

'If I had to choose just one plant from the whole herb garden', wrote Elizabeth David in 1954, 'I should be content with basil.' So would many other English-speaking cooks who were introduced to French and Italian cuisines by pioneers like Elizabeth David and Patience Gray. They discovered that the flavours of the Mediterranean basils are so distinctive—some call them addictive—that no substitutes are possible. In fact, dishes like the famous basil pesto of Genoa and the pistou of Provence are built around this herb, especially the sweet basil (*Ocimum basilicum*) and the smaller-leafed bush basil (*O. minimum*).

The basil genus evolved in tropical and sub-tropical regions, so England could never offer ideal conditions for culinary basils. As a food historian, however, Elizabeth David was aware that the 16th- and 17th-century English herbalists were familiar with several varieties, and she herself had grown basil successfully in rooftop boxes in London. Why, then, was basil so rare in English cookery? she asked. This is an intriguing question, considering that 19th-century British gardeners grew thousands of similarly tender annuals for bedding out in their summer flower gardens.

The unpopularity of basil in Britain before the late 20th century is not the only puzzle involving this herb. There are some questionable beliefs about its origins and early history, as well as little agreement about its properties, even two millennia ago when it was first described. The impression gained from the classical sources is that basil was still a relative newcomer. Several herb writers have stated that 'basil' originated in India. It would be more accurate to say that India is just one possible homeland of several of the basil species, including the widespread hoary basil (*O. americanum*, also known as *O. canum*) and *tulsi*, the sacred or holy basil (*O. sanctum*). East Africa is definitely the place of origin of the camphor basil (*O. kilimandscharicum*), while the homeland of the most common culinary basil (*O. basilicum*) cannot be pinpointed any closer than 'probably Africa'. As for the little bush basil (*O. minimum*), which is found only in cultivation, nothing is known of its wild progenitors. There are even some exclusively American basils, such as the mosquito-repellant *O. micranthum*.

Another common belief is that basil was an important culinary herb in ancient Greece and Rome, and that it was planted with abuse and curses in order to procure a good crop. Like most fables, this story has undergone significant changes in the course of transmission. The Greek writer Theophrastus originally stated that it was cumin that should be cursed at the time of sowing. Three hundred years later Pliny applied the comment to basil, adding that the earth should be rammed down around the seeds. Later still Palladius declared that it was rue that had to be cursed! There were good reasons for firming the soil around basil, which had nothing to do with superstition. Theophrastus observed that if the soil was left in a loose condition the seed usually rotted. The Roman writer and poet Columella was more explicit: firming would stop the seedlings being scorched by the early summer sun when they germinated, as well as protecting them from ants and 'ground fleas'. Theophrastus also discovered that basil should be watered only in the heat of the day, important advice for a sub-tropical plant which is easily damaged by having cold water lying on its leaves.

The Greeks initially called the basil plant *ókimon*, and it was referred to as early as the 5th century BC as being attractive to slugs. This word became the Latin *ocimum*, which provides our genus name. Later the Greeks adopted a new name, *basilikón*, meaning 'royal', and it is possible that this renaming reflected the introduction of a new type of basil from Asia. In late Latin this word became confused with the word for a basilisk or serpent (*basiliscus*), and the herbalists duly recounted contradictory stories about the plant's properties as an antidote or its propensity to generate scorpions! Despite numerous references in classical literature, there is very little evidence that basil was eaten as a culinary herb. Apicius's Roman cookbook mentioned it just once, added fresh to a pea and vegetable soup. Even as a medicinal plant, there were warnings that over-consumption could dull vision and impair digestion. So why was it grown in the gardens of ancient Greece and Rome? It seems to have been valued primarily for its scent, although we can only speculate which scent was dominant at this period—was it anise, citrus or cinnamon?

The Middle East and India provide a parallel case, for in those regions basil is seldom used in the kitchen, but grown for its religious associations and perfumed leaves. In South-east Asia, however, the number of varieties of at least three basil species suggests a long history of culinary use. Several modern cultivars were introduced to the West from Thailand in the 20th century, including anise and licorice-flavoured *O. basilicum* varieties, and the lemon and lime-scented *O. americanum*.

So when did basils become important in Western European cuisines? They were seldom mentioned in mediaeval vocabularies or recipe collections, and were described in other texts as examples of sweet-smelling rather than culinary herbs. In the 16th century, basils were regarded as good for strewing on floors, and were grown in both gardens and pots. In 1597 John Gerard classified the basils he was familiar with by size, smell and colour: the little bush basil smelled of cloves, the middle-sized basil of lemons, while the large-leaved basil and its purple variant were simply sweet. Significantly, John Parkinson chose to discuss basils under the heading 'The Garden of pleasant Flowers', not 'The Kitchen Garden'. He was emphatic that the 'ordinary Basill is in a manner wholly spent to make sweet, or washing waters, among other sweet herbes, yet sometimes it is put into nosegayes'.

During the 17th century basils were increasingly added to food, but not so much in England as in France and Italy. John Evelyn would permit only sparing use of the tender tops in his 'sallets', and it was occasionally mentioned as a suitable pot-herb 'for broth or for stewing meats'. The situation was clearly different in northern Italy, for in 1724 Richard Bradley, professor of botany and writer on cooking and gardening, reported that 'His Royal Highness the Grand Duke of *Tuscany* presented me one year with above fifty different Sorts of *Basils*'.

British food writers contributed to the unpopularity of basils by presenting them as generally unacceptable. John Dicks wrote in 1769, 'These plants have a strong scent like cloves, too powerful for most persons', while William Hanbury in 1770 thought that their odour 'would be highly refreshing, could we have it in a less degree'. Considering that contemporary cooks were happily using garlic, horseradish and actual cloves, it is tempting to conclude that the perception of basil as over-powering was based on a preexisting prejudice. Phillip Miller had noted in 1768 that basil was employed 'particularly by the French cooks, who make great use of it in their soups and sauces'. By 1822, Henry Phillips declared that 'The French are now so partial to the flavour and qualities of this plant, that its leaves enter into the composition of almost all their soups and sauces'. If jingoism lay behind the poor status of basil in England, it certainly wasn't the only herb affected. Nor was its reputation helped by the publication in 1820 of John Keats's poem 'Isabella or The Pot of Basil', in which the head of her murdered lover was buried under a basil plant!

Eventually, food writers like Elizabeth David inspired English-speaking cooks to take a fresh look at the Mediterranean basils. In places where Mediterranean and South-east Asian cultures have come together, such as Australia and the American West Coast, there have been even more opportunities for an exchange of basil species and varieties. Horticulturists have discovered and disseminated natural crosses of *O. basilicum* and *O. kilimandscharicum*, such as 'African Blue', as well as deliberately hybridising *O. basilicum* with the Asian *O. americanum*. With so many species and cultivars to work with, and such a range of flavours already represented in the genus, basils have an exciting future.

in a sunny position, and you should be rewarded with fresh basil out of season. Another technique followed by some cooks is to lift garden-grown basil plants that have not flowered and, with a minimum of root disturbance, transfer them to pots filled with a free-draining potting mix. Prune the stems back to lower leaves and bring inside. Regular light harvesting of these indoor basil plants will keep them compact and bushy. Feed occasionally with liquid fertiliser at the correct strength. Remember to keep well watered, as heated rooms can dry plants quickly.

HARVESTING

We cannot stress enough the importance of keeping basil plants well trimmed to encourage a bushy habit and to prevent flowering. This ensures that leaf production is at its maximum, resulting in the best flavoured and textured leaves. Start early, as once buds have formed trimming encourages the formation of more buds and not leaves.

Your first basil harvest can be the thinnings from your garden rows or containers. Start picking from bigger plants when they are about 15–20 cm tall. Cut each stem back by a third to a half, just above a leaf pair. Don't tear the leaves from the plants as this may damage the soft stems—

use scissors. Handle the pickings gently as they bruise and darken easily. Pick just before they are required in the kitchen.

Despite our best intentions, we sometimes end up with basil flowers. Although these are coarse-textured and not as aromatic as the leaves, we use them as pretty garnishes.

Food writers disagree as to whether it is worth drying basil for use out of season. Dried basil has a different taste to the fresh, with a much more pronounced mint flavour. We think that basil is a valuable dried herb for winter pizzas, breads and rich tomato sauces. When dried well it retains much of its flavour and even some green colour. We find that freezing is not satisfactory, as it blackens the leaves unacceptably. Pesto frozen in small lots is another good preservation method. Basil leaves, especially large ones, are succulent and slow to dry. Either tie stems in small bunches and hang in a warm and airy place, or snip leaves from stems to lie flat on racks in a slow oven or dehydrator. As natural drying may take 2–3 weeks or even longer, it is important to keep the leaves away from light and dust. Cover bunches with large brown-paper bags with a few ventilation holes. See page 16. Once the leaves are dry, pick them from the stems and store whole in airtight and light-proof containers. Crumble the leaves just before adding them to food.

IN THE KITCHEN

Pick leaves from the stems and either shred with the fingers into small pieces, if the leaves are large, or leave whole for smaller-leaved varieties. Alternatively, large basil leaves may be stacked and rolled and then sliced finely into thin threads or chopped. Use a very sharp stainless steel knife to reduce damage and resulting discolouration. Always prepare basil just before it is required.

Basil may be added to dishes to be served hot before cooking, giving a delicious mellow flavour which is subtle and different from the more pungent raw herb. Quite large quantities can be used in this way. We like to add smaller amounts of fresh basil to the finished dish just before serving.

For those cooks without home-grown supplies, we recommend that you look out for living basil in small pots. These last well on the kitchen windowsill, providing a high quality product. Several basil varieties are available,

including purple, lemon and Genovese. If you have to store cut basil, recut the stem ends and place in a container with about 5 cm of water. Place in a shady and cool position and remember to keep the water topped up. See page 20.

HOW TO USE BASIL
- The use of basil in pizzas and pasta sauces needs no introduction. Both fresh and dried basil leaves can be added before cooking, and fresh leaves can be added as a garnish to the cooked dishes—providing the famous and much-loved flavour.
- Basil enhances many vegetables, especially the summer ones we associate with Italian cuisine—zucchini, aubergine, capsicum and, of course, tomatoes. Don't be timid about using it with other vegetables—in particular, cucumber, beans, broccoli, mushrooms, carrots, sweet corn, potatoes and all roasted or barbecued vegetables.
- There is no substitute for fresh basil in salads. Always add at the last minute to prevent discolouration and ensure maximum flavour. Add basil to mixed green salads (the purple variety is striking), vegetable salads (in particular tomato), chicken or fish salads (in both Western and Eastern styles) and pasta and rice salads.
- Make basil vinegar (see page 17). Purple basil produces a pretty pink-coloured vinegar. Use for vinaigrettes, mayonnaise and marinades.
- Basil butter (see page 18-19) has many uses: on freshly cooked corn cobs, in sandwiches with sliced tomatoes, as a garnish on tomato soup, with baked jacket potatoes, and with any boiled or steamed vegetables.
- Make the famous pesto sauce (see recipe on page 29). The home-made version has a superior flavour to commercial brands. Use pesto in the traditional ways, tossed with hot pasta and stirred into minestrone soup. Also use it as a topping on hot vegetables, such as green beans, broccoli, carrots, cauliflower, aubergine, potatoes, peas, spinach, zucchini and tomatoes. Spread pesto onto bread and top with slices of tomato. Stir it into hot rice and add to mayonnaise and vinaigrettes. Some members of our family have been known to add it to almost anything edible.
- Make lemon basil the dominant herb in rice salads.

We include chives and parsley too. Add extras such as olives, toasted nuts, dried tomatoes and diced celery and moisten with a vinaigrette made with basil vinegar and olive oil.

- Fill an omelette with chopped basil, tomatoes and grated cheese (see recipe on pages 46–47).
- Basil with chopped dried tomatoes and grated cheese makes a tasty grilled sandwich filling.
- Make a purple basil cheese ball and decorate it with an assortment of tiny flowers or petals. In a food processor combine 250 g of cream cheese, 100 g grated Cheddar cheese or other favourite cheese, 50 g of softened butter, 3–4 tablespoons of chopped purple basil (or substitute green basil), 1 clove of garlic (very finely chopped), 1 tablespoon of port wine and seasoning. Spoon onto a sheet of plastic food film and shape into a ball, enclose and chill for 2–3 hours. Just before serving, press the edible flowers, such as heart's-ease, calendula petals, chive blossoms, borage flowers, onto the surface. Serve with crackers, vegetable sticks or baguette slices.
- Add chopped basil and dried tomatoes and/or olives to your regular bread dough.
- Mary's favourite comfort food is a sandwich made with freshly baked white bread, a thickly sliced ripe tomato still warm from the sun, a basil leaf torn into small pieces and plenty of ground black pepper.
- Add an unusual but delicious flavour to fruits. Infuse sugar syrup with lemon basil leaves. Use with peaches, apricots and berries.
- Make a simple tomato salad with thickly sliced, firm but fully ripened tomatoes, dressed with extra virgin olive oil, lemon juice, a pinch of salt and caster sugar, scissored chives and torn fresh basil leaves.
- Use lots of chopped basil to flavour sautéed courgettes and tomatoes. To serve 4, cut 500 g of courgettes into 5 mm slices. Sauté the slices in 2 tablespoons of oil in a large frying pan over a moderate heat until they are almost tender. Peel 4 medium-sized tomatoes (if time permits) and chop roughly. Add to the courgettes with a finely chopped clove of garlic. Cook slowly until the tomato is soft but not mushy. Season with pepper and salt and add 2–3 tablespoons of chopped fresh basil.

PESTO
Makes 1 small jar

There are many good recipes for pesto, using a variety of ingredients, including ones where other herbs are included or replace the traditional basil. Some substitute different nuts for the usual pine nuts, and some include extras such as dried tomatoes. For this book we decided to look back to the traditional recipes from Genoa, and start again. Our reference was *The Classic Italian Cookbook* by Marcella Hazan, first published in 1973, which won the prestigious André Simon Memorial Fund Prize in 1980.

Marcella Hazan, a respected writer and teacher of Italian cooking, explains that Genovese basil sauce, known as pesto, is made from fresh basil, garlic, cheese and olive oil. In Genoa they use equal quantities of Parmesan cheese and a pecorino cheese made from sheep's milk. The traditional recipes do not include pine nuts but most modern versions do. We decided to follow Marcella Hazan's instructions and make our pesto in a mortar and pestle. This was hard work, as we expected, but worth the effort. Instructions are also given for making pesto in a blender or food processor, and this is the preferred method when making large quantities for the freezer.

2 tablespoons pine nuts
1 clove garlic, peeled
50 g freshly harvested basil leaves, stripped from the stalks
25 g grated Parmesan cheese
1 tablespoon grated pecorino cheese, optional (Whitestone in Oamaru, New Zealand make an excellent local variety)
4 tablespoons extra virgin olive oil (avoid oil with a strong flavour: it may be rancid)
2 tablespoons softened butter, optional

Using a mortar and pestle, crush the garlic first and then the pine nuts until well broken up. Add the basil leaves, torn into small pieces. You may need to add the leaves in 2 batches if your mortar is on the small side. Grind the ingredients to form a paste. Add the cheese and continue grinding until the mixture is evenly blended. Measure the oil into a small jug and pour a few drops at a time into the basil mixture. Beat with a wooden spoon between additions. Finally beat in the butter, if used. Spoon into a small jar, cover tightly and store in a refrigerator for up to a week.

PESTO MADE IN A BLENDER OR FOOD PROCESSOR
Makes 2 small jars

This recipe makes twice as much as the previous one and is designed to be frozen. Marcella Hazan suggests omitting the cheese for frozen pesto, as a fresher taste is achieved when this is added after thawing. If this larger batch of pesto is not to be frozen but used within a few weeks, transfer it to a small bowl and beat in 50 g freshly grated Parmesan cheese. This gives a better texture than processing it with the other ingredients.

100 g freshly harvested basil leaves, stripped from the stalks
25 g pine nuts
2 cloves garlic, peeled and crushed
125 ml olive oil (keep extra virgin olive oil for pesto to be eaten immediately, not frozen)

Process all the ingredients in a blender or food processor until a smooth paste is obtained. You will need to stop from time to time to scrape the ingredients down from the sides. Spoon the paste into small containers for freezing, or cut pieces of plastic food film, approximately 20 cm square, and place in medium-sized muffin pans. Fill the lined pans with pesto and loosely fold the plastic food film over the top to seal. When frozen, remove from the pans and transfer to a freezer bag.

When required, thaw overnight in a refrigerator. Beat in 1–2 tablespoons of Parmesan, depending on the quantity of thawed pesto.

Marcella Hazan offers a good tip for mixing pesto into cooked pasta: thin it with a little hot pasta water before adding.

SOUPE AU PISTOU
Serves 4 as a main-dish soup

This is our version of the classic French vegetable soup which gets its name from the bright green basil sauce (the French version of pesto) called pistou. You can vary the vegetables depending on what is in season.

1/2 cup dried haricot beans, soaked overnight in plenty of cold water
2 tablespoons oil
1 onion, chopped
1 clove garlic, very finely chopped
400 g can peeled tomatoes in juice
1 tablespoon tomato paste
3 cups chicken stock
2 medium-sized waxy potatoes, scrubbed or scraped and diced
2 carrots, peeled and diced
2 small sticks celery, sliced
2 courgettes, diced
100 g green beans or snow peas, cut into 2 cm lengths
1 bay leaf
salt to taste
black pepper

Pistou
2 cloves garlic, finely chopped
1 cup loosely packed basil leaves
3 tablespoons extra virgin olive oil

freshly grated Parmesan cheese as topping

In a large saucepan, heat the oil and sauté the onion and garlic until soft. Add the tomatoes plus their juice and break up with a wooden spoon. Add the tomato paste and stir to mix in. Add the stock. Drain the haricot beans and rinse thoroughly, drain again and add to the saucepan. Bring to the boil and simmer for 30–40 minutes, covered, until the beans are almost tender. Add the potatoes, carrots and celery and cook for another 20 minutes. Add the courgettes, bay leaf, fresh beans or peas, and cook for a further 5 minutes or until the haricot beans and the other vegetables are tender. Taste for seasoning.

Make the pistou by pounding the garlic and torn basil leaves with a pestle in a mortar until a paste is formed. Gradually work in the oil to form a smooth sauce. Pour into a small bowl for serving.

Ladle the soup into deep bowls and serve. Offer the pistou and Parmesan to be added and stirred into each bowl.

MUSHROOM & CORN CHOWDER WITH BASIL
Serves 4 as a main-dish soup

Basil is usually associated with Mediterranean-style cooking but this doesn't always have to be the case, as this recipe demonstrates. The chowder has a smooth creamy base with chunks of mushroom (use field mushrooms if you are lucky enough to have some) and sweet yellow corn kernels. We have used a can of corn but fresh kernels scraped off the cobs are even better.

2 tablespoons oil
1 medium-sized onion, finely chopped
2 cloves garlic, very finely chopped
300 g mushrooms, diced
400 g can of whole kernel or cream-style corn, or
2 cups of fresh kernels scraped from the cobs
1 cup chicken stock
2 teaspoons cornflour
1 1/2 cups evaporated milk (one 375 g can)
2 tablespoons dry sherry
black pepper
salt to taste
3–4 tablespoons chopped basil

In a large saucepan, heat the oil and sauté the onion and garlic until soft. Add the mushrooms and cook over a fairly high heat, stirring frequently, until they soften and begin to brown and all the liquid has evaporated. Stir in the corn and chicken stock. Bring to the boil and simmer gently for a few minutes until the mushrooms and corn (if you are using fresh kernels) are cooked. Measure the cornflour into a cup and mix with a little of the evaporated milk until smooth. Pour the remainder of the milk into the soup. Reheat to just below boiling point. Pour in the cornflour mix and stir until slightly thickened. Remove from the heat. Add the sherry, seasoning and basil. Serve immediately.

VIETNAMESE-STYLE CHICKEN & CABBAGE SALAD WITH PURPLE BASIL
Serves 4

Purple basil provides an authentic flavour and visual enjoyment to this simple and fresh-tasting salad. Serve it as a first course or a light main meal.

Poaching liquid
500 ml water
1 tablespoon rice vinegar
1 slice fresh ginger
1 slice lemon
1 leaf rau răm (Vietnamese mint), (optional)
half a small onion, sliced

3 chicken breasts (about 500 g), skins removed

500 g Chinese cabbage, finely shredded
4 spring onions, sliced (include some of the green part)
2 tablespoons shredded purple basil, plus 2 more for garnishing

Dressing
2 cloves garlic, very finely chopped
2 tablespoons peanut oil
1 1/2 tablespoons lemon juice
1 tablespoon fish sauce
2 teaspoons sugar

In a large pan with a lid, combine the poaching ingredients. Bring to boiling point and add the chicken. Lower the heat and maintain just simmering. Cover the pan and cook the chicken for about 10 minutes or until tender. Use a slotted spoon to transfer to a plate to cool.

Meanwhile, place the cabbage, spring onions and first 2 tablespoons of basil in a large bowl. As soon as the chicken is cool enough to handle, slice it thinly across the grain. Add to the cabbage mixture. Combine the dressing ingredients and pour over the salad. Toss gently to mix thoroughly.

Spoon the salad into a serving bowl and garnish with the extra basil. Serve immediately or chill for up to an hour.

FRESH TOMATO & BASIL PASTA SAUCE
Serves 2

The combination of a chilled, colourful and flavoursome sauce to top a bowl of steaming pasta makes a refreshing change from the usual hot versions.

250 g ripe tomatoes, diced into 1 cm pieces
1 clove garlic, very finely chopped
3 tablespoons extra virgin olive oil
1 tablespoon red wine vinegar
1/4 teaspoon salt
black pepper
2 tablespoons chopped sweet basil
freshly grated Parmesan cheese

In a small bowl, combine all the ingredients except for the basil and Parmesan cheese. Cover and chill for 30 minutes.

Meanwhile, cook your pasta and drain. Serve in pasta bowls with the sauce spooned over the top. Sprinkle with the basil and serve immediately. Pass the Parmesan cheese around as an optional extra.

RICH TOMATO & VEGETABLE PASTA SAUCE
Serves 4–6

Use ripe tomatoes for a full-flavoured sauce. Serve with green pasta for an attractive colour contrast.

2 tablespoons oil
1 large-sized onion, chopped
1 clove garlic, finely chopped
1 medium-sized carrot, grated
1 stick celery, finely sliced
750 g tomatoes, skinned and chopped
1 bay leaf
3 tablespoons chopped fresh basil plus extra for garnishing
1–2 tablespoons tomato paste (depending on how intense a flavour you prefer)
1/2 teaspoon salt
1/2 teaspoon sugar
black pepper
freshly grated Parmesan cheese as a topping

Heat the oil in a heavy-based saucepan. Sauté the onion and garlic for a few minutes. Add the carrot and celery and continue to cook for a few more minutes. Add the tomatoes and remaining ingredients except the Parmesan cheese. Simmer gently for about 30 minutes or until thick. Cover with a lid for most of the cooking time. Uncover if the sauce is too thin. Remove the bay leaf.

To serve: boil the required quantity of pasta. While it is cooking, gently reheat the sauce. As soon as the pasta is cooked and drained, dish it up into bowls. Spoon the hot sauce on top. Sprinkle with freshly grated Parmesan cheese and the extra basil, finely chopped.

POLENTA WITH A BASIL, CAPSICUM & TOMATO SAUCE
Serves 2–3

Using one of the fast-cooking polentas, this scrumptious Italian-style lunch or main-meal dish can be prepared in about 30 minutes. The sauce combines cooked tomatoes, capsicum and lots of basil, and then just prior to serving a repeat of the same ingredients is added but not cooked. The result is a flavoursome but fresh-tasting sauce which enhances the creamy polenta and Parmesan cheese.

Sauce
700 g ripe tomatoes
2 small yellow capsicums, deseeded and chopped
1 cup chopped basil
2 cloves garlic, very finely chopped
1/4 teaspoon salt
black pepper

Polenta
2 cups milk
1/2 cup chicken stock
150 g quick-cooking polenta
1 teaspoon finely chopped sage
1/4 teaspoon salt
black pepper
1/2 cup freshly grated Parmesan cheese

Pour boiling water over 500 g of the tomatoes and leave for 12 seconds. Drain and remove the skins. Chop roughly, discarding cores, and place in a small saucepan. Add one of the capsicums, half of the basil, the garlic, salt and pepper. Simmer over a moderate heat for 15–20 minutes or until the mixture is sauce-like. Remove from the heat.

Meanwhile, measure the milk and stock into a heavy-based saucepan. Heat to boiling point. Stir in the polenta, sage and salt. Simmer, stirring constantly until thick. Turn off the heat source, cover the saucepan and allow to stand for 10 minutes. Add the pepper and Parmesan cheese and stir to mix through.

While the polenta is standing, chop the remaining tomatoes (not skinned) and just before serving add them along with the remaining capsicum and basil. Stir to mix and check seasoning.

Spoon the polenta into a shallow serving dish and spread to fill. Top with the tomato sauce and serve immediately.

BASIL BREAD

A tomato- and basil-flavoured bread makes a change from the still popular garlic version.

75 g butter, softened but not melted
1 tablespoon tomato paste
1 clove garlic, very finely chopped
1 tablespoon chopped fresh basil (or 1 teaspoon dried basil)

1 French bread stick or baguette

In a small bowl, combine the butter, tomato paste, garlic and basil. Mix thoroughly.

Cut the bread diagonally part-way through into 3 cm slices. Be careful not to cut right through the base. Spread the slices with the butter and press together. Wrap the bread in aluminium foil and bake at 150°C for 15–20 minutes. Unwrap and bake for a further 5 minutes if a crisp loaf is preferred.

LEMON BASIL FRUIT SAUCE
Serves 4–6

The idea for this recipe came from *Country Gardens* magazine (May 1998). We enjoy it made with lemon basil but the original suggested substituting 'plain' basil (we presume they mean sweet basil) plus 3/4 teaspoon of grated lemon rind.

Dressing
1/2 cup plain yoghurt
1/2 cup low fat or ordinary sour cream
2 tablespoons honey (warmed if stiff)
2 tablespoons orange juice
2 tablespoons lemon juice
3–4 tablespoons chopped lemon basil leaves (reserve a few small sprigs to use as a garnish)

a selection of 3 or 4 prepared fruits to cover a platter or to fill individual small bowls, from strawberries, fresh pineapple, kiwifruit (green and gold), oranges, bananas, stone fruit, colourful apples, pears

Mix all the dressing ingredients together in a small bowl. Cover and chill for at least 1 hour or overnight.

Just before serving, arrange the fruit on the platter or in the bowls. Garnish with the lemon basil sprigs. Pass the sauce around in a small bowl to be spooned over individual servings.

bay

Bay trees (*Laurus nobilis*) can grow to 20 m high, forming beautiful, dark-leaved evergreen specimens. Very few of us have room for one of these. Fortunately for gardening cooks, bay trees are slow growing and respond well to shaping into shrubs or even into statuesque topiary forms. They also make attractive container shrubs which can be easily protected, if needed, during cold winter months. In mild climates they can be used to make permanent edible hedges. Although slow growing, these can be trained higher than 1.5 m.

The common names include sweet bay, bay laurel and sweet laurel. As these reveal, confusion surrounds the identification of the culinary bay. The garden trees with which it may be confused are the Portuguese laurel (*Prunus lusitanica*) and the poisonous cherry laurel (*P. laurocerasus*). The leaf of the cherry laurel is a glossy green and that of the Portuguese laurel a darker green. When you hold either of these leaves up to the light only the main side veins are visible, and if you tear a leaf in half there is no obvious smell. The leaf of the culinary bay is dark-coloured when older (like the Portuguese laurel) but when held up to the light an intricate network of veins and veinlets becomes obvious. When torn, the leaf emits a sweet, spicy fragrance.

Bay leaves dry particularly well, with some food writers even claiming that their flavour is better than the fresh. All keen cooks should have a bay tree and, as Tom Stobart put it, 'No kitchen should exist without bay leaves, and they should be used as a matter of habit.'

VARIETIES

There appears to be quite a variation in leaf shapes among the bay trees we have seen. Mary's treasured pair, one in a tub in a sheltered courtyard and the other coping well with the odd −10°C frost in an open border, have ovate, pointed, flat leaves with smooth, not crinkled, edges. They were propagated from the original small plant given to Mary over 40 years ago and shifted with her three times to new homes. By the time of the last shift her bay, growing beside the compost bins, was racing to equal the height of the two-storeyed house nearby and far too big to shift again. Thirty cuttings were taken and nurtured for 18 months, with the previously mentioned pair being the only two to strike. We may be biased but, having sniffed the aroma of many bays in other gardens, we feel that this particular form is superior. We seldom see our flat-leaved type for sale, instead the crinkly-edged one is the most common.

There are 3 named cultivars listed in British catalogues: *Laurus nobilis* forma *angustifolia*, with narrow leaves; *L. n.* 'Aurea', which has golden leaves; and *L. n.* 'Crispa', with wavy-edged leaves. The latter may be the one we see most often in garden centres.

CULTIVATION

Bay is described as being frost hardy down to −5°C. In our experience, they are hardy to at least −10°C. However, we don't know how they would cope with continuous hard frosts and ground that does not thaw each day. Young plants are far more vulnerable to cold conditions (both frosts and winds) and in marginal climates should be grown on for 2–3 years as movable container plants. Alternatively, young plants that are placed in a permanent outdoor position should be mulched well with straw and provided with a frame and a covering of double frost cloth on cold nights. Fortunately for cooks living in places that experience very hard winters, bay trees thrive in tubs, making them relatively easy to shift to warm places when required.

Bay trees will grow well in either full sun or partial shade. Some midday shade is desirable in hot climates. They prefer a moderately rich, well-drained soil, and will tolerate dry conditions reasonably well. When temperatures reach 30°C plus and humidity is low, a deep watering is beneficial.

Position your outdoor bay where it can grow, unrestricted, to the shape you desire. They make distinctive garden focal points, either clipped as a large shrub or trained as a specimen tree. Ensure that the cook has easy access for picking.

Bay trees are propagated commercially from cuttings. As these may take many months to strike and are then slow growing, it is not surprising that a well-grown bay tree is expensive to buy. Keen home gardeners can also use this method, but ideally would need a heating pad and a controlled environment, such as a misting unit. Clear plastic bags held free of the leaves by wire hoops are a simple alternative. Moisture levels must be maintained and fungal diseases watched for. Take semi-hardwood cuttings at almost any time of the year (see page 14 for more information).

Some old established bay trees sucker at their bases and it is possible, though not easy, to dig these suckers up with some roots attached. If you are successful, pot them up carefully in free-draining mix and cover with clear plastic bags for a few weeks to help prevent excessive wilting. Grow on in pots for a year before planting out.

Propagation from seed is reported to be chancy and difficult.

The main ongoing care required for bay trees in small gardens is regular trimming to maintain size and shape. This is best done in spring to promote new growth. To train a bay into an attractive small specimen tree, encourage it to grow on one central stem by removing any suckers from the base and progressively trimming laterals up to the desired trunk height. The top can then

Bay

BAY

(*Laurus nobilis*)

Before we began writing this book, we imagined that bay leaves had a long and glorious history, in keeping with their symbolic significance in the classical civilisations of Greece and Rome—for bay leaves come from the bay or sweet laurel, aptly named *Laurus nobilis*. Laurel wreaths were worn by winners at Greek games, by victorious Roman generals and emperors, and by the best poets. We perpetuate this symbolism in the award of the baccalaureate, the recognition of the poet laureate, and in the design of the Royal Air Force badge. Sadly, the bay never achieved high honours in the English kitchen, though it has been important in French cuisine for several hundred years.

To some extent this can be attributed to the English climate—extreme winters can seriously damage or even kill bay trees grown outdoors, even in the southern counties. But it may also result from the name 'laurel', which the bay unfortunately shared with several poisonous evergreens introduced to Britain over the past five hundred years: the cherry laurel (*Prunus laurocerasus*), the rose laurel or oleander (*Nerium oleander*) and the deadly mountain laurel (*Kalmia latifolia*).

We shouldn't blame English herbalists for this loose naming, since the Greek and Roman writers had been unable to sort out the varieties of berry-bearing evergreens growing wild around the shores of the Mediterranean. It seems that the Greeks called the sweet bay *daphne*, referring to one of their myths involving the metamorphosis of a beautiful nymph pursued by a god. To escape Apollo, Daphne was turned into a laurel. He subsequently wore her leaves around his head—but was this first laurel wreath a symbol of victory or a consolation prize? The Greek botanist Theophrastus knew of many cultivated and wild forms of laurel, and of its habit of sending up new shoots from its rootstock.

The Romans called the sweet bay *laurus*, along with several other trees and shrubs, some undoubtedly varieties of bay but others separate species. Pliny wrote at length about the confusion, referring to types with pale leaves, crinkled leaves, red berries, blue berries, no berries, dwarf habit or very large size. His description of a shrubby *laurus* with blackish red berries whose leaves produce a burning taste in the mouth may apply to the cherry laurel, which we now know contains a cyanogenic glycoside in its leaves that releases prussic (hydrocyanic) acid in the presence of water and an enzyme. From both their painted frescoes and

writings, it is clear that the Romans used laurels as ornamentals in their gardens, and in wreaths for the many religious and municipal ceremonies in their calendar. Laurels were used far more as medicine than in the Roman kitchen. Apicius gives only nine recipes that required laurel leaves, and seven calling for the berries (*bacae lauri*).

It was this Latin word for berry, *baca* or *bacca*, that gave rise to the English name 'bay' about the 15th century. Before that time the tree was a 'lauri' or 'laurier', and it figured in mediaeval manuscripts as both a forest tree and garden occupant. Its evergreen foliage symbolised everlasting constancy. Strangely, the mediaeval recipe books we have consulted mention neither bay nor laurel.

By 1548, 'baye trees' were described as common in gardens in southern England. They were also grown in pots. When John Gerard wrote his *Herball* in 1597, he referred primarily to the medicinal virtues of the bay laurel, then added: 'The later Physitians doe oftentimes use to boyle the leaves of Laurell with divers meats, especially fishes, and by so doing there happeneth no desire of vomiting: but the meat seasoned herewith becommeth more savory and better for the stomacke'. Over time the medical reasons for adding bay leaves to cooking liquor seem to have been forgotten and the plant was increasingly valued for its flavour.

In 1629 John Parkinson transferred the name 'bay' to each member of the extended family of laurels. Thus the poisonous oleander became the 'rose bay' and the mezereon daphne the 'dwarfe baye'. For him, the poisonous properties of some of the group were overshadowed by their many uses 'both for pleasure and profit, both for ornament and for use, both for honest Civill uses, and for Physicke, yea both for the sicke and for the sound, both for the living and for the dead'. Any culinary value the bays might have was unimportant to him.

During the 17th century, gentlemen flower-fanciers became more interested in the cherry laurel than the bay. Compared with the common bay, it had 'most beautifull large shining green leaves' and was much hardier. It could also be clipped into thick, tall hedges, which were very fashionable in Western European gardens at that period. Its bitter leaves meant that animals left it well alone. Bay trees were sometimes still to be found in the formal parterre garden, clipped into pyramid or round-headed shapes. London gardeners found that the bay coped better with the growing air pollution than the cherry laurel. There was some use for bay clippings in the early 18th-century English kitchen, where French sauces, marinated meat and fish dishes, and braised meats, many flavoured with bay leaves rather than the traditional mace, were being adopted and simplified. Before this, bay leaves were to be found mainly in pickling liquor.

To confuse the question of identification, the practice of adding cherry laurel leaves to food and beverages shows up in the early 18th century. The liqueur known as ratafia was normally made by soaking bruised apricot kernels in brandy for four to five days, before straining off the liquid and sweetening it. In 1736 Professor Richard Bradley revealed a deceased distiller's secret recipe which achieved the same flavour of bitter almonds by soaking the buds of young cherry laurel branches in the brandy. This practice was extended to making custards and creams—laurel leaves were simmered with the milk or cream before the eggs were added. Then at the end of the 18th century a potentially more dangerous modification appeared. Recipes that used to include bay leaves in a marinade now substituted the words 'laurel leaves', as though they were the same. To complete the confusion, pudding recipes from the 1840s changed laurel to bay, obviously in ignorance of the original intention to impart the flavour of bitter almonds.

No wonder Mrs Beeton erred on the side of caution when discussing the bay in her *Book of Household Management*. 'It ought to be known,' she warned, 'that there are two kinds of bay trees,—the Classic laurel, whose leaves are comparatively harmless, and the Cherry laurel, which is the one whose leaves are employed in cookery. They have a kernel-like flavour, and are used in blanc-mange, puddings, custards, &c., but, when acted upon by water, they develop prussic acid, and therefore, but a small number of the leaves should be used at a time.' Mrs Beeton seems to have been unaware that the bay ever had culinary uses. These misunderstandings continued well into the 20th century when a herb writer passed on the suggestion that 'a bay leaf placed under the paper in a drawer will keep silverfish away because it gives off hydrocyanic acid as it dries'. In fact, it is the leaf of the cherry laurel, not the sweet bay, that contains the precursor to this poison, and moisture is needed to release it.

The New Zealand recipe books that our mother used only occasionally called for bay leaves—a single leaf might be specified for an oxtail stew or soup, and three for pickled ox tongue. Our custards were flavoured with vanilla essence, and we left laurel leaves well alone. The reintroduction of the bay to our kitchens was associated with the appearance of oven-to-table casseroles and the French-inspired recipes that accompanied them. By the 1970s serious cooks began to consider the bay tree an essential feature of their herb collections. We may now have reached the point where, for the first time in its long history, the bay is important only in the kitchen.

be rounded into a large ball, or left in a natural form. Bay trees can be cut back without any ill effects.

If maximum growth is required, feed bay trees twice a year, in early spring and again in early summer. Mulch in spring with a good compost or well-rotted manure. In frosty areas, mulch the root area with straw or leaves in autumn. Water well during dry, hot summers.

Scale insects are reported to be a problem for some gardeners. These are best controlled by spraying with an appropriate oil or scrubbing them off with soapy water.

GROWING IN CONTAINERS

Bay makes a handsome container shrub, or small tree, happy to be clipped at regular intervals and rewarding the cook with a handy, year-round supply of fresh leaves. Its requirements are easily met: a free-draining potting mix (5 parts proprietary tub mix to 1 part horticultural grit) in a container large enough to hold its root system and allow some room for growth. It should never be allowed to dry out completely. In the spring it should be given a feed with a liquid fertiliser and, if your bay has outgrown its pot, this should be repeated monthly. It should be positioned outside for most of the year and receive at least half of each day's sunshine. If necessary, it can be moved for the winter months to a frost-free location. A container-grown bay is more vulnerable to frost damage, so remember to give it additional protection if temperatures drop below −5°C.

If your bay is under cover, such as house eaves or on a verandah, and misses out on rainfall, then a regular spraying from the hose will wash its leaves free of dust and city pollution. Until your bay has reached its desired size, it should be repotted into a larger container every 1–2 years. Once fully grown, it will need to be given regular additions of fertiliser, and every 2–3 years a change of potting mix. Remove it from its container and place in a wheelbarrow. Use the hose to thoroughly wet the root ball. Use your hands to gently untangle the roots, and wash away some of the old potting mix. Any very long, tangled roots can be pruned. Replant with a quality tub mix.

HARVESTING

Bay leaves can be picked as required. Harvest individual mature leaves by pulling off with a sharp downwards tug. Older leaves, darker coloured and leathery, have the best flavour. Alternatively, combine harvesting with shaping and use secateurs to prune whole branches.

Bay is one of the best herbs for drying. Cut whole branches and hang them upside down inside brown paper bags in an airy, warm place. Once they are crisp, carefully strip the leaves, without breaking, from the stems. Store in airtight containers away from light. Alternatively, dry individually picked leaves in a dehydrator or in a microwave (see pages 16–17).

IN THE KITCHEN

Bay leaves are added to dishes at the beginning of preparation or cooking and removed at the end before serving. Cooked bay leaves remain tough and are not eaten.

Bay leaves release their flavour best when they are torn. As removing whole leaves from a dish is easier than removing fragments, we suggest that you tear each leaf twice along each side, towards the centre, but without severing the main vein.

There are opposing views about the relative intensity of flavour of fresh and dried bay leaves. Some writers are adamant that the flavour becomes stronger and sweeter when the leaves are dried. In our opinion, the aroma of a torn, freshly picked leaf is much more pronounced than that of a dried one, especially if the latter is more than a month or two old. Our recipes specify fresh leaves, but if you have to use dried ones, add an extra 1 or 2. We suggest a 'use by' date for dried bay of 6 months. If buying, look for green, unbroken leaves.

When trimming a bay tree you may end up with a surplus of leaves to give away. They store particularly well for several months in resealable plastic bags in a refrigerator, and make a welcome gift for any keen cook with no tree of their own.

HOW TO USE BAY LEAVES
- The addition of bay to soups, stew and sauces is well known. Sometimes they are used on their own, or more often included in a bouquet garni (see page 180).
- Bay has a long tradition as a meat flavouring. Insert pieces of bay leaf into slits cut in pork, veal, beef or lamb roasts. Line a baking pan with whole leaves before cooking a terrine or meat loaf.
- Include bay leaves in any meat marinade. Always add bay leaves to the liquor when boiling corned beef, pickled pork or tongue.
- Use 12 fresh bay leaves and 2 cloves of garlic to give a delightful fragrance and flavour to a roast chicken. Loosen the chicken skin from the flesh by working your hand around under the skin, being careful not to tear it. Put 2 bay leaves in the cavity of the bird and insert the remaining leaves evenly under the skin on both sides. Spread thin slices of garlic under the skin as well. Season well with salt and pepper. Tie the legs and wings closely to the body. Place on a greased rack, breast side up, and brush with oil. Roast at 180°C for 55 minutes per kilo. Serve hot or cold.
- Christmas or mid-winter solstice dinner would not be complete without our grandmother's bread sauce to accompany the roast chicken or turkey. Simmer 400 ml of whole milk with a shallot or small onion stuck with 3 whole cloves, a torn fresh bay leaf and 5 peppercorns for 15 minutes. Do not cover. Meanwhile, use a food processor to finely crumble 70 g of crustless white bread. Some purchased breads absorb less liquid than others, so you may have to use extra crumbs. Tip the crumbs into a small bowl. Add 1/4 teaspoon of salt, a pinch of cayenne, a pinch of ground mace, a pinch of freshly grated nutmeg and stir with a fork to mix. Strain the flavoured milk into the crumbs, and stir with a fork. Add a new bay leaf. Cover the bowl and allow to steep until the breadcrumbs have absorbed the milk. Reheat just before serving and stir in

1–3 tablespoons of cream to obtain a thick, sauce-like consistency. Remove the bay leaf.

- Fresh bay leaves impart a subtle flavour to vegetables. Use with carrots, artichokes, potatoes, broad beans, beetroot, cauliflower, broccoli and cabbage. Bay reduces the unpleasant odour of cooking cauliflower. Lay torn bay leaves over seasoned pumpkin or potatoes before roasting in a little oil.
- Bay leaves are equally good when used to flavour sweet foods. Infuse fresh leaves in milk or cream for custards (see page 41), rice puddings, ice-cream and junket (see page 41. Infuse bay leaves in a syrup for poaching pears, fruit compotes or apple sauce.
- Bay leaves are essential in a rich venison casserole, along with crushed juniper berries.
- Add a torn fresh bay leaf to the water for polenta or couscous. Include a leaf in the sauce for macaroni cheese.
- Bay is an essential herb in a court bouillon for poaching fish. The usual ingredients are water, salt, lemon juice, a sliced onion, garlic, a chopped carrot, peppercorns and herbs such as bay, parsley and lemon thyme.
- Marinate olives in oil flavoured with lemon and fresh bay.
- Add 1 or 2 fresh bay leaves to rich tomato sauces for pasta.
- Include bay leaves with the whole spices in pickling vinegar.

AUNT MAUDE'S MEAT PASTE

This recipe comes from our mother's collection. Sadly, we cannot recall who Aunt Maude was but we do remember her meat paste as made by our grandmother. The original recipe included '4 ounces' of butter, some cooked with the meat, and the remainder melted and poured over the paste before storing in a cool larder. Before the days of refrigeration fat was often used as a short-term preservative. Nowadays it is not needed, so can be omitted with no real loss of flavour or texture. Use the paste as a sandwich filling on fresh wholemeal bread, or spread on toast or small savoury biscuits garnished with slices of cherry tomatoes or gherkins.

500 g lean braising steak, cut into small cubes
1/2 a whole nutmeg, freshly grated
1/2 teaspoon ground mace
pinch of cayenne
plenty of black pepper
1/4–1/2 teaspoon salt
1 tablespoon anchovy sauce or paste
2 fresh bay leaves, torn

Put all the ingredients in the top part of a double boiler or small basin that fits over a saucepan. Cover and steam for 3 hours, stirring after 1 hour. Allow to cool a little. Use a slotted spoon to transfer the meat to a food processor and chop finely. Add the gravy and process until smooth. Spoon into a small bowl and store for 2–3 days in a refrigerator, or freeze in small batches.

MARINATED MUSHROOMS ITALIAN-STYLE
Serves 4–6

Bay, lemon and garlic give a tangy flavour to these moreish mushrooms. Serve them with chunks of focaccia bread.

1/2 cup mild-flavoured oil
1/3 cup water
4 tablespoons lemon juice
2 fresh bay leaves, torn
2 cloves garlic, flattened with the side of a knife
6 black peppercorns
1 teaspoon salt
400 g small white button mushrooms

Combine all the ingredients, except the mushrooms, in a large pan with a lid. Simmer for 15 minutes. Strain and return to the pan. Add the mushrooms and simmer, turning them over once, for 5 minutes. Leave to cool in the marinade. Serve at room temperature. Store in a refrigerator for up to 2 days.

LENTIL & VEGETABLE SOUP
Serves 6–8

This hearty and filling soup makes a lunch or main-course meal. The recipe is designed to be flexible so that you can use any available vegetables. The 3 fresh bay leaves release a background warmth and sweetness which permeates the soup and the kitchen during the long slow cooking. Lentil soups often taste heavy—this one is lightened with the last-minute addition of chopped tomatoes, red wine and lemon juice.

1 1/2 cups brown lentils (soak for 2 hours or overnight)
2 tablespoons oil
2 medium-sized onions, chopped
2 cloves garlic, finely chopped
2 teaspoons each of coriander and cumin seeds, freshly roasted and ground
2 teaspoons paprika
6–8 cups vegetables, cut into 1–2 cm pieces
7–8 cups of water, depending on desired consistency
1 tablespoon mushroom stock powder
3 fresh bay leaves, torn
black pepper

1 1/2 cups chopped tomatoes
2 tablespoons red wine or port
2 tablespoons lemon juice
1 tablespoon red wine vinegar
1 1/2 tablespoons brown sugar
salt to taste
chopped parsley for garnishing

In a large saucepan, heat the oil and sauté the onions and garlic until soft. Add the spices and stir-fry for 2–3 minutes. Add the vegetables and continue to stir-fry for a few more minutes. Drain the lentils and add to the vegetables, along with the water, stock powder, bay leaves and pepper. Simmer slowly for 1 1/2 hours, stirring occasionally.

Just before serving, stir in the tomatoes, red wine or port, lemon juice, wine vinegar and sugar. Stir to mix and taste, adding salt if needed. Ladle into large soup bowls and garnish with the chopped parsley.

CHICKEN & POTATO CURRY WITH THREE BAY LEAVES
Serves 6–8

One often sees bay leaves listed in curry recipes from books in English about Indian cuisine. In northern India, the Indian bay (*Cinnamomum tamala*) is the herb or spice that is commonly used. Since Indian bay leaves are not usually available in the West, most writers suggest the leaf of the Mediterranean bay (*Laurus nobilis*) instead. This substitution is acceptable, providing we realise that the taste is not the same. Indian bay leaves are reported to be strongly aromatic and reminiscent of cinnamon. Our curry recipe is rich in sweet spices and lean on chilli, making it typical in flavour of the northern Indian cuisines.

3 tablespoons oil or ghee
one 4 cm cinnamon stick, crumbled
2 whole cardamom pods, flattened with the back of a spoon
3 fresh bay leaves
3 whole cloves
2 large onions, chopped

5 cm piece of fresh ginger, peeled and chopped
4 cloves garlic, finely chopped
1/4 teaspoon commercially prepared chilli
2 teaspoons ground turmeric
1 teaspoon salt
1 tablespoon oil

one large chicken piece per serving (skins removed)
1 1/2 cups water
3 large tomatoes, chopped (or 400 g can of tomatoes in juice)
500–750 g potatoes, peeled and diced
1 teaspoon garam masala (see page 59)

Heat the oil in a large pan. Add the cinnamon, cardamom, bay leaves and cloves. Sauté for a few minutes. Add the onions and sauté until golden.

Meanwhile, grind the ginger and garlic in a mortar and pestle, together with the chilli, turmeric, salt and 1 tablespoon of oil, or chop the ginger and garlic very finely and combine with these ingredients in a cup. Add to the onion mixture and continue cooking for a further 3 minutes. Add the chicken pieces and sauté gently for 5 minutes on each side. Add the water, tomatoes and potatoes. Cover the pan and simmer slowly until the chicken and potatoes are tender. Sprinkle with the garam masala just before serving.

HONEY BAY CUSTARDS WITH A TOUCH OF RUM
Serves 6

These dreamy custards are smooth, rich and a real treat. Baked and served in small ramekins or individual soufflé dishes, they are simple to prepare and can be cooked a day ahead. We like to serve them accompanied with a bowl of fresh blueberries or blackcurrants, to be passed around for each person to sprinkle a few over their custard.

300 ml milk
200 ml cream
2 fresh bay leaves, torn
3 yolks from medium-sized eggs
3 tablespoons clover honey (warmed if stiff)
4 teaspoons rum

Heat the milk, cream and bay leaves together gently in a small heavy-based saucepan until just at boiling point. Remove from the heat, cover, and leave to infuse for about 30 minutes.

Preheat the oven to 180°C. Grease six 150 ml (about 2/3 cup) ramekins or custard cups. In a medium-sized bowl, beat the yolks and honey together until creamy. Remove the bay leaves from the milk and reheat it to almost boiling point. Whisk the hot milk into the egg mixture. Add the rum and whisk again. Pour into the 6 ramekins. Place in a baking dish filled with boiling water to half-way up the depth of the ramekins. Bake for 25–30 minutes. Shake gently to see if the custards are set. Remove from the hot water and cool to room temperature. Chill for 3–4 hours or overnight.

BAY LEAF JUNKET
Serves 2

We were reminded of junket by a recipe that appeared in a London weekend newspaper last year. Obviously, this humble pudding had been rediscovered and was now 'in fashion'. When we were made to eat junket as children, it was served at room temperature so it is not surprising that it was disliked. Served chilled, with a thin layer of cream trickled over it and a generous sprinkling of crunchy demerara sugar, it deserves the high status it now enjoys. The newspaper recipe suggested serving it with ripe figs— we have found that chopped fresh plums, properly ripe, are excellent too.

300 ml whole milk
3 fresh bay leaves, torn
1/2 teaspoon rennet
thin cream
demerara sugar

Pour the milk into a small saucepan, add the bay leaves and leave to infuse for 2 hours. Warm the milk to just above blood heat (43°C: when you dip your finger into the milk it should feel comfortably warm). Remove the bay leaves. Stir in the rennet and pour into 2 small glass or earthenware bowls. Leave at room temperature for 10 minutes and then cover and place in a refrigerator for 2 hours to chill. To serve, pour a thin layer of cream over the top of each bowl and sprinkle with about a teaspoon of demerara sugar.

Chervil (*Anthriscus cerefolium*) is the most delicately flavoured herb of all, and needs to be harvested in handfuls rather than sprigs. An indispensable ingredient in French cuisine, its mild anise flavour and soft texture have recently been rediscovered by many cooks, making it a sought-after and fashionable herb. As it is only rarely available for purchase, home-grown harvest is the only way to ensure a regular supply.

Gardeners who have grown chervil will be quick to point out that it is not easy to provide a year-round supply in sufficient quantities to satisfy kitchen demands. However, with an understanding of chervil's life cycle and cultural requirements, it is possible, in all but the hottest and driest areas, to grow luscious crops during many months of the year. In cooler climates it is one of only a few salad herbs that can be cut in winter and early spring. Gardening cooks in warmer places may have to content themselves with good supplies only during their cooler months.

Chervil has very pretty, fragile, feathery, light green foliage which can be used to advantage in shady corners to please the eye as well as the palate.

VARIETIES

According to most herb writers, there are two types of chervil: plain leaved and curly leaved. We have purchased seed and grown the so-called curly-leaved variety as the only choice in catalogues. Our plants have surprisingly flat leaves considering their description. We have also grown a selected cultivar, 'Brussel's Winter', which is reputed to be slow bolting. Our trial crops of this have certainly produced an abundance of leaves before inevitably running to seed.

It is often our self-sown crops that produce pickings for the longest periods. This is probably due to the fact that the plants are following their natural cycle and are not being expected to be productive out of season.

CULTIVATION

Chervil is a hardy, short-lived annual which grows best in cooler climates and during short daylight hours. As large quantities are required for the kitchen, plan to sow a short row, thinned to 8–10 plants, every 2–4 weeks. In cold climates, sow from early spring until late autumn and provide cover for winter crops for more productive pickings. In mild but not hot areas, it is possible to sow any time that the soil is workable. In warm to hot areas, sow in late summer and autumn for harvesting over winter and spring. Early spring sowings may also be worth trying.

For winter crops, choose a site which receives full sun; summer crops perform better in dappled or half-shade. Grow on the shady side of taller crops or provide a screen to protect the crop from midday and afternoon sun. Chervil does poorly in full shade even during summer heat. Provide shelter from both cold and hot winds.

Well-drained, light soil rich in compost is preferred. As chervil resents heavy wet soils, improve drainage by building up the bed before sowing. Also add lime if the soil is excessively acid.

As a taprooted plant, chervil resents root disturbance so must be grown from seed sown *in situ* (see page 12).

42

Use fresh seed each year or preferably save your own seed for guaranteed excellent germination rates. The seeds require light to germinate, so either leave uncovered but pressed lightly into the soil or sprinkle with a very light covering of fine soil or seed-sowing mix. It is essential to keep the seed moist during the 7–21 days it may take to germinate. One reliable method of providing both light and moisture, suggested by the writers of *Rodale's Illustrated Encyclopedia of Herbs*, is to sow the seed, which is left uncovered, in a furrow 2.5 cm deep. The seed can then easily be kept damp with fine direct watering. This method is worth trying in particularly dry seasons.

Thinning should be done once the seedlings reach 4–6 cm in height and, if they are very close together, it is easier to pinch off at ground level rather than risk disturbing the roots of neighbouring plants selected to grow on. Thin to a spacing of 15–20 cm between plants.

Chervil cannot tolerate hot dry conditions so it is essential to keep the soil moist, but not wet, at all times. A shortage of water will encourage the plants to produce flower stalks sooner than is desirable and thus shorten the productive harvesting period. During extreme temperatures and droughts, cover damp soil with a thick mulch. Not only will the mulch conserve moisture but it acts as an insulator against very cold or excessively hot soil temperatures.

Chervil

In hot, dry weather, chervil leaves and stalks may turn a mauve- or orange-pink colour. This is caused by sunburn and indicates that temperatures are too warm for ideal growth.

Keep plants weed free and side-dress with a liquid fertiliser to promote leaf growth.

Start picking as soon as the leaf stalks reach a useful size, and keep picking to prolong the harvest. Cut back flower stems as soon as they appear, to stimulate more leaf growth.

In cold climates, cover plants with cloches or sow in a glasshouse or tunnel house to encourage plenty of leaf growth for winter harvesting.

Allow one or two healthy chervil plants to flower and set seed. Unless harvested, the seeds rapidly self-sow, which we find is a bonus providing an extra crop with no effort on our part. Don't forget to maintain soil moisture to ensure the production of good quality seed.

GROWING IN CONTAINERS

With the right conditions, chervil grows well in containers. As large pickings are required for the kitchen, sow in a large container or several smaller ones. Sow again as soon as the first crop reaches harvesting size. Provide similar light conditions to those required by garden crops and remember that, as chervil dislikes heat, most conservatories and sunny windows will be too hot. Instead, grow outside in a sheltered courtyard or balcony with partial shade in summer and maximum sun in winter. The potting mix should be free-draining (add extra horticultural grit) and reasonably rich (see page 15).

HARVESTING

Picking can begin when plants are only 8–10 cm high, about 6–8 weeks after sowing the seed. Harvesting early maximises the usefulness of the crop. Always pick stems from the outside, leaving the inner leaves to continue growing. If cut almost to ground level, plants will grow a new crop of leaves. Chervil wilts easily so gather just prior to use.

IN THE KITCHEN

Chervil is best used fresh and raw, as cooking destroys its flavour and colour. When adding to soups, sauces or other cooked dishes, always do so just before serving.

CHERVIL

(*Anthriscus cerefolium*)

How many annuals or perennials do you know with finely divided foliage and tall flowerheads made up of umbels of tiny white flowers? There are dozens, and they range from the deadly hemlock to the delicate chervil. The herbs caraway, parsley and coriander also fit this description, along with sweet cicely, cow parsley, shepherd's needle and wild chervil. Among the generic names applied to these plants are *Chaerophyllum*, *Scandix* and *Anthriscus*, all three derived from Latin and classical Greek. Following the system of the plant taxonomist Linnaeus, we call our garden chervil *Anthriscus cerefolium*, a combination of these old names. But doing so does not mean that, when Pliny referred to *caerefolium* and Columella to *chaerophylum*, they were describing garden chervil. Similarly, when the Greek writer Theophrastus referred to *anthryskon* as an uncultivated pot-herb and *skandix* as a wild plant, modern translations of these words as chervil and wild chervil should be treated as tentative.

Regardless of how these ancient names should be matched to the range of chervil-like plants, we can say that none were important culinary plants in the ancient Mediterranean civilisations. If mentioned at all—and they are absent from Apicius's cookbook—they were described as lowly, the food of refugees or the poor. Pliny was more interested in wild chervil's reputation for reviving virility in the aged than its role in the kitchen.

It may be significant that the ancestor of our garden chervil was not native to Greece or Italy, but had evolved further north in the Caucasus and south-west Russia. It grows best in temperate conditions with adequate moisture, and is capable of overwintering in open ground in many British gardens. This capacity may explain why garden chervil became much more popular in Central and Western Europe than in the Mediterranean cuisines. In France it achieved the same level of popularity as parsley did in England. Comparing the two, the food writer and Francophile Waverley Root described chervil's odour and flavour as 'more subtle, sweetened by a suggestion of fennel overlaying the parsley taste, and more assertive—which may account for its lack of favor among Anglo-Saxons, easily frightened by tastiness'. This was not always the case, for chervils were mentioned in mediaeval documents on both sides of the English Channel.

In the 16th century, common chervil was one of many pot-herbs, seldom singled out in recipes. The Elizabethan herbalist John Gerard was more interested in the culinary virtues of sweet cicely (which he knew as great chervill, or myrrhe). John Parkinson reinforced this ranking in 1629, writing that the common garden chervil was 'much used of the French and Dutch people, to bee boyled or stewed in a pipkin, eyther by it selfe, or with other herbes, whereof they make a Loblolly'. However, in the second half of the 17th century, garden chervil became an important ingredient of 'small sallets', spring and winter salads composed of young seedlings of cress, mustard, chervil, lettuce and radishes. These remained popular through the 18th century, with chervil being valued for its 'fine biting tast[e]'. All 18th-century commentators classified it as a 'hot' salad herb, an interesting contrast to 20th-century descriptions of its 'delicate flavour'.

The decline of the salad in 19th-century Britain left chervil without a significant place in English cuisine. Herbs that survived this downturn were often those that continued in use as garnishes. In this respect chervil could not compete with parsley, which wilts less readily when picked and discolours less quickly when exposed to heat. On the Continent, however, chervil had much wider usage: it was a key ingredient in the German green sauce, in the French *omelette aux fines herbes*, in ravigote sauces, and Belgian soups.

Renewed interest in international cuisines among English-speaking peoples has brought chervil back into their cookbooks. However, its delicate foliage makes it unsuitable for the handling and marketing that most supermarket produce undergoes. Thus, what started over two millennia ago as a food of the poor has now achieved gourmet status because of the decline of the kitchen garden, its traditional home.

Use chervil as tiny sprigs of leaf, plucked from stems, whole in salads and as a garnish. Stalks and leaves can be chopped or scissored. Use handfuls rather than sprigs in order to appreciate chervil's delicate, slightly sweet aniseed flavour. It will not overpower equally delicate foods. You can afford to be generous in using it.

HOW TO USE CHERVIL

- Sprinkle freely over cooked vegetables, especially peas, tomatoes, aubergines, spinach, asparagus, avocados, carrots, cucumber, mushrooms, potatoes, corn and green beans.
- Add to egg dishes (see pages 46–47 for omelette recipes).
- Garnish simple fish dishes with sprigs or scissored chervil.
- Use by the handful, coarsely scissored, in green salads or potato salads.
- Sprinkle scissored chervil on cream soups.
- Small sprigs make a delicate-textured garnish for canapés.
- Serve cooked, sliced beetroot with sour cream or yoghurt, flavoured with Dijon-style mustard, scissored chives and plenty of chervil.
- Make chervil vinegar (see page 17).
- Preserve the fresh flavour of chervil for a month or two by making herb butter (see pages 18–19) and freezing it in small blocks.
- Add finely chopped chervil to vinaigrette dressings.
- Chervil is an essential ingredient in the classic French herb mixture called fines herbes (see page 180).

SALAD OF CARROTS & COURGETTES WITH A CHERVIL DRESSING
Serves 2 as the only accompanying salad to a main dish, or 4 with other salads.

The flavour of both carrots and courgettes is enhanced with the generous addition of chervil. This is a very fresh-tasting salad which goes well with most main dishes. Make it ahead to save last-minute preparation and to ensure the best flavour.

200 g fresh young carrots, thinly sliced
200 g small green or yellow courgettes, thinly sliced

Dressing
large handful chervil leaves and stalks, roughly scissored
4–5 chives, scissored

3 tablespoons white wine vinegar
1 tablespoon lemon juice
1/3 cup mild-tasting olive oil
black pepper
1/4 teaspoon salt
1/2 teaspoon sugar

Blanch the carrots for 3 minutes and the courgettes for 1 minute (the vegetables should be tender-crisp). Refresh each vegetable with cold water and drain. Pat dry with paper towels.

Combine all the dressing ingredients in a medium-sized bowl and whisk to blend. Add the vegetables and stir to coat well. Chill in the refrigerator for preferably 2 hours or longer for the flavours to blend.

SAUCE RAVIGOTE
Serves 4

The cold version of the classic French sauce ravigote is basically a vinaigrette flavoured with lots of chervil, parsley, chives and tarragon. Other additions may include capers, gherkins, anchovies and sieved hard-cooked egg yolks. Our version is an adaptation of the recipe from Elizabeth David's *French Provincial Cooking*. The eye-catching green colour is perfect with grilled salmon. Serve it also with grilled chicken, other types of fish and steamed vegetables. Use a food processor to simplify the method.

50 g mixed freshly gathered herbs (a good handful each of
chervil and parsley and 4 or 5 sprigs of tarragon and
4 or 5 chives)
4 tablespoons olive oil
2 teaspoons tarragon vinegar (or white wine vinegar)
2 teaspoons lemon juice
black pepper
3 anchovy fillets, drained
1 large gherkin (about 50 g), drained and chopped
1 tablespoon capers, drained

Process the herbs, except the chives, until evenly chopped. Add the oil, vinegar, lemon juice and pepper. Process to form a thick sauce. Add the scissored chives, anchovies, gherkin, and capers. Process briefly to mix well. Serve at room temperature or chilled.

POOR MAN'S AUBERGINE CAVIAR

This favourite dip of the 1970s is worthy of revival. The original recipes were derived from the traditional 'caviars' of Georgia and Moldavia, former republics of the USSR. Our version includes a handful of chervil, which enhances the flavour of the aubergine, toasted nuts to provide substance, and poppy seeds to resemble caviar. We serve the spreading dip in the aubergine shells, as they are too beautiful to discard. Surround the filled shells with sticks of brightly coloured raw vegetables and wedges of toasted pitta bread.

1 medium-sized aubergine (about 400 g)
juice of 1 lemon
2 tablespoons olive oil
1 clove garlic, finely chopped
1/4 cup whole almonds, dry roasted
1/4 cup whole or broken cashews, dry roasted
1/2 cup sour cream
pinch cayenne pepper
1/4 teaspoon salt
1 tablespoon poppy seeds
a small handful chervil, chopped

Cut the aubergine in half lengthwise. Using a sharp teaspoon, carefully remove most of the pulp, leaving about 1 cm intact to ensure that the shells keep their shape. Use about 2 teaspoons of the lemon juice to brush the insides of the shells to prevent excessive browning.

Cut the aubergine flesh into chunks. Heat the oil in a frying pan and sauté the flesh and garlic until soft and lightly browned (about 10 minutes). Allow to cool a little.

Chop the nuts in a food processor until fine. Add the aubergine flesh and garlic, sour cream and seasoning. Process until well mixed. Add the remaining lemon juice and poppy seeds. Pulse briefly until mixed. Spoon into the shells. If possible, chill for 2 hours before serving.

The classic combination of chervil and eggs has long been appreciated by the French. We have included recipes for both a French or flat omelette and a simple puffy omelette. Fill with either chopped chervil or fines herbes and add a complementary vegetable from our list of suggestions to make a simple and satisfying light meal.

Cook both omelettes in a small electric frying pan or non-stick pan with a lid (about 24 cm diameter).

FRENCH OMELETTE
Serves 2

3–4 eggs
1 tablespoon water for each egg
pinch salt
black pepper
1 tablespoon butter
small handful chervil, scissored or chopped, or
similar quantity fines herbes
optional fillings (see below)

Beat the eggs, water, salt and pepper together lightly. Heat the frying pan to a moderate temperature. Add the butter and tilt the pan to allow the melted butter to coat the base evenly. As soon as it starts to sizzle, pour in the egg mixture. Cover the pan and cook until the egg is set and the base is golden brown. Remove from the heat. Mark a line down the centre of the omelette. Add the chopped chervil or fines herbes to one side. Top with the chosen filling, if desired, and carefully fold the other half over the filling. Cut in half and lift or slide each section carefully onto a plate. Serve immediately.

PUFFY OMELETTE
Serves 2

ingredients as for previous recipe

Separate the eggs. Place the whites and the salt in one bowl and the yolks, pepper and water in a second bowl. Beat the whites to the stiff-foam stage (the peaks will fold over). Without washing the beater, beat the yolk mixture until very thick and light coloured. Gently fold the yolks into the whites: do not overmix. Heat the frying pan to a moderate temperature. Add the butter and tilt the pan to allow the melted butter to coat the base evenly. As soon as it starts to sizzle, pour in the egg mixture, using a spatula to spread evenly. Cover the pan and cook over a moderate heat until the egg is set, well risen and the base is golden brown. Remove from the heat. Fill, fold, cut and serve as for the French omelette.

Fillings

- asparagus, cut into short lengths and blanched
- tomatoes, skinned (if time permits) and chopped
- yellow or green courgettes, sliced into thin rings and sautéed for a few minutes in a little oil until tender-crisp
- spinach or young silverbeet, cooked and well drained
- sugar peas, blanched
- baby broad beans, blanched
- mushrooms, sliced and sautéed in a little oil
- finely shredded lettuce
- finely grated Parmesan or tasty Cheddar cheese

CREAM OF MUSHROOM SOUP WITH CHERVIL
Serves 4

This simple everyday soup is so delicious that it appears as though considerable cooking skill and effort are involved. The sophisticated flavour comes from a tablespoon of good quality dry sherry and a handful of fresh chervil, added just before serving.

2 tablespoons oil
1 shallot or small onion, chopped
1 clove garlic, very finely chopped
350 g mushrooms, washed and roughly chopped
1 medium-sized potato (about 200 g), peeled and sliced
500 ml chicken stock, home-made, or 375 ml pack of commercial liquid stock made up to 500 ml with water
375 ml can evaporated milk or cream
1 tablespoon dry sherry (good quality Spanish sherry is worth using)
black pepper
salt to taste
small handful chervil, chopped (reserve a few small sprigs for garnishing)
1 tablespoon chopped parsley

Heat the oil in a large saucepan, add the shallot and garlic and sauté without browning for a few minutes until softened. Add the mushrooms and potato and sauté for a few minutes more. Pour in the stock. Cover and simmer for 20–30 minutes or until the potato slices are very tender. Purée the soup in a liquidiser for the creamiest result, or a food processor, or push through a sieve. Return the purée to the saucepan, add the evaporated milk or cream, sherry, pepper, and salt if needed. Reheat gently without boiling. Remove from the heat and stir in the herbs. Serve immediately. Garnish with a sprig of chervil floating on the surface.

FISH WITH CHERVIL
Serves 2–3

The delicate flavours of fish and chervil are best appreciated in simple dishes. In this quickly prepared example, the fish is baked in cream or unsweetened evaporated milk and flavoured only with lemon juice, chervil and a little freshly roasted and ground coriander seed.

2 tablespoons oil
500 g fresh fish (preferably delicately flavoured)
2 tablespoons lemon juice
1/2 cup canned evaporated milk or cream
1/4 teaspoon salt
black pepper
1/2 teaspoon coriander seeds, dry roasted and ground
small handful chervil, chopped

Pour the oil into a shallow ovenproof dish, large enough to hold the fish fillets in one layer. Tip the dish to spread the oil. Lay the fillets in the dish. Sprinkle the lemon juice evenly over the fillets. Pour the evaporated milk or cream over the fillets and season with the salt, pepper and coriander. Bake at 180°C for about 20–30 minutes or until the fish flakes easily when tested with a fork. Be careful not to overcook. Sprinkle the surface with chervil and serve immediately.

chives

It is hard to imagine summer salads or creamy spring vegetable soups without finely chopped chives (*Allium schoenoprasum*). We would miss their sweet, mild onion flavour (the most subtle of all the onion family) and their fresh green colour when sprinkled on food as a garnish.

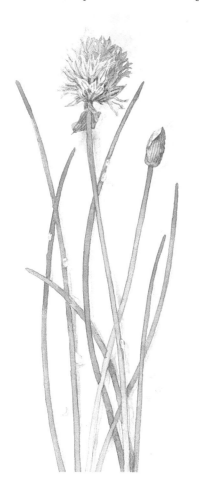

Many gardening cooks also value their pretty pink-mauve flowers, not only as attractive garden plants but as tiny, delicately flavoured florets, separated from the pom-pom shaped heads and scattered over salads. The whole flowerheads can also be used to flavour wine vinegar and to give it an appealing pink tint.

Fortunately, in most climates chives are with us for a long season, from early spring until late autumn. They are a perennial, growing from tiny, deep-set bulbs which multiply quickly into large clumps. Their hollow tubular leaves emerge early (ahead of most other perennial herbs) and, with good care and harvesting techniques, they will keep the kitchen supplied with the best quality shoots for many months. In hot climates, chives may die down in summer to reappear in autumn.

It is wise to remove flower stalks as they appear, to keep up leaf production. If you plan to harvest flowers as well, and want to enjoy their beauty in the garden, then grow many more clumps. Chives make charming and productive edgings to flower or vegetable beds, or may be used as informal groups in any mixed border. Chives also make pretty patio pot subjects—again, plan to have some exclusively for leaf production and others for flowers.

VARIETIES

Chives are sometimes called onion chives to distinguish them from the unrelated garlic chives (see page 76).

We have grown two selections of chives: a fine-leaved type, which is likely to be the one found in old established gardens and is reputed to have the better flavour and texture; and a newer, taller-growing and more vigorous

CHIVES
(*Allium schoenoprasum*)

The 20th-century herb pioneer Eleanour Sinclair Rohde once performed a very interesting experiment with a clump of chives which had been left undivided to the point where it measured nearly 40 cm across. She split the clump, obtaining 780 individual bulblets, and planted them out separately. After a few months they had multiplied sixfold. This experiment demonstrated not only how quickly chive edgings can be made, but also how tolerant chives are to years of neglect.

This easy-care member of the onion family has other star qualities. During its winter dormancy it will survive in frozen ground, emerging with the spring thaw to provide shiny green shoots for omelettes and salads. Its hardiness is not surprising given that the distribution of the species in the wild extends to a latitude of 70° N, well into Arctic regions. Wild chives exist right across the northern hemisphere, including both the old and new worlds. At lower latitudes it is increasingly restricted to damp mountainous areas, reaching its southernmost extent in northern India. Survival in the wild seems to have depended on a winter dormancy period.

Recent analysis of the species' DNA has revealed distinct sub-groups: Scandinavian specimens differ from those of southern and eastern Europe, while as a group the European forms are distinct from the Asian. Botanists have distinguished several subspecies, including the giant *sibiricum* (from Siberia) and *laurentianum* (from eastern North America). However, in gardens these readily interbreed. It is now believed that chives were brought into cultivation in many places.

Chives' climatic preferences cast some doubt on claims that they were grown in ancient Mediterranean gardens. Though there is no evidence of the presence of chives in classical Greece, the Romans had a plant called *porrum sectile* or *sectivum* ('cutting leek') which has often been identified as the chive. Their other *porrum*, a headed form called *porrum capitatum*, is usually translated as 'leek'. Columella gave detailed instructions for growing *porrum sectile*, advising spacing at about 10 cm intervals and delaying cutting until the plant has grown up. After each cutting, the plant should be manured, watered and weeded. This reads like the treatment we give to chives, but does this prove that *porrum sectile* were chives? To preserve his singing voice, the emperor Nero ate only *porrum sectivum* preserved in oil on fixed days every month—but should we visualise tiny tubes of chives sliding down his throat or something more substantial? If there were no other candidate for the role, this would be a reasonable identification. However, there was a much more ancient 'cutting leek' in the eastern Mediterranean, the Egyptian kurrat leek (*Allium ampeloprasum* var. *kurrat*), which for several thousand years had been cultivated for cutting every three to four weeks. The kurrat may have been happier growing in southern Italy than the chive.

Mediaeval manuscripts provide little help in fixing the earliest cultivation of chives. Again the problem lies in the name. *Chive* was a northern form of the Old French *cive*, derived from the Latin word *cepa*, meaning 'onion'. Increasingly, the name applied to green leafy forms of onion and to smaller species of the genus *Allium*. However, late mediaeval recipes using 'cive(y)', such as the 15th-century 'Civey of Coney [rabbit]', reveal on closer inspection that they are accompanied with fried minced onions, not chives.

Not until the 16th century is the evidence for chive cultivation convincing. In John Gerard's words, their leaves are 'like to little rushes' and they have 'both the smell and taste of the Onion and Leeke'. 'Cives are set in gardens', he went on, 'they flourish long, and continue many yeares, they suffer [put up with] the cold of Winter'. In some areas, they were called 'rush leeks' or 'rush onions' because their slender leaves were hollow, like rushes.

Slow to appear in gardening texts, chives took even longer to be specified as ingredients in recipes. In 1629 John Parkinson wrote that chives are 'shred among other herbes for the pot' as well as 'put into a Sallet among other herbes, to give it a quicker rellish'. British gardeners sometimes provided winter protection for the plants in order to have them in late winter salads before spring onions were ready. However, few recipes in English books called for chives in cooked dishes. In one late 17th-century recipe, some 'minced cives and parsly' were added to a 'white Hash, or ffricassee of Roasted veale, chickins or Rabets'. In two recipes from a 1744 collection chives again accompanied parsley, in the stuffing for a whole cabbage and in a topping for baked mushrooms. To Mrs Cole's 1789 recipe 'To Make an Amulet [omelet]' was added the note that some people 'put in clary and chives, and some put in onions', but parsley was the usual herb. Over the next hundred years chives lost status to the point where Mrs Beeton considered them 'old-fashioned' and grown only in 'old-fashioned gardens'.

In Scotland, however, chives were more appreciated. Mrs MacIver's 1789 recipe book specified chives in several lamb dishes, including 'A Pudding of Lamb's Blood', 'A Lamb's Haggies [haggis]' and 'To dress a Lamb's Head'. Over a century later, the early ethno-botanist E. Lewis Sturtevant observed that 'Chives are much used in Scotch families and are considered next to indispensable in omelettes and hence are much more used on the Continent of Europe, particularly in Catholic countries'. According to Tom Stobart, in the 1970s you were more likely to see bunches of chives for sale in the market stalls of Germany, Austria, Switzerland and Scandinavia than south of the Alps.

In the history of chives, England and North America play a peripheral part. Though the climate was favourable for cultivation, the taste of chives was not esteemed. Dislike of raw onion flavours (and fear of 'onion breath') persisted through the 19th and well into the 20th century. Writing about English salads in 1940, Eleanour Sinclair Rohde said 'it is customary to serve the grass [chives] finely snipped up in a separate little dish, for some people dislike Onion flavouring in any form'. The herb writer Florence Ranson had to explain in 1949 that 'as they are not so rich in sulphur as onions, they will not cause digestive disturbances'.

Fortunately, the English obsession with the bodily effects of alliums has declined, and chives are now welcomed into herb gardens and the fashionable ornamental potagers. We can't help wondering, however, how often the edible flowers of the new varieties such as 'Forescate' or 'Profusion' are actually eaten. Other varieties, however, bred with thick leaves for freezing or drying by the food industry, are infiltrating our diets in packet soups and sauces. We prefer to snip them fresh from the cook's garden.

---

variety, which may have rather tough lower sections to its leaves. Both sorts are available from time to time from garden centres, but they are usually unidentified, being labelled only as chives. You need to see both types together to know which one you are buying. 'Small', 'medium' and 'large' forms are listed in one Australian catalogue (see page 188 for a list of seed suppliers). The Royal Horticultural Society (UK) web-site listed 16 chive cultivars in early 2001, including white and pink forms. How many of these have been selected for culinary purposes is not stated.

CULTIVATION

According to *Rodale's Illustrated Encyclopedia of Herbs*, chives are natural inhabitants of moist pastures and stream banks. This tells the gardener that cultivated chives are likely to need a moist site too. They grow best in light, slightly acid, humus-rich soil. Like most members of the onion family, chives must be grown in free-draining beds to prevent bulb rot.

In temperate regions, chives are happiest to grow in full sun, though they will tolerate some afternoon shade. In very hot, dry climates, they may require more shade. They prefer an open situation and dislike being over-crowded, either by chive clumps nearby or other plants.

Avoid planting chives where any other member of the onion family has grown in the last 3 years. This helps to prevent the spread of bulb rot diseases.

Garden writers from cool climates sometimes suggest speeding up the emergence of the new season's leaves in early spring by covering the dormant clumps with cloches in late winter. Chives are very hardy, being able to withstand extremes of high and low temperatures. While dormant, the bulbs do not appear to be harmed by heavy frosts.

By far the easiest method of obtaining many chive plants quickly is by division of an established clump in early spring, just as the first leaves emerge. In warm climates the task can also be done in autumn. Dig deeply to carefully lift a whole clump. Tease off small groups of 6–10 healthy-looking bulbs and replant them in a new position. A great many new clumps can be obtained in this way. Space these mini-clumps 25 cm apart for fine-leaved chives and 40 cm for the larger types. Border plantings may be positioned a little closer.

Chives also grow well from fresh seed, though the process takes longer before harvesting can begin. In most climates it is best to raise the seedlings under cover. Sow seed in pots (10–15 cm diameter) filled with moist potting mix. Sprinkle about 20 seeds evenly over the surface and cover with fine mix. Chives germinate best in dark conditions so cover the pot with a circle of black plastic. Keep moist but not saturated. The recommended germinating temperature is 16–21°C, so a little bottom heat will speed the process, which should take 10–14 days. Don't thin the seedlings: just plant them out in a clump.

Outdoor sowings should be delayed until soil and air temperatures warm. Sow 10–20 seeds in a little group, 1 cm deep. Firm the soil over the top and keep moist. Clumps should be positioned 20–40 cm apart, depending on the variety grown (see pages 48–50).

Small chive clumps in pots are usually available from garden centres and specialist nurseries. Self-sown chives seedlings in the wrong position can easily be transplanted.

It is important to keep newly established clumps weed free as it is almost impossible to remove entangled grasses from a large clump.

Chive clumps that are being picked frequently must be given extra nutrients if they are to keep producing new shoots. Any yellowing of the leaves may be a symptom of a deficiency. Two to three doses of a liquid fertiliser during the growing season, and an extra dose following a full trim, is beneficial.

Maintain moisture levels and be particularly vigilant when the weather is hot and dry. An annual mulch of good compost will slow the evaporation loss.

A productive herb garden should include a minimum of 3 clumps. This will allow one plant in turn to be trimmed back to 5 cm from the soil surface, fed with a liquid fertiliser and left for a few weeks to grow a new set of fresh young shoots. Young leaves have the best texture and flavour.

It is best to remove flowerheads as they form from clumps designated for maximum leaf production. If you

Cut chives back regularly to encourage the production of young shoots.

allow your chives to flower for decorative reasons, be sure to remove the spent flowers before they drop their seed. Self-sown seedlings can prove a nuisance.

Small black aphids can be a pest. Use soapy water or a strong jet of water to blast them off. Treat the surrounding ground too. If rust appears, cut back the clumps to 5 cm from the surface of the soil. The new growth is generally rust free. In spring, clear last season's decayed leaves from around the emerging plants.

Chive bulbs increase rapidly to the point where they become overcrowded and leaf production deteriorates. This can occur as soon as 2 years after planting, but generally lift and divide clumps every 3–4 years. Always replant in fresh soil.

GROWING IN CONTAINERS
Chives are both 'thirsty and hungry' pot subjects. They do not like being overcrowded and require good air circulation to prevent disease—so don't include them in mixed herb plantings. Chives do well in temperatures ranging from 12–21°C, so during summer, in most climates, they are best outside on a sheltered patio or balcony. Two or three clumps, each in a 15–20 cm pot, will provide sufficient leaves for a small household. Use a good potting mix plus horticultural grit (5:1) for better drainage. Either buy small potted clumps from a garden centre or specialist nursery, or acquire a few bulbs from the division of a large garden clump. Keep the pots moist by applying water as soon as the surface shows signs of drying. Feed regularly with liquid fertiliser at the recommended strength for container-grown plants.

Harvest by cutting off the individual leaves about 2–3 cm from the surface of the soil. If this is done carefully, it is possible to remove just the large leaf from each bulb, leaving the small replacement one to grow in its place. Don't cut too hard or too often.

As chives require a dormant period in winter, place the pots in a cool place outside and allow them to die down. Water sparingly during this period.

If you have chive clumps in the garden, you may like to pot up some bulbs in autumn, leave them outside until they die down and experience some cold temperatures, then bring them inside to a warm, well-lit place. The reward for this effort could be earlier harvests of leaves.

HARVESTING
Young chive leaves are the most tender and have the mildest flavour. Snip individual leaves with scissors 5 cm from the surface of the soil. Flower stems are tough and should be discarded. Regular harvests encourage fresh growth.

Whole flowerheads or umbels are too large and strong tasting, but the florets, picked from the umbel, make a delightful, dainty and delicately flavoured garnish. Pick the heads before they become too papery.

IN THE KITCHEN
We prefer to slice chives finely in order to release the maximum flavour. Large chive pieces are unattractive and can be tough and difficult to eat. As it is hard to snip chives finely enough with scissors, we prefer to use a sharp knife on a board. Check the lower sections of the leaves from the larger chive varieties for tenderness, discarding the tougher parts, as for asparagus. Line a small bundle of chive leaves up on the board and slice finely into 2–5 mm sections.

Always add chives to hot dishes just before serving. They can be warmed through but too much heat will result in loss of flavour and colour.

The tiny chive florets can be easily snipped from the flower stalk. Holding the stalk in one hand and a pair of scissors in the other, make a 'V'-shaped cut with 2 snips upwards into the flowers. The individual florets will then fall from the stem. Use florets to garnish cool dishes or sprinkle over hot foods just before serving.

HOW TO USE CHIVES
- Like parsley, chives blend with most other herbs and can be used to flavour any savoury dish. Use whenever a mild onion flavour is appropriate.
- Add finely sliced chives to freshly cooked vegetables, just before serving. Chives team particularly well with sweet corn, tomatoes, potatoes, courgettes, cucumber, beans, cauliflower, asparagus and carrots.
- Chives have a special affinity with beetroot. Use them to enhance the first tender beetroot of the season, especially golden ones. Trim and scrub the beetroot and place them in a casserole dish. Add about 2 cm depth of boiling water, cover tightly and bake in a hot

oven (210°C) for 45–60 minutes, until tender. Drain and allow to cool. Use your fingers to rub off the skins, roots and stalks. Cut into wedges if round, or thick slices if cylindrical. Pour 2 tablespoons of oil into a sauté pan and add the beetroot and some seasoning. Heat through gently. Just before serving, add the grated rind and juice of half a lemon and 3 tablespoons of finely sliced chives.

- Chives are a member of the classic herb combination fines herbes (see page 180).
- Chives are a favourite garnish for soups. Sprinkle directly on top or over a dollop of sour cream or yoghurt. Try with asparagus, potato, pumpkin and tomato soups.
- Chives add a delicate onion flavour and colour contrast to a salmon pâté. We follow a popular recipe from Joan Bishop's column in the *Otago Daily Times* (27 October 1987). In a food processor, process 100 g of smoked salmon (any skin removed), 150 g of cream cheese, 1 tablespoon of lemon juice, 2 tablespoons of softened butter, and a little black pepper until smooth. Add 3 tablespoons of finely sliced chives and process just long enough to mix through. Spoon into a small bowl and serve with toasted pitta bread wedges or slices of fresh brown bread.
- Combine chunks of cucumber, ripe tomatoes and feta cheese with finely sliced chives. Add a sprinkling of extra virgin olive oil and some seasoning.
- Most egg dishes benefit from a sprinkling of finely sliced chives added just before cooking is complete. Add to scrambled eggs (see recipe on page 54), omelettes (pages 46–47) and baked eggs. The old favourite, stuffed eggs, just wouldn't be the same without chives.
- Chives accompany other herbs in cheese spreads, balls and dips. Use instead of basil in the recipe on page 29.
- Make chive butter to serve with cooked vegetables, grilled lamb or fish, or jacket potatoes. A general recipe for herb butter is given on page 19.
- Chives are indispensable in mixed leaf salads. When seasonally unavailable, we substitute spring onions or tree onion leaves, which appear several weeks earlier than the first chives.
- Combine chives with cherry tomatoes in a simple warm dish. Sauté 1 or 2 cloves of finely chopped garlic in a little olive oil for 2 minutes. Add the tomatoes, cut in half, and sauté for about 2 minutes longer. Add plenty of finely sliced chives and some seasoning and serve immediately.

CHICKEN SCALOPPINE WITH HERBS
Serves 2

Scaloppine is the Italian word for thin slices of meat, usually veal, which are lightly cooked in oil or butter until golden and tender. They are often seasoned with lemon juice and chopped herbs.

Chives are our favourite herb for this dish, though parsley, dill, basil, tarragon, lemon thyme, oregano and mint are delectable too.

This is one of the quickest, simplest and tastiest ways of cooking chicken breasts.

2 chicken breasts (approximately 300 g), skinned
2 tablespoons flour
1/4 teaspoon salt
black pepper
1–2 tablespoons oil
1/2 cup white wine
grated rind and juice from half a lemon
3 tablespoons finely sliced chives

Place the chicken on a sheet of plastic food film on a board. Cover with another sheet and pound them with a meat pounder until spread and about 5 mm thick. Combine the flour and seasonings on a plate. Coat each side of the chicken, shaking off any excess.

Heat the oil in a large, heavy-based frying pan or electric pan and lightly brown and cook the chicken on both sides until tender. This will take only a few minutes. Use tongs to lift the pieces onto a plate and keep warm. Drain off any excess fat from the pan. Lower the heat and add the wine, scraping in any browned bits from the base. Simmer until reduced a little. Add the lemon rind and juice and stir to mix. Check the seasoning. Return the chicken to the pan and sprinkle with the chives. Serve immediately.

PERFECT SCRAMBLED EGGS
WITH CHIVES
Serves 2–3

Scrambled eggs is one of the simplest and best ways of cooking eggs, but sadly its reputation has been tarnished by all too frequent over-cooking. The secret is to remove the partially cooked egg mixture from the heat before it is completely set to allow the heat of the pan to finish the cooking.

We vary the chopped herbs that we add to the eggs just before serving. Chives are our favourite, either alone or as part of a fines herbes mixture. For a gourmet breakfast, serve the chive-flavoured scrambled eggs on toasted English-style muffins and arrange a few thin slices of smoked salmon and a small dollop of sour cream on top. A sprinkling of tiny chive florets is an equally appealing garnish.

4 large eggs
1/2 cup milk
1/4 teaspoon salt
black pepper
2 tablespoons butter
2–3 tablespoons finely sliced chives

Optional garnish
thin slices of smoked salmon
sour cream
chive florets

In a small bowl, beat the eggs, milk, salt and pepper until well mixed. In a heavy-based, non-stick frying pan or electric pan, melt the butter but don't brown.

Pour in the egg mixture and cook over a low heat. Gently lift the mixture as it sets, keeping it in large soft masses. Do not allow it to brown on the bottom. Remove from the heat while some egg mixture remains liquid. Stir in the chives and serve over hot toast. Garnish as desired.

coriander

Those of us who grew up before fresh leaf coriander (*Coriandrum sativum*) was rediscovered find it either appealing or appalling. If you love it, you become mildly 'addicted' to it and work hard to secure a regular supply. If you hate it, don't despair, time may change your opinion. It is an indispensable herb in many cultures. Educate your taste buds by eating it cooked—this softens the flavour, as in the Bevy's sautéed chicken and coriander recipe on page 60. The mildest and best-flavoured fresh coriander is from broad-leaved young plants.

Coriander leaves and roots are classified as herbs but the dried seeds of the same plant are a spice. Don't try to substitute ground seeds for fresh leaves, as their flavours are totally different.

VARIETIES

When growing coriander for leaf production, choose a variety selected for the superior quality and quantity of its broad basal leaves and 'slow to bolt' habit. This type produces large lush leaves for several weeks before its mature finer foliage appears and it flowers. The seed packet will be labelled as 'cilantro' or 'leaf coriander'. This type will also produce seed if allowed to flower.

CULTIVATION

Coriander is a hardy annual which grows happily in a large range of climates. It will grow in hot, dry places as well as tolerating light frosts. However, leaf production is easiest for the gardener in cooler temperatures. If coriander is water-stressed or temperatures are too hot, it will bolt to seed in just a few weeks, giving only a very short period for leaf harvesting. This problem can be overcome with successive sowings 2 weeks apart.

Light, free-draining soil containing plenty of coarse compost provides the best growing conditions. Full sun is desirable when temperatures are cooler and daylight hours short, but partial shade is preferable in hot climates. Sited by a path edge, the leaves will release their fragrance when lightly brushed.

As coriander is taprooted, disturbance will prematurely trigger it to run to seed. This is why plants bought from garden centres often bolt and as a result fail to produce sufficient leaves for harvesting. The only way to ensure adequate supplies is to grow coriander from seed in short rows in the vegetable garden or herb plot. The seed is long lived if stored in a cool, dry place. We have found it economical to buy seed in bulk in a 100 g pack from a mail-order seed merchant, to ensure that seed is always available for successive sowings during spring, summer and autumn. Autumn sowings produce the longest harvest period. Mary grows her best leaf coriander in an unheated glasshouse or under cloches during winter. Her garden regularly experiences up to −10°C frosts and the temperature in the glasshouse drops to just below zero.

Sow the seed 1 cm deep, 2–3 cm between seeds and

CORIANDER
(*Coriandrum sativum*)

'I know of no other herb that is quite so provocative', said Elisabeth Lambert Ortiz, the author of authoritative books on both Mexican and Japanese cooking. She was referring to its capacity to divide the world into coriander users and abusers. Mexicans, Peruvians, Indians, Afghans, Egyptians, Moroccans and Portuguese rank among the passionate users of both the aromatic dried seedheads (technically fruits) and the young green leaves. The Thai even consume the root, grinding it into a paste with garlic for their distinctive green and red curries. Many other cultures use the dried fruits as a spice, but regard the green leaves as inedible. The latter opinion is often expressed in strongly abusive language. John Gerard (1597) referred to 'the venemous quality of the leaves', calling it a 'stinking herbe'. Olivier de Serres (1605) perversely included it in his flower garden, because its leaves, rubbed between the hands, enhance the good scents of the other flowers. John Evelyn (1699) did not consider it a suitable salad herb, because it is 'offensive to the Head'. Twentieth century writers have described it as 'intensely foetid', 'objectionable', 'disagreeable', 'nauseating' and 'nasty'. The same writers usually prop up this opinion by pointing out that the word 'coriander' comes from *koris*, the classical Greek term for a bedbug, and the plant was so named because it smells like bedbugs.

Should we accept this derivation? The term *ko-ri-ja-da-no*, found in lists of spices from Late Bronze Age (1415–1100 BC) Aegean texts written in Linear B, suggests a very ancient origin, before the Greek language developed. When the supposed connection with bedbugs was thought up in the 16th or 17th century, Linear B had not yet been discovered, let alone deciphered. Nor is it evident in classical Greek or Latin literature. Perhaps it is a case of spurious etymology dreamed up by a coriander-hater?

Does fresh coriander really smell of bedbugs? In his 1977 book *Herbs, Spices and Flavourings*, Tom Stobart wrote: 'Most readers will not have experienced the joys of bedbugs, but if they have travelled rough in the East, they may be in a position to judge. There is really little similarity.' A Thai colleague has recently confirmed this opinion. The distinctive smell emanates from aliphatic aldehydes in the oil canals of the leaves and on the outside of the green, unripe fruit. As the fruit ripens to a chestnut colour, these canals flatten and the strong-smelling oil evaporates, leaving just the aromatic spicy oil which fills the oil canals in the centre of the fruit.

Coriander has a long history as a food plant in the eastern Mediterranean and Middle East. The wild form is probably a native of Greece and Asia Minor. As an annual plant growing in rather open oak forest and scrubland, it was adapted to germination at the onset of winter rains and growth through the cooler months, followed by rapid flower and seed development during the short spring before summer drought set in. Most of the varieties grown today retain this propensity to bolt. The earliest archaeological evidence for coriander fruits comes from a cave in Israel, possibly before 7000 BC. Whether or not this finding is confirmed by further discoveries, we know that by 1500 BC coriander was used in considerable quantities throughout the Middle East and eastern Mediterranean. Its name was inscribed in cuneiform script on clay tablets found at the Old Babylonian cities of Mari and Karana, about 1815 BC, along with black and white varieties of cumin, fenugreek and saffron. Large quantities were listed in the Mari records, raising the possibility that the leaves were used as well as the fruits. Documents from Late Bronze Age sites around the Aegean also list coriander along with spices such as cumin and fennel. The coriander at the palace of Knossos on Crete was described as coming from Cyprus, from where coriander seed has been identified in the 13th-century BC site of Apliki. The earliest record for coriander in Egypt is from 1550 BC. By the time that half a litre of coriander seeds was placed with other burial goods in Tutankhamun's tomb in 1327 BC, coriander had become the dominant flavouring spice that today characterises the cooking traditions of North Africa and other Arab nations. Since these culinary cultures also use fresh coriander leaves, it is highly likely that these too were eaten by the young Tutankhamun, Agamemnon or King Midas.

The Mycenaeans pressed coriander oil for perfumed unguents, and by the time of classical Greece and Rome there was a long list of medicinal uses. The famous Roman cookbook of Apicius called for coriander in numerous recipes. In many cases the context suggests that it was the fruit; however, Margaret Visser has recently argued that the Romans made a type of coriander pesto with the green leaves.

This broad range of uses continued into the Middle Ages. Barbara Santich calls mediaeval cooking the original Mediterranean cuisine, inheritor of a time-honoured tradition of spicy dishes flavoured with the dominant spices coriander and cumin. One mediaeval specialty was the comfit, in which sugar-coated seeds of fennel, caraway, anise and coriander were offered at the conclusion of a meal to aid digestion. The same seeds were often employed to flavour wines and preserves. These usages persisted in England through to the end of the 16th century. Then the plant disappears from the gardening manuals. Only its dried fruits were retained, mentioned in recipe books as optional ingredients for seed cakes, 'Shrewsberie' cakes, 'cracknell' biscuits and spiced wine. By the late 17th century, coriander was grown in the drier counties of England primarily for fruits to flavour 'strong waters' such as gin, and gripe mixtures. In Eastern Europe coriander oil was pressed for use in perfumes, liqueurs, medicines, and eventually for industrially prepared foods. Varieties were developed with a significantly higher oil content.

Only one European culinary tradition continued to use fresh coriander leaves through to the 20th century. In Portuguese cuisine, according to Margaret Visser, the plant is 'all but indispensable'. Curiously, the Spanish do not use fresh coriander, which makes the plant's popularity in parts of Central and South America hard to explain. While there is no mystery about its use in Brazil, which was influenced primarily by the Portuguese, the success of *cilantro*, as coriander is known in Spanish-colonised Mexico and Peru, raises more questions. Elisabeth Lambert Ortiz speculated that, when Columbus reached America, Arab influences on Spanish cooking may still have been important. This view was supported by Elizabeth David's discovery of 16th-century potage recipes calling for green coriander in a Catalan cookbook. Alternatively, the plant may have reached Mexico and Peru via the Manila galleons, trading between the Philippines and the New World across the Pacific. Filipinos remain heavy users of green coriander. In fact, apart from Japan, most cooks in Asia were familiar with fresh coriander long before Columbus.

The Indian subcontinent was using coriander by at least 400 BC, with writers of Sanskrit texts calling it by names borrowed from earlier Asiatic languages. The same names occur in Malay and Indonesian, indicating the early spread of the plant through South-east Asia. By about 100 BC it had reached China, early in the Han dynasty. Its green leaves became the most common garnish in soups, while the dried fruits contributed to the spicy dishes of Szechuan.

The last two centuries have seen coriander return to European cuisines after several centuries of neglect. First, British colonial experiences in India led to the introduction of curry powder to British kitchens from the late 18th century on, and this blend of spices can contain up to 40% ground coriander. The second wave of influence involved migrants to Britain, France and Germany from coriander-loving countries such as India, Pakistan, Algeria, Turkey and the West Indies. Their desire for fresh coriander led to a sharp increase in local production. At the same time, European cuisines opened themselves to cosmopolitan influences. The critical step in the rehabilitation of coriander was the renaming of fresh coriander greens as Chinese parsley, Indian parsley, Arab parsley, even Afghan parsley, a process which occurred in German and French as well as English. Undoubtedly the change of name drove out the taint of bedbugs!

in rows 20 cm apart. Keep well watered. Germination is slow, taking up to 25 days (see page 12). Some writers suggest soaking seed overnight as a way of hastening germination but we have not found this necessary. Two plants emerge from most seeds (which are strictly speaking fruits containing twin seeds). Thinning is optional: we thin when plants are large enough to be of use in the kitchen. Plants intended for seed production should be thinned to 20 cm spacing.

To maintain optimum moisture levels in the soil, cover the surface of damp soil with a mulch. Weekly watering with a liquid fertiliser based on fish or blood and bone promotes luscious leaf growth over a longer period. Pinch out any centre stalks which are beginning to produce fine leaves, as this will help to prolong broad leaf production.

It is well worthwhile allowing two or three well-grown plants to flower and set seed. Fresh home-grown dried coriander seed is markedly superior to the purchased product. In a windy garden it is wise to stake and tie your plants as they get taller. Continue to provide ideal growing conditions to obtain a good crop of fat seeds. Watch the seed heads closely as the seed will fall without warning. Cut when roughly two-thirds of the seeds change from green to light brown and smell pleasant. Don't wait until they are all brown, as the seed heads will shatter before you harvest them. However, a few dropped seeds can be a bonus, as they germinate easily and provide a continuing supply of leaves.

GROWING IN CONTAINERS

Choose a container with a large surface area (30–40 cm wide) with a depth of 10–20 cm. Fill with free-draining damp mix (5 parts coarse potting mix to 1 part horticultural grit). Sow coriander seeds 2–3 cm apart and 1 cm deep. Keep damp but be careful not to over-water as coriander resents having 'wet feet'. Don't thin plants, instead harvest while still young by shearing with scissors. When all used, pull up the remaining stalks, renew the potting mix and start again. Plant several containers in succession to ensure a continuous supply. Place containers where they receive good light with warmth in winter and cooler temperatures in summer, outside or in a well-lit conservatory. Avoid direct sunshine through glass.

HARVESTING

Pull thinnings and young plants whole, roots and all, to use in Thai recipes. When a little larger, snip young stems with broad leaves with scissors or fingers to use fresh as required. When mature, fine-leaved foliage begins to appear; the plants should then be harvested without delay as their flavour rapidly becomes too pungent.

To harvest seed, cut heads with enough stalk to enable them to be bunched 4–6 together, placed in a paper bag, tied and hung upside down in a dry, warm and airy place. Alternatively, hang the whole plant by its roots, with a sheet of plastic underneath to collect the seeds. When dry, these can be stripped or shaken off the stems, sieved and stored in airtight, light-proof containers in a cool place.

IN THE KITCHEN

If necessary, store bunches of stems and leaves or small whole plants in a refrigerator (see page 20).

For garnishing, use small stems and leaves attached, or snip off individual leaves. When chopped coriander is required, we find that scissoring does less damage.

Coriander leaves lose their fresh, unique flavour when dried or frozen, so aim for a year-round fresh supply if possible.

For seeds, use them whole or ground just before they are required. The seeds are easier to grind and release a superior flavour if lightly dry roasted first. Use a small, heavy-based frying pan over a gentle heat. Shake the pan or stir the seeds to prevent scorching. They will be sufficiently roasted when they emit a fragrant aroma and have darkened slightly in colour.

HOW TO USE LEAF CORIANDER

- Sprinkle scissored leaves over meat, fish, chicken or vegetable curries just before serving.
- Add leaves to stir-fries just before serving.
- Sprinkle scissored leaves over hot chilli dishes with a Mexican or Caribbean flavour.
- Sprinkle leaves or scissored leaves on spicy soups such as lentil or black bean.
- Use scissored leaves sparingly in tomato or pasta salads.
- Add to Middle Eastern-style lamb casseroles.
- Use in sandwiches: thin slices of cold roast beef and tomatoes with a little Asian-style sweet chilli sauce and scissored leaf coriander; or mashed avocado, shredded cooked chicken and scissored leaf coriander.
- Add scissored leaves to pickled beetroot salad.
- Add scissored leaves, stem and roots to marinated mushrooms.
- Cook young green beans and serve tossed with butter or olive oil, lemon juice, black pepper and scissored leaf coriander.
- For a delicious chilled soup, process avocados with lemon juice, coriander leaves, and red-skinned onion until smooth. Pour into a bowl and stir in yoghurt, liquid vegetable stock and tomato juice. Garnish with extra coriander leaves.
- Make an Indian-style green masala to serve as a condiment (like mustard) with chicken, fish or vegetable curries. Process a 3 cm piece of fresh ginger (peeled and chopped), 3 cloves of garlic (peeled and chopped), 3 fresh green chillies (seeds removed and flesh chopped) and a small handful of young coriander leaves and stems in a small food processor or blender, adding sufficient water to make a coarse paste.
- Make your favourite stuffed-egg recipe using a little garam masala (see page 59), scissored chives and leaf coriander.

Start harvesting coriander at the seedling stage.

Coriander at a good size for harvesting.

- Use the dainty white flowers to garnish soups, salads and vegetable platters.

HOW TO USE CORIANDER SEED

- Use fresh home-grown coriander seeds to make your own garam masala (the flavour is superb): 2 tablespoons of coriander seeds, 1 tablespoon of cumin seeds, 1 teaspoon of black peppercorns, 2 cinnamon sticks (5 cm long), 1/2 teaspoon of whole cloves, 16 cardamom pods, half a whole nutmeg. Dry roast all the spices, except the nutmeg, separately in a small frying pan over a gentle heat until slightly darker and smelling aromatic. Remove the seeds from the cardamom pods and place in a heavy mortar, coffee-grinder or electric blender along with the other roasted spices. Grind them to a fine powder. Finely grate the nutmeg and mix in. Store in an airtight container away from light.
- Use roasted seeds to flavour cooked beetroot, and orange marmalade.
- Use whole or lightly crushed roasted seeds in ratatouille.
- Add freshly roasted seeds to flavour terrines and pâtés.
- Sift 1/2–1 teaspoon of ground coriander seeds with the dry ingredients when making gingerbread, banana and carrot cakes.

- Add 1–2 teaspoons of lightly crushed coriander seeds to apple pies.
- Replace the cinnamon in fruit crumbles with ground coriander seeds.

FRESH CORIANDER & MINT RELISH
Serves 6–8 as an accompaniment to spicy Indian or Middle Eastern-style dishes.

1 large handful fresh coriander leaves, stalks and roots
small handful mint sprigs
2 cloves garlic, peeled and roughly chopped
3 tablespoons lemon juice (about 1 1/2 lemons)
1 red chilli, deseeded and the flesh roughly chopped, or
1 teaspoon commercially prepared chilli
3 tablespoons mild-flavoured oil
100 g peanuts, roasted (see page 21)
1/4 teaspoon salt

Place all the ingredients in a food processor and pulse until very finely chopped. Spoon into a small bowl and chill until required.

BEVY'S SAUTÉED CHICKEN
& CORIANDER
Serves 2–3

This simple, Thai-inspired dish can be made with chicken breasts in the time it takes to cook the rice. Alternatively, slower-cooking cuts of chicken may be used and the time increased accordingly. Serve over jasmine rice with lightly cooked green beans, courgettes or pak choi.

handful of fresh coriander (4–5 plants including roots)
2 onions, roughly chopped
3 cloves garlic, sliced
slice fresh ginger (about 3 cm diameter)
2 tablespoons cooking oil
1 teaspoon turmeric
1/4–1/2 teaspoon chilli powder (according to taste)
salt to taste
1/2 cup plain yoghurt
400 g can whole skinned tomatoes in purée, or equivalent in fresh tomatoes, chopped (skin if time permits)
500 g chicken breasts, skinned and cut across the grain into 1 cm thick slices, or chicken drums or thighs, skinned and left whole

1 1/2 teaspoons garam marsala (see page 59)
fresh coriander leaves for garnishing

Using a food processor, finely chop the first 4 ingredients.

Heat the oil in a sauté pan and lightly cook the processed mixture for a few minutes. Add the turmeric, chilli and salt and cook for a few minutes longer. Stir in the yoghurt, and tomatoes with their juice. Break up the tomatoes with a wooden spoon. Bring slowly to simmering point. Add the chicken and cook very gently with a lid on until tender. Chicken breasts will take about 15 minutes and drums or thighs 30–45 minutes.

Stir in the garam masala and garnish with coriander leaves.

Salsa is the Mexican word for sauce, and fresh leaf coriander is an essential ingredient in many salsa recipes. We have included two we make often: one green, using green tomatoes, and the other based on red tomatoes. Choose the colour and flavour best suited to the food it is to accompany. Make salsa 3 to 4 hours ahead to allow flavours to blend.

GREEN SALSA
Serve with grilled or pan-fried fish or chicken, barbecued steak, tostadas or burritos

half a small cucumber (about 200 g), peeled if skin is tough, seeds discarded if large, and flesh cut roughly into chunks
1 small stick of celery, cut into chunks
1 large green tomato, core discarded and flesh cut into chunks
1–2 small green chillies, deseeded and chopped
small handful fresh coriander leaves, stalks and roots, roughly sliced
3 spring onions, trimmed and sliced
1 clove garlic, peeled and crushed
2 tablespoons mild-flavoured olive oil
1 tablespoon lemon juice
1/4 teaspoon salt or to taste
black pepper

Place all the ingredients in a food processor and pulse until finely chopped. Tip into a serving bowl and chill for 3–4 hours. Stir just prior to serving.

RED SALSA
Serve with taco chips, tortillas, Mexican bean dishes, spicy sausages, kebabs

1 red capsicum, seeds discarded and flesh roughly chopped (if time allows, grill whole capsicum and peel off charred skin)
1 small red-skinned onion or shallot, roughly chopped
1 clove garlic, peeled and crushed
2 small red chillies, deseeded and flesh roughly chopped, or 2 teaspoons commercially prepared chilli
3 medium-sized ripe tomatoes, cut into quarters and cores discarded
small handful fresh coriander leaves, stalks and roots, roughly sliced

1 tablespoon mild-flavoured olive oil
1 tablespoon dry sherry or red wine
1/4 teaspoon sugar
salt and black pepper to taste

Place all the ingredients in a food processor and pulse until finely chopped. Tip into a serving bowl and chill for 3–4 hours. Stir just prior to serving.

GUACAMOLE

Fresh leaves of coriander, or *cilantro* as the plant is called in Mexico, are a basic flavouring ingredient in Mexican cooking. Guacamole, generously flavoured with coriander and chilli, features in many meals: as a salad, a sauce, a filling for tacos, or simply spread on warm tortillas.

2 ripe avocados
2 spring onions, finely sliced, or 1 shallot, or 1/2 small red-skinned onion, peeled and finely chopped
1 clove garlic, peeled and crushed
1 medium-sized ripe tomato (skin if time permits), finely chopped
1 fresh green chilli, deseeded, flesh very finely chopped, or 3–4 drops Tabasco sauce
1/4 teaspoon salt
juice of 1 lime or half a lemon
1–2 tablespoons finely chopped fresh coriander leaves and stems

Split avocados in half and remove the stones. Peel. Place in a bowl and mash with a fork until broken up but not too smooth. Add remaining ingredients and mix well. Taste and adjust seasoning by adding more salt, lemon juice or chilli to taste. Serve immediately in a small bowl.

CORIANDER FRUIT SALAD
Serves 4

Young, freshly picked coriander leaves add an unusual and refreshing flavour to winter and spring fruit salads. Ground coriander seed enhances the coconut cream dressing.

2 oranges, peeled, cut into segments and each cut into 2 or 3 pieces
2 bananas, peeled and sliced
2 kiwifruit, peeled and cut into small pieces
200 g peeled fresh pineapple, cut into small cubes, or use a drained can of pineapple pieces in juice
juice of half a lemon (other half required for dressing)
1 tablespoon scissored coriander leaves plus extra tablespoon for garnishing

Dressing
70 g can thick coconut cream
1 tablespoon honey (warmed if stiff)
1/2 teaspoon coriander seeds, lightly dry roasted and then ground with a mortar and pestle
juice of half a lemon

Combine fruits, half the lemon juice and coriander leaves in a bowl.

Whisk dressing ingredients together.

To serve, spoon fruit salad into individual bowls. Drizzle the dressing over the top and garnish with additional scissored coriander leaves.

dill

Dill (*Anethum graveolens*) is often called the fish or pickle herb. It is a favourite of the Scandinavians, Germans and peoples of central and eastern Europe, plus many Americans with their dill pickles. We think it deserves to be included more often in Western kitchen gardens and used in a much wider variety of dishes. Its delicate, refreshing, slightly sour taste enhances many more foods than just the well-known fish and pickles.

As a short-lived annual herb, dill has to be sown from seed each year. This is not difficult and, unlike many herbs, the leaves, flowers and seeds all have a role in the kitchen— a good return for effort and garden space.

Dill and fennel are sometimes confused as their leaves are similar and they both go well with fish. Dill (an annual) has blue-green leaves, grows to about a metre tall, and has a single hollow stem rising from a single taproot. Fennel (a perennial) has yellow-green (or bronze) leaves, grows well over a metre tall, and has many solid stems rising from a branched root system. Although dill and fennel leaves can replace each other in some dishes, they do taste distinctly different. Dill has a pungent, pleasantly sour tang with just a hint of aniseed, while fennel is sweeter with a definite aniseed taste. We think that dill is the more delicate, in both flavour and texture, making it worthwhile spending the extra time each year in growing it.

A bonus of having a good crop of dill in the garden is the flowers, which add a light, airy touch to natural-looking flower arrangements. They last very well in water.

VARIETIES

It is worth looking out for named cultivars of dill, as these are likely to have been selected for leaf production. We have grown both 'Bouquet' and 'Fernleaf', which are excellent compact varieties, and 'Dukat', which is reported to be more tolerant of heat and is slower to bolt. If you can't locate a source of these, the species which is readily available does well in most gardens.

Dill in the vegetable garden after a heavy dew.

DILL
(Anethum graveolens)

Dill is one of those herbs that self-seeds, conveniently and not aggressively, so you might expect it to 'hang out' in your garden from year to year. But early one summer you will look for it in vain—it will simply have vanished. Its history in the West is marked by similar disappearances.

As dill is an annual 'weed' of cereal crops—it is adapted to being supported by their stems—the nature of its distribution before the birth of agriculture is rather uncertain. Some writers point to an origin of the genus *Anethum* in south or south-west Asia, while others include the Mediterranean basin. The difficulty lies in distinguishing wild from feral plants that have escaped from cultivation. Although cereals such as wheat and barley have been cultivated for more than ten thousand years, there are no archaeological finds of dill seed until the late 2nd millennium BC in Macedonia. Dried sprigs of dill were reported from a tomb of similar age in Egypt.

Two other umbelliferous plants of somewhat similar taste or appearance—fennel and anise—were known to early farmers in the Middle East, so the identification of words like the Ancient Egyptian *imst* and the Assyrian *simru* as dill, rather than fennel or anise, is problematic. Even the classical Greek word *ánethon*, from which we get the genus name, is frequently translated as both dill and anise.

By the time of the Roman botanical texts, there is a clearer separation. When Pliny the Elder said that *anesum* and *anetum* were grown for use in the kitchen and by doctors, we can be reasonably sure that the first referred to anise and the second to dill. The latter's medicinal applications as outlined by Pliny included the treatment of hiccoughs, and the relief of gripes and indigestion, precisely those properties recognised in the traditional dill water given to babies and young children. Apicius gave about 25 recipes with dill as an ingredient. A few called for dill seed, but generally the *anetum* was included in a bouquet of fresh herbs (often including leeks and coriander) added to the liquid in which meat was simmered, or to barley or pea soups. Supporting evidence for dill's widespread use in Roman times is archaeological finds from Roman sites as far afield as Britain and Germany.

Presumably dill continued to be used in Europe after the collapse of the Roman Empire. The English word 'dill' is closely related to German *dill*, Swedish *dill*, Dutch *dille* and Danish *dild*. In Old Norse, spoken over a thousand years ago, *dilla* meant 'to lull', a probable reference to the medicinal properties of dill seeds. Dill has such a prominent place in the cuisines of northern and central–eastern Europe that we can assume that it was also grown for the kitchen. However, it practically vanished from the kitchens of western Europe, judging from the mediaeval recipe collections. The seed was still of medical significance, but may well have been restricted to physic gardens or even imported, as anise was, from warmer countries.

Not all 16th- and 17th-century garden writers in France and England included dill in their manuals, and sometimes it was mentioned solely as a herb to distil. It was the rise of the cucumber, and the desire to preserve its fruits for winter use, that raised dill's profile in England. The Elizabethan writer Thomas Hill wrote of a method of layering them with salt, vinegar, fennel and marjoram. In 1629 John Parkinson described dill as an alternative to fennel: 'The leaves of Dill are much used in some places with Fish, as they doe Fenell; but because it is so strong many doe refuse it. It is also put among pickled Cowcumbers, wherewith it doth very well agree, giving unto the cold fruit a pretty spicie taste or rellish'. Allen Paterson thinks that dill was originally added to correct the windiness of the cucumbers, as a sort of 'adult gripe water'!

Thus dill pickles evolved, crossing the Atlantic with the early colonists and growing in popularity. When you examine a list of modern dill varieties, the United States stands out as a dill-friendly nation. They have developed varieties especially for the size of their seedheads, which are the preferred portion of the plant in American dill pickles. Other centres of dill production such as Germany, Poland and Scandinavia have emphasised oil content, or high leaf production combined with resistance to bolting. The Scandinavian specialty gravlax (cured salmon) uses sugar, salt, gin or vodka, white pepper and copious quantities of dill leaf in the processing. Mutton or lamb is often layered with dill sprigs in a Norwegian hotpot.

Other countries have also made much use of this plant. Indians have a distinctive variety of *A. graveolens* known as 'Sowa', which produces seeds of greater pungency and bitterness. As an ingredient of some curry powders, this clearly has to be assertive rather than lulling in its action. Dill is a popular herb in the Balkans, Turkey and Iran, being served in pilafs and koftas, and with yoghurt and sour cream. Its acceptance in the West in other dishes besides pickles is related to a growing interest in so-called ethnic cuisines.

CULTIVATION

Dill's most important requirement is adequate moisture throughout its entire, relatively short life span. Like most herbs, it resents water-logged, heavy soils and does best if grown in the rich, humus-filled beds of a productive vegetable garden. Lack of water may prevent germination, cause the delicate young seedlings to shrivel, and encourage the plants to produce flowers prematurely at the expense of a leaf crop. Built-up beds suit it well, too—providing excellent drainage and consequently warmer soil temperatures in spring, and allowing for an early start with seed sowing. Good drainage is also the key to avoiding attack by a root fungus which may cause seedlings to die.

Dill requires full sun in most climates, though a few hours of afternoon shade is probably beneficial in hot places.

Dill developed as a field plant and is happiest growing with grasses and other tall plants which provide it with support. Choose a sheltered position, or be prepared to stake the metre-high plants which topple easily when their flowerheads develop. We have noticed how happy the odd self-sown dill plant is when tucked up against our broad beans or growing among the garlic.

As a hardy annual which resents having its taproot disturbed, dill has to be raised from seed sown *in situ* (see page 12). In hot weather, it is inclined to run to seed in a matter of 6–8 weeks, so successive sowings of a small number of seeds every 2–3 weeks is the ideal. The first sowing can be made as early in spring as soil conditions permit. If a crop is intended for flowers to use in dill pickles or for seed production for drying, plan to sow between mid- and late spring.

The seeds, which are large and easily handled, germinate best with soil temperatures between 15 and 21°C. They need some light, so only barely cover them. The most important requirement for good germination rates is adequate moisture. Ensure that the seedbed is damp before sowing and avoid having the surface dry out until well after good sturdy seedlings have emerged. In very hot climates, summer sowings of dill are unlikely to be successful, so instead plan your crops for the cooler seasons, including winter. Sow in short rows, spaced 40 cm apart and thin seedlings when 5 cm tall to a 25–30 cm spacing. The thinnings should be used in the kitchen.

In the right conditions, dill self-sows freely—not always where you want it, but the resulting plants are invariably vigorous. Some gardeners assist this process by deliberately scattering ripe seeds around the garden at harvest time.

A rich compost mulch applied around young seedlings helps to maintain crucial moisture levels and provides nutrients. If leaf harvesting is frequent, feed dill plants with a liquid fertiliser—fish emulsion works well. During dry weather, apply extra water to maintain moist soil conditions. Dill plants that are deprived of moisture will be short lived and will not provide harvests of luxuriant leaves for the kitchen.

Dill plants being grown on for flower and seed production should be staked before they are tall enough to be damaged by wind. Either stake each individual plant or position a few stakes on either side of the row and tie twine between them at appropriate heights as the plants grow.

If leaf production is the main purpose of your dill crop, remove flower stems as they form, to extend the period of prime foliage production by a few weeks. The immature buds can be eaten with the leaves.

GROWING IN CONTAINERS

Dill is not the ideal container plant, as its long taproot needs to be accommodated and its moisture requirements may mean that daily attention is essential. However, with deep pots, a foolproof watering system and the time to re-sow at regular intervals, dill in pots is attractive. If you have several plants in production, good supplies of leaves and flowers can be expected.

Sow seeds directly and thin to 3–5 plants per 20 cm pot. For a continuous supply of dill for the kitchen, have 2–3 pots under cultivation and start a similar number when these are half grown. Use a moisture-retentive potting mix. Feed with liquid fertiliser at half strength following harvests to boost further leaf production. Water whenever the soil surface begins to dry. Container-grown dill which is allowed to flower may need staking.

HARVESTING

Harvesting can begin as soon as plants reach about 12–15 cm tall. Cut leaves close to the main stalk. The leaves have their best texture and most appealing flavour before the plants produce seeds. Once flowering starts, the leaves are sparser and stronger tasting. The flower buds can also be harvested and used like the leaves.

Allow some plants to produce flowers to use as a pretty and flavoursome garnish. Also, flowers are the traditional herb addition to pickles, especially gherkins. For the best flavour and appearance, snip flowers for pickles when the heads are carrying both flowers and unripe seeds at the same time.

To harvest seeds for drying, wait until at least half of the seed on each umbel begins to turn pale brown and ripen. The immature seeds will ripen as they dry. Cut the stems, with enough length to be tied in bunches. Handle them gently to avoid dropping too many seeds. Hang upside down in a warm, airy place, with the tops in a loosely tied paper bag or with paper or a tray underneath to catch falling seed. Most of the seeds will fall from the stalks while the remainder will drop when shaken. Store in airtight and light-proof containers in a cool place and use within 6 months for the best flavour.

Dill flowers make a pretty and flavoursome garnish and addition to pickled vegetables.

IN THE KITCHEN

To release its full flavour, dill should be scissored or chopped fairly finely with a sharp knife. Heat causes loss of colour and flavour, so with hot foods add dill just before serving. If dill has to be added during cooking, provide extra freshly picked leaves to add at serving time.

Dill leaf has a milder flavour than the more pungent seeds, which can be used fresh or dried.

Snip the small flowers from the umbels to use as an attractive garnish with a distinctive dill flavour, or add whole umbels to pickles.

Make dill vinegar by the general method given on page 17. Use unripe dill seeds, not dried ones, for maximum tang. Leaves and flowers can also be added. We usually include a few flowers in the bottles of vinegar before sealing, as these look pretty on pantry shelves.

HOW TO USE DILL

With fish

- Make a simple lemon, butter and dill sauce to pour over steamed or grilled fish. Melt a tablespoon of butter in a small saucepan. Add a finely chopped shallot and sauté until softened. Add the grated rind and juice of a lemon and bring to simmering point. Lower heat and gradually whisk in 3 tablespoons of butter, cut into small pieces, a few at a time until a sauce-like consistency is obtained. Remove from the heat and stir in 3 tablespoons of scissored dill and seasoning to taste.
- Add dill to a roux-method white sauce, and for added richness stir in a little sour cream just before serving.
- Bake a whole fish or thick fillets or steaks on a bed of dill branches.
- Add dill to fish parcels: fillets of fish topped with extras such as chopped tomatoes, capsicums, mushrooms, seasoned and then wrapped in aluminium foil and baked.
- Make gravlax, the Swedish way of curing salmon with a mixture of salt, sugar, gin or vodka and dill.
- Top grilled or barbecued fish with dill butter (see pages 18–19).
- For contrast, serve a chilled dill sauce with cooked fish. Combine 1 cup of plain yoghurt with 3 tablespoons of scissored dill and 1 teaspoon of Dijon-style mustard.
- Make a fish pâté by combining smoked salmon or other fish with cream cheese, a little melted butter, lemon juice, black pepper and scissored dill.

- Sprinkle dill on fish soups and chowders.
- Add scissored dill to the white sauce when making a fish pie.

With other foods

- Dill complements many vegetables, particularly cabbage, turnips, cucumber, carrots, onions, potatoes, tomatoes, beetroot, cauliflower, Brussels sprouts, courgettes, mushrooms and broad beans.
- Use traditionally in Middle Eastern-style pilafs, couscous, tabbouleh, etc.
- Try dill instead of mint with lamb, as an equally famous traditional herb.
- Home-pickled gherkins are far superior to most purchased varieties. The recipe for a simple method is in our first book, *The Cook's Garden*.
- Garnish Danish open sandwiches with tiny sprigs of dill. Cut thin slices of wholegrain bread into easily handled pieces, spread generously with butter, or herb butter, or cream cheese, then layer with an assortment of sliced meats or fish, cooked new potatoes, hard-boiled eggs or pâtés, garnish with sliced tomato, onion rings, caviar and dill.
- Dill is a favourite salad herb—its delicate, sour taste enhances many salad greens.
- Add dill to your favourite potato salad dressing.
- Make a simple cucumber salad by coating thin slices of cucumber with a dressing made by combining a teaspoon of salad oil, a teaspoon of wine vinegar, 1/4 teaspoon salt, black pepper and a teaspoon of scissored dill. Alternatively, combine 1/2 cup of sour cream or yoghurt, or a mix of both, with salt and black pepper to taste and a tablespoon of scissored dill.
- Dress hot cooked beetroot with a small diced onion or shallot sautéed in oil until just soft, plus a cup of sour cream, lemon juice, seasoning and scissored dill.
- Garnish soups, especially potato, pumpkin, tomato and fish chowders, with a generous sprinkling of scissored dill.
- Add dill to cheese dips and spreads.
- In the Greek style, add dill to cooked spinach dishes.
- Combine with grated cheese for an omelette filling (see pages 46–47), or sprinkle on scrambled eggs.
- Dill seed flavours many northern European breads. Add a tablespoon of dill seed to your everyday breadmaker wholemeal recipe.
- Dill seeds enhance cooked cabbage — try our method of pan steaming. Heat 2 tablespoons of oil or butter in a large frying pan with a lid. When hot, add the shredded cabbage and a teaspoon of dill seeds, plus 4 tablespoons of water. Cover and steam for a few minutes only, until tender-crisp. Season with pepper and salt if necessary. If fresh dill is available, use it to garnish each serving.

NANCY'S CARROT SPREAD

The basis for this recipe comes from our book *More from the Cook's Garden*. It has developed over the years to include different combinations of fresh herbs. Currently, dill, mint and parsley are preferred. The spread is quickly made in a food processor and is delicious with fresh wholemeal bread.

100 g Cheddar cheese
4 medium-sized carrots, cut into chunks
3–4 stems dill
2 sprigs mint
1 stem parsley
black pepper
2 spring onions, trimmed and roughly chopped
1 teaspoon olive oil

Using the grating disc, grate the cheese and tip out onto a plate. With the metal blade in place, process the carrots, dill, mint, parsley and pepper until finely chopped. Add the cheese, spring onions and oil. Process until well mixed. Spoon into a small bowl. Store in a refrigerator for up to 2 days.

BORSCHT
Serves 4–6

There are many versions of this classic Russian soup. What they all have in common is beetroot, sour cream and lots of dill. A food processor will make short work of chopping the vegetables.

2 tablespoons oil
1 large onion, finely chopped
1 large carrot, peeled and finely chopped
2 medium–sized beetroot, peeled and finely chopped
piece of broccoli, or section of cauliflower, or wedge of cabbage
(approximately 200 g), divided into tiny flowerets, or for
cabbage sliced
1 tart apple, cored and finely chopped
2 medium-sized potatoes, scrubbed and finely chopped
3 cloves garlic, finely chopped
1 teaspoon paprika
2 tablespoons tomato paste
750 ml beef stock
250 ml water
1 bay leaf
black pepper

salt to taste
1 teaspoon sugar
1 tablespoon lemon juice
2 tablespoons chopped parsley

Topping
1/2–3/4 cup sour cream or yoghurt
2 tablespoons scissored dill

In a large saucepan, heat the oil and gently sauté all the vegetables, garlic and the apple, adding them as they are prepared. Once they have softened a little, add the paprika, stir to mix and cook for a further 2 minutes. Add the tomato paste, stock, water, bay leaf and pepper. Stir to mix well. Cover the saucepan and simmer for an hour, stirring occasionally.

Make the topping while the soup is cooking. Combine the sour cream or yoghurt with the dill, cover and chill in a refrigerator.

Taste the soup for salt and add the sugar, lemon juice and parsley. Ladle the soup into bowls and pass the dill-flavoured sour cream around to be spooned into each bowl and stirred in to mix.

RUSSIAN-STYLE VEGETABLE SALAD
Serves 2–4

This refreshing dill-enhanced salad uses readily available vegetables. Steam them just long enough to be cooked while still retaining their colour. Substitute other vegetables as available for those specified in the recipe, to make a total weight of approximately 800 g.

150 g carrots, peeled and cut into bite-sized chunks
300 g small new potatoes, cut if necessary into
bite-sized chunks
200 g broccoli or cauliflower, divided into small flowerets
150 g green beans, sliced into chunks

Dressing
1/2 cup mayonnaise (preferably home-made)
2 tablespoons wine vinegar
1/4 teaspoon salt
1 teaspoon Dijon-style mustard
2 tablespoons chopped pickled gherkins
1 tablespoon capers
2 tablespoons scissored dill

Steam the vegetables individually until just tender. Tip into a large bowl and leave to cool.

Whisk the mayonnaise, wine vinegar, salt and mustard together until smooth. Add the pickled gherkins, capers and dill. Stir to mix.

Pour over the vegetables and stir gently to coat. Spoon into a serving bowl, cover and chill for 1–2 hours or up to 12 hours before serving.

SMOKED SALMON & DILL
PASTA SAUCE
Serves 2

This divine pasta sauce can be made in the time taken to cook the dried pasta.

150 g dry pasta
1/2 teaspoon salt

1/2 cup sour cream
1/2 cup fresh cream
1/2 teaspoon finely grated lemon rind
1 tablespoon lemon juice
2–3 spring onions, trimmed and finely sliced
black pepper
2 or 3 stems dill
200 g smoked salmon, skin discarded, and flesh sliced thinly
across the grain

Half fill a large saucepan with water, add the salt and bring to the boil. Add the pasta and cook for the recommended time. Drain.

Meanwhile, in a small bowl, combine the sour cream, fresh cream, lemon rind and juice, spring onions and black pepper. Chop or scissor the dill.

As soon as the pasta is cooked and drained, return it to the saucepan and gently stir in the cream mixture. Fold in the salmon and half the chopped dill.

Serve in pasta bowls with the remaining dill sprinkled on top.

ROAST LAMB WITH DILL
Serves 4-6

This dill and yoghurt marinade produces a tender, succulent and well-flavoured roast. The tang of the dill permeates the meat and the cooking time is reduced as the joint has been boned and then butterflied. Ask your butcher to do this for you. Serve with minted new potatoes or rice.

1.5–2 kg boned shank end of leg of lamb, butterflied

Marinade
1 cup plain yoghurt
1 shallot or half a small onion, chopped
2 cloves garlic, very finely chopped
1/4 cup roughly chopped parsley
1/2 cup roughly scissored dill
1/2 teaspoon salt
black pepper

Trim as much fat from the meat as possible. In a small bowl combine the marinade ingredients. Spread the meat flat, with the side that had the skin uppermost. Spoon half of the marinade evenly over the surface. Turn the meat over and place in a glass or ceramic dish. Coat with the remaining marinade. Cover and place in a refrigerator for at least 4 hours, or up to 12 hours.

Preheat the oven to 230°C. Put a rack in a roasting pan and place the meat with the inner surface uppermost. Cook in the oven for 15 minutes. Lower the temperature to 190°C and roast for 20 minutes. Turn the meat over and roast for a further 20 minutes. The meat will be pink at the centre, and this may be the preferred stage for serving. If you would rather it was cooked right through, give it another 20 minutes. Remove from the oven and allow to stand at room temperature for 20 minutes before carving. Scrape up the pan juices and serve with the meat—they are too good to be discarded.

BEEF STROGANOFF
Serves 4–6

Dill, sour cream and mushrooms are the characteristic ingredients of a stroganoff.

400 g button mushrooms, sliced
1 large onion, chopped
3 tablespoons butter or oil
2 tablespoons flour
2 tablespoons brandy
1 tablespoon Dijon-style mustard
1 tablespoon tomato paste
2 teaspoons horseradish cream
1 cup beef stock
150 g pottle sour cream (use one of the low-fat versions)
black pepper
500 g rump steak, cut across the grain into thin strips

Garnish
1/2 cup thick yoghurt
several stems of dill

In a large pan, fry the mushrooms and onion in 2 tablespoons of the butter or oil until lightly browned and the juices have evaporated. Lower the heat and stir in the flour. Cook for 2 minutes. Add the brandy, mustard, tomato paste and horse-radish. Stir to mix. Gradually pour in the stock and stir continuously until boiling. Remove from the heat. Add the sour cream and pepper and stir until combined.

In another, heavy-based frying pan, brown the meat in two batches in the extra butter or oil. Add to the mushroom sauce. Reheat gently.

Serve over pasta with a dollop of yoghurt and a generous sprinkling of dill.

DILL & CHEDDAR MUFFINS
Makes 30 mini-sized muffins

Mary likes to have a batch of these moreish mini-muffins in the freezer ready for impromptu nibbles at any time. Serve warm with a small piece of extra Cheddar or cream cheese inserted into the centre, plus a quarter-slice of tomato. Alternatively, serve cold filled with sour cream, a tiny sprig of dill and a piece of smoked salmon. Garnish the plateful with extra dill sprigs. The basic recipe for the cheese muffins comes from Lois Daish's book *Good Food*.

2 cups white flour
3 teaspoons baking powder
1/4 teaspoon salt
black pepper
pinch chilli powder
pinch mustard powder
2 tablespoons scissored dill
150 g Cheddar cheese, grated

2 eggs
200 ml milk
75 ml oil

Preheat the oven to 200°C.

Sift the flour, baking powder, salt, pepper, chilli powder and mustard into a large bowl. Stir in the dill and cheese.

In a small bowl, beat the eggs, milk and oil. Pour into the dry ingredients and stir until just combined. Do not over-mix.

If necessary, lightly grease your muffin pans. Using a teaspoon, three-quarters fill each pan. Bake for 15 minutes or until well risen and golden brown. Loosen the muffins and remove from the pans onto a rack to cool. Use within a few hours or freeze.

fennel

Bold and beautiful, bronze fennel is currently a fashionable architectural garden plant. But how many gardeners know that its feathery leaves, crisp stalks, buds, flowers and seeds are all edible and share a sweet anise flavour, making it an equally valuable culinary herb?

The common green fennel is a rampant weed in some temperate countries, and so is often despised by many who have not even tasted it. Others who do enjoy using it can't see the point of growing it in the garden if roadside supplies are handy. A risk with eating these wild fennels is that they may have been sprayed with weedkillers and, if near a busy road, are likely to be coated in traffic pollutants. Another risk is mistaking fennel for the very poisonous hemlock (*Conium maculatum*), which grows in similar situations. Fennel has green stems with feathery leaves, yellow flowers and a sweet anise smell. Hemlock has purple blotches on its stems, parsley-like foliage, white flowers and a light 'mousy' smell. All parts of hemlock are toxic and should not be touched.

Fennels (*Foeniculum vulgare*), bronze fennel in particular, make attractive and rewarding garden plants, requiring only a minimum of care. They are perennials which thrive in most garden situations and grow upwards of 1.3 m tall, making them very suitable for the back of the border. Alternatively, if grown only for leaf harvests, they will make a pretty row beside other vegetables.

In the garden setting, fennel and dill are sometimes confused. We have listed the differences in our chapter on dill (page 62). If in doubt, taste the leaves—fennel's sweet liquorice flavour will be evident.

VARIETIES

It is important to distinguish between the herb fennel and the vegetable fennel. The latter is known as Florence fennel or finocchio (*F. vulgare* subsp. *vulgare* var. *azoricum*) and has leaf stalks swollen at the base, rather like celery. It makes a delightful vegetable and deserves to be better known, but its feathery leaves, which look the same as the herb fennel, are lacking in the characteristic and desirable sweet anise taste.

There are 3 commonly grown forms of the herb fennel: the so-called wild fennel (*F. vulgare* subsp. *vulgare* var. *vulgare*), which has slightly bitter leaves and less anise flavour; sweet fennel (*F. vulgare* subsp. *vulgare* var. *dulce*), with sweet, liquorice-tasting leaves, flowers and seeds; and bronze fennel (*F. vulgare* subsp. *vulgare* 'Purpureum'), which has a similar taste to sweet fennel but has attractive bronze-purple foliage.

As it is difficult to distinguish between the 2 green herb fennels, and therefore possible to purchase the wild one lacking the sweet anise flavour, we recommend that cooks buy the bronze form.

CULTIVATION

Fennel grows best in a sunny place with deep, well-drained, moisture-retentive soil. It likes lime, so incorporate a cup of dolomite lime per square metre, if necessary, at planting time. As fennel dislikes heavy clay soils, which inhibit root development, you may need to add extra amounts of coarse compost and horticultural grit to the bed prior to planting. The addition of compost to all soil types will ensure adequate moisture retention and reduce the amount of watering required. Fennel roots can rot if the ground is not free draining, so build up beds if needed. Fennel will tolerate hot dry positions but its foliage will be sparse. As Jekka McVicar says, fennel grown in good soil looks like 'a dome of green or purple candyfloss'. In very hot areas, some afternoon shade may be beneficial.

Fennel can be propagated by either sowing seed or dividing established roots. Small plants are also available from garden centres and specialist nurseries.

Seed is best sown *in situ* as early in spring as soil conditions, temperatures and frosts permit. Germination will be slow if temperatures are too low. Alternatively, sow seed indoors in individual containers. Sow 3–4 seeds per container and thin to 1 healthy seedling. Bottom heat (15–21°C) will speed germination (see page 11). When planting out, it is important to avoid disturbing the roots, so transplants should be small and not rootbound. This applies to purchased plants as well, which should be no larger than a seedling.

To sow directly in the garden, use shallow drills 45 cm apart and cover the seeds no deeper than 5 mm (see page 12). Keep constantly moist until the first leaves appear, in 10–14 days. Progressively thin to 45 cm apart, if growing for flowers and seeds, or 20–30 cm apart for maximum leaf production. It is important to plant or sow as early as possible in spring to allow time for flowering and seed ripening to occur before winter approaches. For leaf production only, successive row sowings through spring and early summer ensure continuous harvests.

Dividing an established root can be a heavy task, as the root system may be massive. Divide into healthy portions taken from the outside of the clump. Replant in rows or as specimen plants in a shrub and flower border.

Look out for self-sown plants as, if these appear in suitable locations, they are a gardener's bonus.

Maintain adequate but not excessive moisture levels during active growth, and occasionally apply a liquid fertiliser such as fish emulsion or well-rotted manure or compost. Avoid watering from mid-autumn, once growth

Bronze fennel in spring

Green fennel

appears to have ceased.

For maximum leaf production, remove flower stems as soon as they form. Cutting some shoots to the base at intervals will also help maintain supplies of lush feathery leaves.

FENNEL
(*Foeniculum vulgare*)

For most of our gardening careers, we knew of only two fennels. There was the tall green form growing wild along roadsides and railway embankments, which we were advised not to touch in case it had been sprayed with weed-killer. The other fennel was the elegant bronze form which decorated ornamental herb gardens and perennial borders. We seldom ate either. We were introduced to a third fennel in the 1970s, the challenging vegetable known as Florence or bulbous fennel which Mary succeeded in growing in her Christchurch garden. Botanists agree that these belong to a single species, but there is less consensus as to whether they are different subspecies or just different varieties of the same subspecies.

European food writers describe three sorts, according to their culinary properties: bitter, sweet, and Florence fennel. Those who are familiar with Italian cuisines may mention another sort called *carosella*—its peeled stalks are eaten just before the flowers develop. It is considered to be a separate subspecies, *piperitum*, while the other three are just different varieties of the same subspecies, *vulgare*. Thus the full name of the common fennel is *Foeniculum vulgare* subsp. *vulgare* var. *vulgare*, as if to remind us what a vulgar plant it is! The sweet fennel is var. *dulce*, and the Florence fennel is var. *azoricum*.

Though sweet fennel has been listed in our local herb catalogues, we are uncertain whether this is the true *dulce* variety known around the Mediterranean. It is supposed to lack bitterness and to have a delicate aniseed flavour in both seeds and foliage. The seeds are said to be longer and heavier than those of the common fennel. In Anatolia (Turkey), where fennel is a native, the sweet variety is preferred for garden cultivation and is treated as an annual. After the ripe seedheads have been gathered, the roots are dug out, washed and sliced, then sun dried or used fresh in fruit and vegetable salads.

For many centuries gardeners in more northerly parts of Europe tried to grow this improved sweet fennel. It was first mentioned as a distinct variety in 9th-century France. By the 16th century, both French and English writers recommended sweet fennel, though it was clearly not at home in colder regions. John Gerard wrote that it 'doth not prosper well in this countrey, for being sowen of good and perfect seed, yet in the second yeere after his sowing it will degenerate from the right kinde, and become common

Fennell'. Eventually, English gardeners gave up on it, and by the 19th century it was so little known that writers began confusing it with the bulbous Florence fennel.

Fennel has been a significant herb in Mediterranean countries since the Bronze Age. In Mycenaean Greece (about 1300 BC) it was called *ma-ra-tu-wo*, and by the time of Homer (8th century BC) it had given its name to a place in Greece called Marathon, presumably a field of wild fennel. In 490 BC this was the site of a battle between the invading Persians and the Greeks. The Athenian athlete Pheidippides ran to Sparta to get help, taking two days to cover the 240 km. This was the original 'marathon' run, not the shorter 42.195 km distance from the battle site to Athens commemorated in the modern Olympic event. Statues of Pheidippides show him with a sprig of fennel in his hand. Nearly 2500 years later, the Greeks still call this plant *márathon*.

The Romans adopted another name for the fennel plant, *foeniculum*, from its rather obscure connection with hay, *fenum*. Some etymologists argue that it smells like new-mown hay, but to us the smell is not similar. We wonder whether wild fennel was thus named because it grew as a weed in hay fields and was included in the fodder, just as the garden plant cornflower took the general English name for a cereal crop (corn) in which it sprang up as a weed. Whatever the association, to the Romans fennel was a useful but not a high status herb. They used its seeds in stuffings, soups and sauces, its fresh foliage in soups and with artichokes and chick-peas, and they pickled its tender young stalks. Medicinally, they recommended it for indigestion and dim vision.

These medicinal virtues were appreciated in the Middle Ages, when there was an extensive trade in fennel seeds. Chewed, they relieved hunger pangs while fasting. Palace accounts show that 3.85 kg were purchased for just one month's use by the occupants of the king's wardrobe in 14th-century England. Was this a sign of diligent fasting or widespread dyspepsia? Mediaeval recipes called for fresh 'fenkel' in soups, and ground fennel seeds and salt pressed into flattened veal steaks before grilling. In Mediterranean countries, mediaeval cooks were using 'the white part of fennel', which suggests that they already had a form of bulbous Florence fennel, or were blanching the young stalks, as the French were doing in the 16th and the English in the 17th–18th centuries.

Traditionally, fennel has been considered an

accompaniment to fish. In Britain this goes back to the 17th century at least, as John Parkinson made clear in 1629: 'Fenell is of great use to trimme up [garnish], and strowe upon fish, as also to boyle or put among fish of divers sorts, Cowcumbers pickled, and other fruits, &c'. He also noted the use of fennel seed in apple pies and in bread, two practices which could be revived. For nursing mothers, fennel leaves in a butter-based sauce served over mackerel 'cause great Quantities of Milk'. By the 19th century this sauce for mackerel was the only form in which fennel reached British tables, other than as a garnish. It is interesting that, while southern Europeans selected fennel varieties to be crisp salad ingredients or cooked vegetables, northern Europeans and Americans turned to celery and celeriac for these purposes, relegating fennel to the status of a second-rate, rather weedy herb.

Although Florence fennel has acquired gourmet ranking with the recent popularity of Mediterranean cooking styles, so far this is the only variety of fennel to be rediscovered by English-speaking cooks. Sweet fennel and *carosella* may yet be adopted in southern hemisphere countries where the climate is warm. Fennel seeds themselves could be much more widely used. With a food pedigree of over three millennia, and extensive use in cuisines from the Mediterranean across to India and Malaysia, they deserve another try.

If aphids become a problem, knock them off with a strong spray from the garden hose.

In colder climates, fennel dies right down to the ground in winter. Cut the dead or old stalks back to the base in late autumn.

Fennel is a relatively short-lived perennial, seldom lasting beyond 6 years. To maintain maximum vigour it is wise to dig up the roots, divide and replant every 3–4 years.

GROWING IN CONTAINERS

Bronze fennel makes a particularly attractive outdoor pot plant. A deep pot is required to accommodate the large root system and daily water will be required. Use a coarse potting mix with the addition of horticultural grit (5:1) to improve drainage. Feed regularly to maintain good growth and stake if required. Repot each year to maintain health and vigour.

HARVESTING

In warm climates, fennel leaves may be available all year, but the most tender and luxuriant harvests of leaves are in spring. In colder places, cooks need to be patient and not pick too heavily from the new shoots as they first appear. Growing several plants will allow earlier and larger harvests, as taking one or two sprigs from each plant is not harmful. Cut feathery fennel leaves off at ground level when small, but when larger snip off from the stems. Young stems and fleshy sheaths are edible, so can be harvested along with the leaves.

Pick whole umbels of buds or yellow flowers and snip from these in the kitchen.

Harvest seeds green and immature for immediate use, or brown and ripe to dry for long-term storage. Inspect the umbels regularly so that the seeds can be gathered before they drop. They will gradually turn from yellowish green to brown and then fall in even the gentlest breeze. The seeds ripen over a long period, so harvesting needs to be ongoing. Some writers suggest harvesting while the seed is still light green to avoid unwanted seedlings next spring. If you choose this method, watch seeds carefully while drying, as they are likely to perspire and if left damp may grow mould.

Fennel leaves lose so much flavour when dried that this is not worth doing.

IN THE KITCHEN

Feathery fennel leaves may be scissored or chopped. Their flavour is most intense if they are gathered immediately before use and, as much character is lost with cooking, they should be added to hot dishes just before serving. Two tablespoons to 1/4 cup of scissored fennel leaves for 4–6 servings will add the characteristic flavour.

Tender stems may be sliced thinly and added to salads or cooked dishes. Peeling before slicing is optional. The tender and fleshy sheaths may be chopped and used like the leaves and stems.

Snip flower buds and flowers from the umbels to scatter over both cooked and uncooked dishes.

Green or ripe seeds can be used either whole or

chopped. If ground fennel seeds are required, dry roast brown seeds until they begin to darken slightly and smell wonderful, before attempting to grind them with a mortar and pestle or in an electric coffee-grinder or blender. The roasting makes them easier to grind and enhances their flavour. Chopped and ground seeds go a long way: half a teaspoon may be sufficient for 4–6 servings. Use a full teaspoon of whole green or dried seeds.

HOW TO USE FENNEL

- Like dill, fennel is most often used in fish dishes. Add to stuffings, sauces, court bouillon for poaching fish, marinades, stews, chowders. Simply lay a large sprig in the cavity of a whole fish for baking, or add to a traditional potato-topped fish pie.
- Our favourite fennel and vegetable combinations include: seeds with parsnips and pumpkin; chopped leaves with Florence fennel, courgettes, tomatoes, aubergine, carrots and new potatoes; either seeds or leaves with cabbage, beetroot, onions and potatoes.
- Use the first little sprigs of spring fennel in mixed-leaf salads. Later, include sliced, tender stems for added crunchiness.
- Fennel adds another dimension to egg dishes. Stir scissored leaves into scrambled eggs just before serving, combine with cheese to fill omelettes (see pages 46–47), and add to egg sandwiches.
- Use fennel buds and flowers snipped from the umbels over grilled fish, tomato, carrot, bean and potato salads, and on chilled soups, especially cucumber.
- Use scissored fennel as an alternative to mint or coriander in hummus and lentil dishes.
- Add scissored fennel to spreads or dips based on cottage cheese, cream cheese, yoghurt or vegetables.
- When barbecuing, add fennel stalks to the hot coals, or wrap fish with damp fennel leaves before placing on the rack.
- Make fennel and cheese scones: use your favourite cheese scone recipe and add 1/2 teaspoon of chopped fennel seeds and 3 tablespoons of scissored fennel leaves.
- Use fennel buds and flowers to replace dill in pickles.
- Use fennel seeds in Italian-style cooking: in rich tomato sauce, sausages, roast pork, pizza crust or focaccia.
- Enhance breads with fennel seeds, either green or dried.

For example, the Swedish Limpé is a dark rye bread flavoured with fennel seeds, orange zest and treacle. For extra flavour and ease of grinding, dry roast the seeds. Mary makes a Limpé-style loaf in her breadmaker with the following ingredients: 2 teaspoons of Surebake yeast or 1 1/2 teaspoons of instant yeast, 200 g of baker's flour, 80 g of wholemeal flour, 40 g of ryemeal, 1 teaspoon of instant coffee powder, 1/4 teaspoon of salt, 1/2 teaspoon of fennel seeds (dry roasted and ground), grated rind of 1 orange, 4 teaspoons of oil, 1 1/2 tablespoons of treacle and 180 ml of warm water. Set the breadmaker to the wholemeal cycle.

- Make a traditional apple pie, layering the filling with 2 teaspoons of chopped fennel seeds and half a cup of sugar to every 500 g of sliced cooking apples.

SPANISH-STYLE BEAN & POTATO SOUP
Serves 4 as a main-dish soup

Saffron turns this white bean and potato soup a cheerful shade of yellow and the fennel seeds and salami impart a warming and spicy flavour.

1 cup dried haricot beans, soaked overnight in plenty
of cold water
2 tablespoons oil
1 medium-sized onion, finely chopped
2 cloves garlic, very finely chopped
1 bay leaf
1 teaspoon chopped fennel seeds
1/4 teaspoon saffron threads, crushed
1/4 teaspoon deseeded and finely chopped red chilli
500 ml chicken stock
1 cup water
500 g small waxy potatoes, cut into quarters or eighths
depending on size
70 g piece of spicy salami, skinned and diced
4 tablespoons dry sherry
salt to taste

In a large saucepan, heat the oil and sauté the onion and garlic until soft. Add the bay leaf, chopped fennel seeds, saffron and chilli and stir over a gentle heat for a few minutes. Drain and rinse the soaked beans and add to the saucepan. Add the stock and water. Cover and simmer for 30–40 minutes or until the beans are almost tender. Add the potatoes and continue simmering for about another 15 minutes, or until they are tender but not broken. Add the salami and sherry and salt to taste. Reheat. Serve garnished with scissored fennel leaves, in season, or otherwise chopped marjoram or parsley.

FENNEL & SALMON PASTA SAUCE
Serves 2

This creamy-tasting but low-fat sauce is flavoured with the traditional partnership of salmon and fennel or dill.

1 tablespoon oil
1 small onion or shallot, finely chopped
220 g can salmon, drained
1 tablespoon cornflour
1 cup canned evaporated milk (the low-fat version is good)
black pepper
2 tablespoons lemon juice
1 tablespoon scissored parsley
1 tablespoon scissored young fennel or dill leaves, plus extra for garnishing
freshly grated Parmesan cheese (optional)

200 g dried pasta

In a small saucepan, sauté the onion or shallot in oil until soft but not brown. Add the salmon and break up with a spoon. In a small container, mix the cornflour with 2 tablespoons of the measured evaporated milk until smooth. Pour the remaining evaporated milk into the saucepan. Heat gently to just below boiling point. Pour in the cornflour mix and continue stirring until thickened. Remove from the heat. Stir in the pepper, lemon juice and herbs.

Cook the pasta in a large saucepan of boiling, salted water until tender. Drain. Dish up into individual bowls or onto plates and top with the sauce. Garnish with fennel leaves and pass around Parmesan cheese to be added if desired.

FENNEL DRESSING
Makes sufficient to dress a salad for 4–6

This versatile dressing transforms any vegetable-based salad into something special. We enjoy it with potato, broad bean, green bean, carrot and broccoli salads and coleslaw. Make an hour or two ahead, coat the selected cooked or raw vegetables, cover, and stand in a refrigerator to allow the flavours to mingle. It can also be used spread on small pieces of toast topped with smoked salmon or gravlax.

1/4 cup mayonnaise (home-made is best)
2 tablespoons sour cream or crème fraîche
2 teaspoons balsamic vinegar
1 teaspoon wholegrain mustard
1 clove garlic, very finely chopped
black pepper
3 tablespoons chopped or scissored fennel leaves

In a small bowl, use a whisk to combine all the ingredients. Store in a refrigerator and use within 2 days.

garlicCHives

Although we have grown garlic chives (*Allium tuberosum*) for many years, enjoying their attractive, tidy, strap-like, dark green, foliage and starry white flowers, we seldom used them in the kitchen, finding their taste rather overpowering and their texture too tough to use, like chives, in salads or egg dishes. More recently, we read about their use in Asian kitchens and learnt that they are usually briefly cooked—in stir-fries or soups. Our garlic chives were picked spasmodically throughout the year, so some leaves were invariably older and tougher. The Asian cultivation methods favour rapid growth, resulting in tender and milder-tasting leaves. In Asian markets, garlic chives are often sold complete with their small, tight flower buds. If the flowers are open they are considered too old to eat.

We have now 'rediscovered' garlic chives, growing them quickly in ideal conditions, and enjoying their mildly garlic, Asian flavour.

Garlic chive florets have a mild, sweet, almost rose-like aroma and pleasant flavour. They can be tossed into salads or added at the last minute to garnish cooked dishes.

VARIETIES

Garlic chives are also known in English-speaking countries as Asian chives and Oriental chives. So far we have been unable to obtain any named cultivars, though varieties have been selected especially for leaf production and others for buds and flowers.

CULTIVATION

Garlic chives grow in a wide range of soils, though they do best in light, fertile soil, rich in organic matter. Built-up beds provide the necessary good drainage and depth of soil for their long roots. Incorporate plenty of compost or well-rotted manure before planting.

Garlic chives are very hardy, tolerating heavy frosts, though leaf growth is likely to die down. They prefer full sun but will grow in light shade.

Garlic chives are slower growing than chives and can remain in the same site for 4–5 years. They develop thick

rhizomes. In all but the coldest climates, they provide leaves all year round. Three to four established clumps is sufficient for a small household.

The quickest method of obtaining plants is by dividing an established clump in spring or autumn. Dig a whole clump and carefully separate into small clumps of about 3 rhizomes and replant in fresh soil. Discard older roots in the centre of the clump.

To raise from seed follow the same method as for chives (see pages 50–51). The seed should be fresh, as it loses viability quickly.

Do not harvest from garlic chive clumps within their first year. Plants obtained by division or raised from seed need time to become established. Keep newly planted clumps weed free, and mulch to maintain moisture levels. If watering is required, ensure that it penetrates well, as deep rooting should be encouraged.

Tidy garlic chive clumps each spring by removing old leaves and clearing debris from the surrounding soil. Apply a fresh mulch.

Remove flowering stems from clumps less than 2 years old. Flowers from older clumps should be picked before their seed ripens, as self-sowing can be a problem, with the resulting progeny becoming invasive.

Garlic chives will benefit from several applications of liquid fertiliser during spring and summer.

GROWING IN CONTAINERS

As a slower-growing herb, garlic chives make tidy container plants. The pots should be deep (at least 20 cm) and filled with free-draining potting mix (see page 15). Keep moist and feed with liquid fertiliser at the correct strength every 6 weeks and after major harvests.

HARVESTING

Like chives, established garlic chive clumps can be cut back several times during late spring and summer. This encourages the development of fresh tender leaves. Alternatively, individual leaves can be snipped as required. Cut just above the soil level, as the lowest portions of the leaves are the most tender.

Pick flower stems complete with tight buds to use in stir-fries. The white flowerheads can also be picked for the kitchen.

GARLIC CHIVES
(*Allium tuberosum*)

Even more tolerant of cold and at least as long-lived as ordinary chives, garlic chives (also known as Chinese chives) were relatively unknown in Western countries until the later 20th century. Calling them chives is rather misleading, for they have solid, keeled leaves instead of hollow tubes. They grow taller and have tuberous rhizomes instead of bulblets, hence the species name *tuberosum*. The wild form occurs in Assam (India) and Nepal to the west, across China and northern Thailand, as far east as Japan and the Philippines.

Domestication probably occurred much earlier than with Western chives, judging from the greater diversity of uses and varieties selected to suit these. Certain forms have been chosen for their tender flower stalks, which are eaten before the white star-like flowers start to open. Others, with broader leaves, are grown in the dark and sold as pale, drooping bundles of tender leaves, which are often eaten with fried noodles. The aim of the producers of *jiu cai*, *gau tsoi* and *nira*, as this plant is known in Mandarin, Cantonese and Japanese respectively, is to grow it as fast as possible for maximum tenderness. Westerners often find the flavour fairly strong and more like garlic than chives, possibly because it has been accentuated by slow growth. Statements that the plant is a substitute for chives have also encouraged its use raw, whereas in most Asian cuisines the leaves and flower stalks are lightly cooked. The introduction of the plant with a misleading name has had a profound affect on its use and acceptability.

IN THE KITCHEN

As the leaves of garlic chives tend to be tougher and more strongly flavoured than chives, we prefer to add them to cooked dishes such as stir-fries. When using them as a garnish, we either stir-fry briefly in a little oil or blanch them. The cooking time should be just long enough to soften the leaves without loss of colour.

Using a sharp knife and a board, slice lined-up groups of leaves into short lengths of 2–3 cm for stir-fries or

1–2 cm for a garnish. Stems with buds can be treated in the same way.

The florets should be snipped from the heads and used in salads or cold dishes, or added to hot dishes at the very last minute.

HOW TO USE GARLIC CHIVES
- Garlic chives make an attractive and tasty garnish in Asian-style or -flavoured dishes.
- Use garlic chives in Asian dishes to help provide that authentic flavour. They are especially needed for stir-fries, roll-ups or spring rolls, soups, dumplings and tofu dishes.
- The florets make a pretty addition when tossed into salads, added at the last minute to steamed or sautéed vegetables, or used as a garnish on baked potatoes, herb butters or vegetable and cold meat platters.
- Garlic chives, sliced and briefly blanched, make an attractive and tasty garnish on a wide range of Western dishes: cheese omelettes, frittatas, soups, pasta sauces, pizzas, meat and vegetable casseroles—in fact, on any robust-flavoured savoury dish.

Snip the starry-white florets to use as a garnish.

Garlic chives

PUMPKIN SOUP WITH AN ASIAN FLAVOUR
Serves 4–6

We developed this recipe to make use of plentiful supplies of garlic chives. To emphasise their distinct Asian flavour, we incorporated other appropriate seasonings. The result has proved to be a 'hit'.

2 tablespoons peanut oil
1 large onion, roughly chopped
2 cloves garlic, chopped
1 slice fresh ginger, chopped
800 g pumpkin (after removal of skin and seeds), chopped into chunks
1 litre chicken stock
1 tablespoon 'mild' sweet chilli sauce
1 tablespoon fish sauce
3 leaves rau răm, (Vietnamese mint) or use coriander stalks and roots
black pepper
salt if needed

Garnish
1 tablespoon peanut oil
1/4–1/2 cup sliced garlic chives
plain yoghurt (optional)

In a large saucepan, heat the oil and gently sauté the onion, garlic and ginger until soft. Add the pumpkin. Pour in the stock and add the chilli sauce, fish sauce, rau răm or coriander and seasoning. Cover and simmer gently for 30–45 minutes or until the pumpkin is tender. Discard the rau răm leaves.

Purée the soup in a blender or food processor until very smooth. Return to the saucepan. Heat the second measure of peanut oil in a small saucepan and stir-fry the garlic chives briefly, until just softened but still bright green. Ladle the soup into bowls and sprinkle with the garlic chives. Pass the yoghurt around in a small bowl.

GARLIC CHIVE RICE SALAD
Serves 2–4

This recipe demonstrates the charms of garlic chives as a tasty and attractive garnish. Other vegetables may be substituted for the ones listed.

2 cups cooked long-grain white rice (start with 2/3 cup raw rice)
1/2 cup cooked peas (or sliced and blanched asparagus or beans)
1 medium-sized carrot, peeled, cut lengthwise into quarters, thinly sliced and blanched for 3 minutes
1 yellow capsicum, deseeded and diced

Dressing
3 tablespoons peanut oil
2 tablespoons lemon juice
1 teaspoon sweet chilli sauce
1 clove garlic, very finely chopped
1/4–1/2 teaspoon salt
black pepper
1 tablespoon chopped basil

Garnish
1 tablespoon peanut oil
3 tablespoons sliced garlic chives
roasted cashew nuts (optional), (see page 21)

In a large bowl, combine the first 4 ingredients.

In a small bowl, combine the dressing ingredients. Pour over the rice mixture and toss gently to mix through. Spoon the salad into a serving bowl.

In a small saucepan, heat the garnish measure of peanut oil and stir-fry the garlic chives briefly, until just softened but still bright green. Sprinkle over the salad with the cashews.

lemon balm

Lemon balm (*Melissa officinalis*) enjoys the reputation of being one of the easiest herbs to grow and is commonly found in most herb gardens. Why, then, is it not more popular in the kitchen? Maybe it is just too familiar or not currently in fashion. Whatever the reason, we think it is time for cooks to rediscover this delightful herb. We love its lingering lemon aroma in the garden (it always appears on plant lists for fragrant gardens) and plant it close to paths where we can brush against the foliage. In the kitchen its value lies in its sweet and subtle lemon flavour with a hint of mint and honey.

Lemon balm is a perennial. Its tall stems (60–120 cm) die back in winter to a basal mound of shoots. In cold winters it may die back completely. Its roots are hardy, though gardeners in areas with very hard frosts are advised to cover the plants with straw. It has pretty heart-shaped or oval leaves, pale green, or variegated green and gold, or plain gold. Its pale cream-coloured flowers are undistinguished but much loved by bees.

Although it looks like, and is, a member of the mint family, it is without runners. However, it does spread into large clumps and can self-sow aggressively. These offspring are easily removed if in the wrong place.

VARIETIES

We have grown 2 varieties: the green-leaved *Melissa officinalis*, and the variegated green and gold *M. o.* 'Aurea' (also called 'Variegata'). The gold-leaved form is called *M. o.* 'All gold', and we have read about one called 'Quedlinburger Niederliegende', which is reported to contain more of the essential oils that give this herb its citrus flavour.

The variegated form tends to revert to green during summer. Cutting back frequently promotes new growth of green and gold leaves.

The gold form scorches easily in summer heat, and we have noticed some minor leaf-edge browning in our variegated form after unseasonal heat in early summer.

As far as we know, all forms have a similar flavour.

CULTIVATION

Lemon balm is a first-choice herb for a semi-shaded position. The green-leaved variety will cope with full sun but afternoon shade is important for the others. Maximum flavour development is assured with at least half a day of full sun.

Lemon balm is not particular as to soil type, but certainly produces larger and more tender leaves when grown in fairly rich, well-draining moist soil in the vegetable garden. As it is shallow rooting, it appreciates extra water during dry spells.

Lemon balm can be propagated by seed, or by division of an established plant—by far the easiest method. Many small, rooted pieces can be obtained from a single large

LEMON BALM
(*Melissa officinalis*)

To the ancient Greeks, *melissa* meant honey bee. Such was the love for honey and knowledge of bee-keeping in the classical world that the Greeks and Romans recognised a category of 'bee-plants'. Lemon balm, or balm as it used to be called, ranked highly, gaining the title *melissophyllon* or 'bee leaf'. If hives are rubbed over with this plant, reported Pliny, the bees will not swarm away, 'for no flower gives them greater pleasure'. Honey was more than a luxury food—it had numerous medical uses—so lemon balm may initially have acquired its healing reputation by association. It was to be found growing wild in damp and shady places around the Mediterranean and across western Asia, and has always shown great ability to perpetuate itself without the gardener's assistance. There is no evidence that the ancient Mediterranean civilisations consumed it as food, except in the value-added product we know as honey.

Knowledge of the plant seems to have been lost in Western Europe until Arab writers advocated its medicinal use in Spain in the 11th century AD. Gradually it penetrated northern Europe. By the 16th century a particularly fragrant form was reported growing in Germany, and it was widely used in England for strewing on floors and as an ingredient of herbal cordials and cosmetic 'waters' like cologne. There was still no mention of it in any recipes, however.

Perhaps it was the growing market for citrus fruit in Western Europe, creating a desire for lemon flavours in food, that simultaneously enhanced the reputation of lemon balm. Its English name, a shortened form of balsam (a rare and expensive Eastern resin), must also have helped its image. With the insight of a modern marketing expert, John Parkinson wrote in 1629: 'I verily thinke, that our forefathers hearing of the healing and comfortable properties of the true naturall Baulme, and finding this herbe to be so effectuall, gave it the name of Baulme, in imitation of his properties and vertues'. Both John Parkinson and John Gerard likened its scent to the citron, a primitive form of lemon.

By the end of the 17th century, lemon balm was an ingredient of broths, salads, cordials and ales, though its advocates never dissociated its culinary uses from its medicinal virtues. The most enthusiastic description of the plant appeared in John Evelyn's book on salads, *Acetaria*, published in 1699. He insisted on adding its tender leaves to mixed salads, and putting freshly gathered sprigs in wine—in his words, lemon balm was 'Cordial and exhilarating, sovereign for the Brain, strengthning the Memory, and powerfully chasing away Melancholy'. On reading his testimonial, I promptly made a cup of lemon balm tea to assist the writing of this book!

Soon, however, its very commonness saw it lose favour among the fashionable set. The anonymous writer of *Adam's Luxury and Eve's Cookery* (1744) declared that this herb 'is so common in every Old Woman's Garden, that it is almost needless to say any thing of it'. By 1822 John Claudius Loudon concluded that 'It is now little used, unless for making a simple balm-tea . . . and for forming a light and agreeable beverage under the name of *balm wine*'. The stigma of 'country' associations persisted throughout the 19th century. A 'coarse-looking' plant which was a 'general favourite in the country' and 'in high repute amongst village doctresses' was unlikely to attract the attention of upper-class households with town houses. In 1932 a leading American herb writer, Louise Beebe Wilder, went so far as to call it 'a determined weed, too rampant to admit to the garden'. She suggested that lemon verbena had 'largely taken its place'. But country people found this hardy perennial balm undemanding and reliable. When they needed a sprig for a spring salad or a summer drink, when they required a handful for a pot of tea to drive away the blues, lemon balm was on hand.

The spread of variegated and golden forms has made lemon balm more acceptable to modern herb gardeners. Variations with floral-mint and lime scents have been discovered and propagated. The plant has shaken off its role as a poor man's lemon thyme, or wartime substitute for lemons in marrow jam, and now has a distinctive part to play in dishes requiring fresh-looking, fresh-tasting leaves gathered directly from the garden.

plant. Divide in spring or autumn into small pieces, each with 3–4 buds. Plant out in a fresh site, 45 cm apart (see page 13).

Only green-leaved lemon balm can be raised from seed. The seed is fine and should be sown in spring in a good quality seed-sowing mix in small pots. It needs light to germinate, so don't cover the seed. The ideal soil temperature for germination is about 20°C, so some bottom heat may be required. Germination takes 7–14 days. Keep moist but not wet. Prick seedlings out into individual pots as soon as they are large enough to handle, and start hardening off (see page 11).

An alternative method, suggested by some herb writers, is to sow *in situ* in late autumn, with germination the following spring. The seed should be left uncovered. When the seedlings are large enough to be handled, they should be thinned or transplanted.

Another easy method is simply to allow one lemon balm plant to flower and set seed. Young self-sown plants will be evident by late the following spring. These can be transplanted. Self-sown plants from variegated or gold-leaved forms are likely to be green.

Small households will need 2–3 lemon balm plants to allow a rotational system of cutting back to ensure ongoing harvests of young leaves for the kitchen.

Lemon balm requires very little maintenance. It can be cut back fully 2 or 3 times during summer to encourage fresh young leaves. Cut back no lower than 5 cm from the ground. If only one cut is scheduled, make it just before flowering. Variegated and golden forms will need to be cut back to retain their colour.

After major harvesting or trimming, apply a liquid fertiliser. Don't overdo this, however, as the plant will produce lush large leaves which may be lacking in flavour.

Rust is reported to be an occasional problem. The solution is to cut the stems back to just above ground level, and dispose of the cuttings along with any fallen leaves. The new foliage should be rust free. We have seen minor amounts of mildew, which can be treated with a baking soda spray after first thinning the plant to allow

Variegated lemon balm

Green-leaved lemon balm

better air circulation.

Provide extra water during hot dry spells, but don't overdo this, as lemon balm does not require as much water as mints.

Tidy plants in late autumn or early spring by removing dead stems and dropped leaves. Apply a fresh mulch of good compost.

Lemon balm plants that are harvested from frequently will lose vigour after 3–4 years and require replacing. If you have 2 or more plants, one can be divided each year to provide continuity of supplies.

GROWING IN CONTAINERS

Lemon balm with its bushy, upright growth habit makes an attractive container plant. Pot up in spring in a good free-draining mix (see page 15). Keep plants moist but not saturated during the growing season. Allow the container to become almost dry during winter. Repot in early spring, dividing the root if too large for the pot. Harvest evenly by snipping off some of the growing sprigs. Have several pots of lemon balm to avoid over-picking.

HARVESTING

To allow young lemon balm plants to establish well, limit or avoid harvesting during the first year.

Cut lemon balm sprigs, at any length, back to just above a pair of leaves. Use scissors to cut small individual sprigs, or secateurs if doing a major revival trim.

Young sprigs harvested in spring and early summer, before hot weather starts, are the most tender for salads and for sprinkling on dishes just before serving. Older leaves are fine for infusing, when they are removed before serving.

Lemon balm loses some flavour and colour when dried but can be enjoyed for herb tea blends during winter. Cut long stems on a dull but dry and cool day just as the flower buds are forming. Handle them gently to prevent bruising. Either tie in small bunches to hang upside down in a darkish, dry and airy place, or snip off the leaves and dry them on a rack in a slow oven, dehydrator or microwave (see pages 16–17). It is important to dry lemon balm quickly and in the dark to prevent black dis-colouration. When crisp, strip the leaves from the stalks and store whole in airtight, light-proof containers.

IN THE KITCHEN

Lemon balm leaves should be snipped from the tough stems. Very young, tender leaves can be torn rather than chopped for salads. Nibble a piece or two to check that their texture is acceptable. If even slightly tough, they are better finely chopped, though do this just before serving as the cut edges tend to blacken.

Lemon balm can be left as whole sprigs, complete with the soft stems, in infusions for tisanes, teas or fruit drinks, or as part of a cooked dish. They remain intact when cooked and are relatively easy to remove before serving.

Lemon balm has a much stronger aroma than flavour. In cooked dishes, 12 sprigs 5–8 cm long would not be excessive. When chopped for salads or when sprinkled on cooked dishes, use 1–4 tablespoons for 2–4 servings.

HOW TO USE LEMON BALM

- Lemon balm is most commonly used in drinks, particularly as a tisane (see pages 19–20), in iced tea (see recipe on page 85), fruit punches and wine coolers. Garnish fruit drinks with tiny sprigs or float a variegated leaf on top of each drink in a tall glass. Use a generous amount for tisanes, as lemon balm loses flavour in hot water. We like to add a little lemon juice to sharpen the taste.
- Make a lemon balm rum fruit punch. Half a day before serving, infuse 4 large sprigs of lemon balm (lightly bruised) in 1 cup of pineapple juice, 1/2 cup of freshly squeezed orange juice, 1/3 cup of dark rum, and a dash of Angostura bitters (optional). Cover and store in a refrigerator. To serve, half fill 2–3 tall glasses with ice. Strain the punch and pour into the glasses until they are three-quarters full. Add sparkling mineral water to fill. Stir and then garnish each glass with a lemon balm leaf—a variegated one is eye-catching.
- Lemon balm teams up well with most vegetables, particularly carrots, beetroot, peas, cucumber, asparagus and courgettes. Sprinkle it over the freshly cooked vegetables, along with a squeeze of lemon juice, butter and black pepper, just before serving.
- Make herb butter with lemon balm (see pages 18–19) to serve on cooked vegetables, baked or grilled fish or chicken.
- Make an orange salad with lemon balm: arrange slices

of orange with finely diced green capsicum, drizzle with vinaigrette and sprinkle with 1–2 tablespoons of finely chopped lemon balm.

- Lightly cook a pan-full of flat mushrooms, cultivated or wild, in a little butter until tender. Season and thicken slightly with cornflour mixed to a paste with water. Serve on toast and sprinkle with freshly chopped lemon balm.

- Make a tangy lemon balm vinaigrette to serve with vegetable salads: whisk together 1 finely chopped small shallot, 2 tablespoons of chopped lemon balm, the grated rind and juice of a lemon, 2 tablespoons of white wine vinegar, 1/2 teaspoon of sugar, 1/2 teaspoon of Dijon-style mustard, 4 tablespoons of mild-tasting oil, 1/4 teaspoon of salt and black pepper.

STIR-FRIED COURGETTES WITH LEMON BALM
Serves 2

We use both yellow and green courgettes to make this extra fast, fresh-tasting side dish. We cut the courgettes into thin sticks with a julienne disc on a food processor. Although slower, this job can also be done by hand; or, alternatively, simply slice the courgettes thinly. The lemon balm adds a refreshing and subtle citrus flavour.

300 g courgettes (mixed green and yellow if possible)
1 tablespoon oil
1 clove garlic, very finely chopped
salt and black pepper to taste
2–3 tablespoons finely chopped, tender lemon balm leaves

Trim the courgettes and cut into thin sticks or slices. In a sauté pan, heat the oil and briefly cook the garlic until soft but not brown. Add the courgettes and stir-fry for a few minutes until tender-crisp. Remove from the heat. Season and sprinkle with the lemon balm. Stir through gently and serve immediately, or cool to room temperature and serve within 1 hour.

BAKED FISH WITH LEMON BALM
Serves 2–3

Simplicity of flavours is the key to the success of this recipe. Use the freshest fish fillets available: we enjoy blue cod for its 'melt in the mouth' tenderness and ability to hold together in serving, but any firm, white-fleshed fish with a delicate flavour would be suitable.

2–3 large shallots, or equivalent quantity of red-skinned onion, chopped finely
1 tablespoon oil
12 sprigs lemon balm with stems
500 g fish fillets
1/4 teaspoon salt
white pepper
1/3 cup white wine
extra lemon balm for garnishing

In a small pan, sauté the shallot or onion until soft. Remove from the heat.

Spray a shallow baking dish, large enough to hold the fish in a single layer, with oil. Lay in it 6 lemon balm sprigs with their stems pointing outwards. Lay the fish on top and sprinkle with seasoning. Spoon the shallots evenly over the fish. Top with the remaining 6 lemon balm sprigs. Pour in the wine. Bake in a hot oven (220°C) for 7–12 minutes, depending on the type of fish and the thickness of the fillets—the fish will be cooked when a creamy white juice comes from the flesh. Be careful not to overcook: remember that the fish will continue to cook for a few minutes after it is removed from the oven. Baste once after 5 minutes' cooking.

Discard the lemon balm—you should be able to pull the bottom sprigs free without disturbing the fish. Serve the fillets and shallots on to individual plates and garnish with freshly chopped lemon balm.

LEMON BALM SALSA
Serves 2–4

A cooling green salsa to serve with spicy foods such as curries or Cajun-style grilled meats. We prefer to chop the vegetables by hand to achieve a chunkier salsa; using a food processor makes it more like a sauce. Prepare no more than an hour or two before required—if left for any longer, it may become too liquid.

2 tablespoons sunflower seeds, roasted (see page 21) and
coarsely ground in food processor
1 small shallot or 2 spring onions, finely chopped
200 g piece of cucumber, cut lengthwise into quarters, large
seeds discarded and flesh finely diced
2 kiwifruit, peeled and finely diced
2 tablespoons lemon juice
1 tablespoon oil
fresh green chilli to taste, deseeded and finely chopped
3 tablespoons finely chopped lemon balm
1/4 teaspoon salt
black pepper

Combine all the ingredients in a small bowl. Stir just before serving.

RHUBARB & LEMON BALM
Serves 6–8

Lemon balm is known for its ability to sweeten tart fruits. In this recipe it reduces the amount of sugar required and imparts a gentle lemon tang. Rhubarb cooked in the oven retains its shape, colour and flavour.

1 kg rhubarb, trimmed and cut into 2 cm lengths
12 sprigs lemon balm, 5 cm long
3/4 cup sugar

In a deep casserole, layer the rhubarb, lemon balm sprigs and sugar. Cover and bake in a moderate oven (180°C) until tender—about 40–50 minutes, depending on the age and variety of the rhubarb. Allow to cool to room temperature. Remove the lemon balm sprigs, which remain tough and intact. Serve with cream or lemon balm yoghurt (see following recipe).

LEMON BALM FLAVOURED YOGHURT
Serves 2–3

This yoghurt has a far more interesting and subtle character than most store-bought flavoured versions. We thank Gillian Painter for the original idea from her *A Herb Cookbook*.

1 cup plain yoghurt
1 tablespoon honey (warmed if stiff)
1 tablespoon very finely chopped lemon balm

Mix all the ingredients together and allow to stand for 15 minutes. Serve with fresh or cooked fruit or with muesli for breakfast. May be stored in a refrigerator overnight.

ICED LEMON BALM & ASSAM TEA
Serves 2

This is a refreshing lemon-flavoured tea to serve on a hot day. We like the slightly malty taste of the Assam tea, but other teas work well too.

1/4–1/3 cup chopped lemon balm
2 teaspoons Assam tea leaves
2 cups boiling water
1 teaspoon sugar
strained juice of 1 freshly squeezed orange

enough ice to two-thirds fill 2 tall glasses
2 thin slices lemon
2 extra sprigs lemon balm

Place the lemon balm and tea into a heated teapot. Pour in the boiling water and stir. Cover and allow to infuse for 5 minutes. Strain into a jug. Add the sugar and stir until dissolved. Pour in the orange juice and stir to mix. Cover the jug and allow to cool. Place in a refrigerator and chill.

To serve, two-thirds fill 2 tall glasses with ice. In each, wedge a lemon slice between the ice. Stir the chilled tea and fill the glasses. Place a tiny sprig of lemon balm on top and insert a straw in each.

Lemon Verbena

When you observe a lemon verbena (*Aloysia triphylla*) bush in winter, it looks so dead that it is hard to imagine it covered in soft green, intoxicatingly lemon-scented leaves and dainty sprays of white flowers. In cooler temperate climates, this deciduous shrub often waits until late spring or early summer before small leaves appear from the bare twigs. We wonder how many gardeners, growing it for the first time, grieve that their plant has died and consign it to the prunings pile.

Lemon verbena tends to be a rather straggly shrub, but makes up for this untidiness with its beautifully scented leaves. It has the most powerful lemon aroma and flavour of any plant, being stronger even than lemons themselves, but without the sour taste. Despite its ugly winter appearance, we like to plant it where we can brush against its leaves. It can grow 2–3 m tall and 1.5 m wide.

In cooler climates, lemon verbena will require protection from frosts. Many northern hemisphere gardeners grow it only in tubs, so that it can be moved under cover before the first frosts. Temperatures below –6°C will kill lemon verbena. Except in very frost-prone areas, southern hemisphere gardeners mostly grow their shrubs outdoors year round, though they may need to choose a warm sheltered position (e.g. against a brick wall) and/or mulch heavily with straw or leaves in winter. Some gardeners treat lemon verbena as an annual, buying new plants each spring. Their growth, once the weather warms, is so rapid that it is possible to obtain good harvests in just one growing season.

LEMON VERBENA
(*Aloysia triphylla*)

This fragrant shrub from temperate South America reached Europe only two to three centuries ago. For such a recent introduction, it has appeared in the botanical literature under a surprising variety of names, including *Lippia citriodora* and *L. triphylla*, *Aloysia citriodora* and *Verbena triphylla*. Herb writers have offered several different versions of the origins of these names, and of the date it was first recorded. A search of the taxonomic sources, however, provides some clarification. It seems that the plant was first classified from specimens growing in European gardens, in particular the Royal Garden at Madrid. A French botanist published a description in 1784, and Spanish botanists in 1785, naming it *Aloysia* in honour of Maria Luisa, princess of Parma and wife of Charles IV of Spain. The plant was later found in the wild by botanists working in South America, who gave it the genus name *Lippia*, in memory of a French-born Italian naturalist, Augustin Lippi, murdered in Abyssinia in 1709.

Before lemon verbena was accepted as a culinary herb, it was fashionable in Victorian gardens as a fragrant ornamental. In England most people grew it under glass, where, if temperatures were warm enough, it behaved as an evergreen. However, Mrs Earle, author of the popular *Pot Pourri from a Surrey Garden* (1897), was able to show that lemon verbena could survive English winters outside, as a deciduous plant. At the time she was writing, the only culinary use recorded in English recipe books was in summer party drinks. Sprigs of lemon verbena should be floated on the top of a champagne cup or claret cup, according to the 1888 edition of Mrs Beeton's *A Book of Household Management*. The Spanish practice of putting a leaf in with tea brewing in a teapot may be somewhat older, since the plant's introduction to Europe was through Spain.

Lemon verbena once had considerable value in the perfume industry. Verbena oil was extracted from the leaves and stems, with the components citral and geraniol giving it a citrus and rose scent. However, it could not be produced in quantity and the resulting high price led to adulteration or substitution with oil extracted from lemon grass. Later it was found that some constituents of lemon verbena oil were powerful skin sensitisers, and could damage the skin when it was exposed to sunlight (known as phototoxicity). Despite warnings from the Research Institute for Fragrance Materials, lemon verbena oil is still promoted on Internet shopping sites for massage, herbal baths and shampoos!

Only in the last two decades have cooks extended their use of lemon verbena beyond beverages. The leaves were initially used, like bay leaves, to flavour foods by infusion, such as syrups and other liquid bases. Now the leaves are being consumed as substitutes for herbs such as lemon grass. It will be interesting to see if this newcomer can hold its own in the kitchen against competition from lemon-flavoured herbs with much more ancient pedigrees. In the Western garden, lemon verbena has been a favourite for well over a century—but given our in-built suspicion of new foods the transition from ornamental to food plant can sometimes take much more than a hundred years.

CULTIVATION

Lemon verbena requires full sun in cooler areas and semi-shade in hotter climates. It grows well in a light, free-draining but moisture-retentive soil. Don't add extra rotted manure or rich compost, as this may encourage lush and soft growth, making the plant more susceptible to damage in cold winters.

Lemon verbena does not normally set seed in temperate climates, so must be propagated from cuttings. Both softwood cuttings, taken in spring, and semi-hardwood cuttings, taken in late summer, are the favoured methods (see pages 13–14). Lemon verbena plants are readily available from garden centres and specialist nurseries. If buying in early spring and you can't locate the stock, ask for help, as it likely that the dead-looking plants will have been deliberately hidden away.

To encourage a bushy shape, pinch out the growing tips frequently. Once established shrubs have started reshooting in late spring, remove dead tips and prune gently to encourage new growth. You can safely cut back an unshapely bush by as much as a third. In frost-prone areas, the shrubs can be cut right back at the beginning of winter and the root area covered with a pile of straw or leaves.

Outdoor lemon verbena shrubs seem to be disease free.

GROWING IN CONTAINERS

In cooler climates, lemon verbena is usually treated as a tub plant—grown outside in a sheltered place during summer and then, before the first hard frosts arrive, shifted under cover for winter and early spring.

Choose a large pot or tub and fill with a standard potting mix lightened with a little horticultural grit (5:1), (see page 15). Pot up in spring and keep growing tips well pinched back to encourage an attractive bushy shape. Lemon verbena likes to be moist but not soggy. During the dormant period, the potting mix should be allowed to nearly dry out. If harvesting frequently, plants will benefit from regular applications of liquid fertiliser at the correct concentration.

Cut container-grown lemon verbena plants back in spring, to within 15 cm of the soil—this will encourage new growth. Repot every 2–3 years.

HARVESTING

Snip short or long sprigs of lemon verbena with scissors, or pick larger leaves from the stems. The light green upper leaves are the most tender. Older darker leaves lower on the stems are tough and may have an excessively strong taste. The highest concentration of aromatic oils is reported to be present just as flowering begins.

Lemon verbena is one of the best herbs for drying. Some writers claim that the dry leaves keep their flavour for years. We enjoy the dried leaves in winter tisanes (see page 19), but prefer fresh leaves for all other purposes.

To dry, hang branches in a dark, warm and airy place until the leaves are crisp. Alternatively, pick large leaves from the stems and dry them on racks in a slow oven, dehydrator or microwave (see pages 16–17). Pack the crisp whole leaves in airtight containers and store away from light. Crumble the leaves just before using.

IN THE KITCHEN

Lemon verbena leaves have a tough texture and are rough on the tongue. They can be used whole but should be discarded before serving. Their most common use, apart from teas, is to flavour syrups for use with fruit. The leaves are added to the hot syrup and allowed to infuse for 30–60

Lemon verbena

Wispy lemon verbena flowers make a dainty garnish.

minutes. Add up to 12 leaves for each cup of water in the syrup. Bruise them lightly by holding them together and gently wringing without tearing.

When lemon verbena is required as a garnish, or is to be incorporated in a dish and not discarded, the leaves should be chopped very finely. As the central vein tends to be tough in older leaves, it should be removed. This is fairly easily done by folding the leaf in half lengthwise with the upper surfaces inwards and pinching the edges together with the thumb and fingers of one hand. Use the other hand to grasp the vein at the stalk end and carefully pull downwards, tearing it from the leaf. The two leaf halves can then be stacked with others and finely chopped.

A food processor can also be used. Having removed their central veins, combine the leaves with sugar (about 1 part sugar to every 2 parts lightly packed leaves). Leave the machine running long enough to make a green crumbly paste. The result can be incorporated into syrups, the cream for home-made ice-cream, custard, fruit purées or any recipe requiring sugar and a lemon flavour. Adjust the recipe to allow for the amount of sugar used in processing. Use the paste cautiously, as the flavour is very concentrated.

Although lemon verbena imparts a strong citrus flavour, it lacks acidity and can taste rather flat. For this reason it is often used in addition to citrus fruits rather than replacing them.

HOW TO USE LEMON VERBENA
- Lemon verbena makes a heady tisane, especially when using fresh leaves. It can also be combined with China or Indian tea to provide a definite lemon scent (see pages 19–20).
- Lemon verbena adds a delightful flavour to cooked fruits, especially rhubarb, gooseberries, nectarines, peaches, plums and apricots. Cook the fruits gently in a syrup infused with lemon verbena, or use the syrup to pour over fresh fruit as a marinade. See page 91 for a lemon verbena fruit salad recipe.
- Use whole lemon verbena leaves in the body cavity when roasting a chicken or baking a whole fish. Leaves can also be laid under and over chicken portions or fillets of fish before baking. Chopped leaves can be incorporated into stuffings for poultry, fish or pork.
- For extra lemon intensity, add a little finely chopped young lemon verbena leaves to lemon curd (lemon honey), lemon meringue pie or lemon flans at the end of cooking.
- Use lemon verbena leaves to flavour cakes. Place whole leaves on the bottom of a lined and greased pan before adding the batter. Finely chopped leaves can be stirred into the batter when preparing carrot, banana and zucchini loaves.
- Add finely chopped lemon verbena leaves to jams. We particularly enjoy their flavour and the pretty green flecks that they add to bright orange citrus marmalade. We use about 1 tablespoon of finely chopped young leaves to each cup of cooked marmalade and add just before pouring into the jars.

SANGRIA
Serves 6

A refreshing wine cooler flavoured with sprigs of lemon verbena and garnished with a spray of the wispy flowers.

1 thin-skinned orange, finely sliced into rounds
half a thin-skinned lemon, finely sliced
750 ml bottle of red wine
1/2 cup Grand Marnier or other sweet orange liqueur
1/4 cup brandy
3 young sprigs of lemon verbena
soda water to serve

Place the citrus slices in a large jug. Add the wine, liqueur and brandy, and stir. Cover and place in a refrigerator for several hours or overnight. Transfer to a clear glass jug and add the lemon verbena sprigs. Stir to mix and chill until required.

Half fill tall glasses with the wine mix, top up with soda water, and decorate each with a slice of citrus fruit and a spray of lemon verbena flowers.

CHICKEN BREASTS WITH LEMON VERBENA
Serves 4

Chicken breasts marinated in wine flavoured with orange and lemon verbena are then grilled and basted with a sauce of lemon verbena, wine, redcurrant jelly, mustard and fresh ginger. The result is succulent chicken with a sweet and intriguing taste.

4 chicken breasts, skins removed

Marinade
3 tablespoons finely chopped lemon verbena leaves
2 tablespoons dry white wine
grated rind and juice of 1/2 orange
2 tablespoons oil
1 shallot or 1/2 small onion, finely chopped
1/4 teaspoon salt
black pepper

Basting sauce
1/4 cup dry white wine
1/4 cup loosely packed lemon verbena leaves, finely chopped
1/4 cup redcurrant jelly, or apricot or plum jam
1 tablespoon Dijon-style mustard
1 slice fresh ginger, finely chopped

Combine all the marinade ingredients and pour over the chicken in a non-metal baking dish. Cover and place in a refrigerator for 3 hours, turning the chicken over after 1–2 hours.

 Meanwhile, prepare the basting sauce. Pour the wine into a small saucepan, add the lemon verbena and bring to the boil. Cover and remove from the heat. Leave to infuse for 10 minutes. Strain through a sieve, pressing as much wine from the leaves as possible. Combine the jelly or jam, mustard and ginger in a small bowl. Stir until smooth. Add the flavoured wine and mix well.

 Heat an oven grill with a grilling rack and pan in place. Lift the chicken breasts from the marinade, and place on the hot grilling rack. Spoon half of the basting sauce evenly over the top surfaces. Grill for about 5 minutes, adding extra sauce part-way through. Turn the chicken pieces and baste. Grill for a further 5 minutes, basting from time to time until all the sauce is used and the chicken is tender and golden. Serve topped with some of the basting sauce spooned from the bottom of the grilling pan.

CREAMY LEMON VERBENA SPREAD OR DIP

Serve this pretty, pale green, lemony spread in a small bowl on a platter, surrounded by bite-sized pieces of fresh fruit. Include a butter knife for spreading. Suggested fruits include: whole strawberries, grapes, halved or quartered stone fruits, apple and pear slices, and plump dried fruit. Include some crisp, plain, sweet biscuits to make a more substantial dessert course. The spread is also delightful as a fruit muffin filling or in fruit-filled croissants for breakfast.

2 tablespoons sugar
1/4 cup lightly packed lemon verbena leaves, centre veins removed (see page 00)
50 g unsalted butter, softened
250 g cream cheese, softened if stiff
grated rind of 1 orange
1 tablespoon Grand Marnier

Pulverise the sugar and lemon verbena in a food processor until very fine (about 1–2 minutes). Add the remaining ingredients and process until evenly mixed and creamy. Spoon into a small bowl and store in a refrigerator for up to 3 days.

LEMON VERBENA SYRUP CAKE
Serves 6

We were introduced to syrup-soaked cakes by Lois Daish with her recipe for Egyptian yoghurt cake soaked with lemon and raisin syrup, which appeared in the *New Zealand Listener*. We have made her excellent recipe so many times that it seemed a good starting-point for developing a lemon verbena-flavoured cake. Serve with thickened yoghurt.

Cake
8 young lemon verbena leaves
2 eggs
1 cup caster sugar
grated rind 1 lemon
1 cup flour
1 teaspoon baking powder
1 cup plain unsweetened yoghurt

Syrup
2 tablespoons butter
2 tablespoons clover honey
grated rind 1 lemon
3 tablespoons lemon juice
1 tablespoon brandy or rum
1 teaspoon finely chopped lemon verbena leaves

Preheat the oven to 175°C. Spray or grease an 18 cm diameter cake pan, and place a round of baking paper on the base. Arrange the lemon verbena leaves in a circle, undersides facing up, on the paper.

Beat the eggs, sugar and grated lemon rind together until very light and high. Sift the flour and baking powder together and beat into the egg mixture. Beat in the yoghurt. Spoon carefully into the cake pan, being careful not to disturb the leaves. Bake for 40–50 minutes until the cake bounces back when pressed and is a rich golden brown on top. (Make the syrup while the cake is cooking.) Leave in the pan for 5 minutes. Loosen the sides and turn out onto a cake rack. Carefully invert onto a flat dish with low sides. Remove the baking paper and immediately pour the warm syrup over the surface.

To make the syrup, combine all the ingredients except the lemon verbena in a small saucepan. Bring slowly to the boil, stirring constantly. Remove from the heat and add the chopped lemon verbena.

LEMON VERBENA FRUIT SALAD
Serves 4–6

Turn a simple fresh fruit salad into something memorable, using whatever fruit is in season, ripe and of high quality. A particlarly delightful combination is grapes, melon, kiwifruit, bananas and plums. Serve with thick yoghurt.

Syrup
1/4 cup sugar
1/2 cup water
9 lightly bruised lemon verbena leaves

Salad
4 cups prepared fresh fruit, cut into bite-sized chunks
lemon juice to taste

In a small saucepan, stir the sugar and water together over a moderate heat until dissolved. Bring to boiling point. Remove from the heat and add the lemon verbena leaves. Cover and infuse for 30–60 minutes. Discard the leaves and put the syrup aside to cool.

No more than an hour before serving, place the fruit in a bowl. Pour in the syrup and stir gently to coat. Taste and add lemon juice, as required, to balance the sweetness of the syrup.

mint

Mint (*Mentha* species) is refreshing in salads and iced summer drinks, balances spicy flavours in North African stews, adds sweetness to rich chocolate cakes, is intriguing in Thai salads along with fish sauce and lemon grass, and comforting in mint sauce with lamb, reminding us of our mother's Sunday roast dinner. Where would a cook be without mint?—sadly deprived, we think!

However, we are never likely to be without mint, as gardeners often have more trouble getting rid of it than getting it started. At the time when many culinary herbs were disappearing from Victorian kitchen gardens, the tenacity of mint and its spreading habits possibly saved it from a similar fate. It hung around in dark, damp corners (often at the base of down-pipes) and was picked occasionally for the classic mint sauce. Happily, in recent years it has been rediscovered by adventurous cooks and is now given an important position in kitchen gardens—though not without its problems. Mint's unruly, rapidly spreading root system presents the gardener with a challenge. Our control methods are discussed on page 96.

VARIETIES
Culinary mints belong to the *Mentha* genus and, although there are only about 25 species, there are literally hundreds of hybrids. Because of this interbreeding, botanists have had, and continue to have, trouble identifying and naming

them. The gardener and cook are left far behind and instead have to rely on senses, not names, when choosing suitable mints for kitchen use. Texture, taste, how the plants perform and seasonal availability should all be considered. We will cover the mints we currently grow, attempting where possible to provide accurate botanical names—at least at the time of writing.

Our two most frequently harvested mints, although looking, tasting and behaving quite differently, share the same botanical name. Our favourite is commonly known as winter mint (*M.spicata* subsp. *spicata*—winter mint form). It has a pleasant spearmint flavour—not over-powering, but definite. In our gardens it seldom suffers from rust (a problem with many mints) and its best attribute is its year-round availability. It is the only mint we know that does not die down in winter.

Our other frequently picked mint is commonly called spearmint (*M. spicata* subsp. *spicata*—spearmint form). Its leaves have a finer texture than those of winter mint and its flavour is more pronounced and sweeter. Some years it suffers from rust, though usually not until it flowers and starts to die down.

We also enjoy growing the tall apple mint (*M. suaveolens*), with its large woolly leaves and soft spearmint scent with a suggestion of freshly sliced apple. Its smaller cousin, pineapple mint (*M. suaveolens* 'Variegata'), has beautiful cream and pale green variegated leaves with, if

MINT
(*Mentha* spp.)

Have you ever wanted to make a collection of mint species in a moist corner of your garden? There are only 25 (or possibly as few as 19) species in the genus *Mentha* and they are nearly all from temperate regions, including Australia, Tasmania, New Zealand, North America and Japan. They range in size from the tiny-leaved crevice-dwelling Corsican mint to the tall hairy horsemint. If you assembled such a collection, you would quickly discover that only a handful of species blend well with food, although all produce essential oils containing menthol. A cook's mint garden would contain a more carefully selected group of species: *M. aquatica*, the watermint, in the wettest portion; *M. longifolia*, the horsemint, at the back of the border; *M. spicata*, the spearmint, along with *M. suaveolens*, the woolly or apple mint, in the middle; and *M. pulegium*, the pennyroyal, at the front. You would probably be surprised by the strong flavours of these species—quite pungent in the case of the pennyroyal and watermint. Traditionally, pennyroyal has been blamed by dairy farmers for tainting milk, and it contains a chemical which inhibits curd formation in cheese-making. Only the spearmint and apple mint would be welcome in the kitchen.

So where are the more acceptable mints, you might ask—Bowles' mint for your classic mint sauce, peppermint for refreshing herbal teas, pineapple mint for fruit salads, and lemon mint for summer drinks? These are hybrid mints of various named and unnamed varieties. They have been giving plant taxonomists headaches for many decades. Back in 1938 Edgar Anderson confessed that 'It is difficult to grow mints without losing faith in botanists'. Even before humans intervened, mints would have been difficult to classify. But gardeners have for hundreds if not thousands of years been digging them up, transporting and transplanting them, letting them run wild again, and allowing species and hybrids to cross and back-cross in combinations that could never have occurred in nature. The botanists' frustration has even led to the mints being accused of uninhibited, almost incestuous, interbreeding.

You can see their point when you study the pedigree of the hybrid spearmint *M.* x *smithiana*. Its ancestry includes watermint, cornmint (*M. arvensis*) and spearmint. Even the species spearmint (*M. spicata*) is thought to be a fertile hybrid of two of the ancestral European species, the horsemint and the apple mint. Whenever you encounter a mint (like spearmint) with stalk-less leaves, you can surmise some horsemint ancestry. Mints with flowers emerging only from their upper leaf axils usually have a cornmint ancestor.

Some of these crosses occurred (and re-occur) spontaneously, because the parent species share the same territory. But a more complex hybrid like peppermint depended on the prior existence of spearmint and its later interbreeding with watermint. This particular hybrid seems to have developed only a few hundred years ago. Bowles' mint might be of more recent origin; it is a sterile hybrid between spearmint and apple mint, officially known as *M.* x *villosa* var. *alopecuroides*. Given the sociability of mints, we can expect more interesting hybrids in the future.

Because several of the parent species are naturally distributed across the temperate zones of Europe and Asia, it is not surprising that mints have been incorporated in human diets for thousands of years. The Assyrians grew one sort of mint (possibly pennyroyal) under the name *urnû*. They would also have been familiar with horsemint and watermint in the irrigation channels leading to their gardens and fields.

The Mycenaeans recorded the name *mi-ta* in their Linear B script, around 1300 BC. In the later Greek language this became *mínthe*, and a typically Greek transformation myth was invented to explain the name. Hades, the god of the underworld, had a liaison with the nymph Minthe. When Hades' wife Proserpine discovered the affair, she trampled the nymph underfoot. Hades then turned the nymph into a mint plant. Does this myth tell us that the Greek *mínthe* was one of the mat-forming varieties? Classical Greek texts give a few more clues: both wild and cultivated mints were known; in one form the seed did not germinate; transplanting and growing from cuttings were common practices; and one mint degenerated if not regularly trans-planted. Since two other names besides *mínthe* appear in the texts (*sisymbrion* and *hedyosmon*, meaning sweet-smelling), it looks as if the Greeks had already selected one or more improved hybrids, and these were possibly sterile and prone to the debilitating mint rust—hence the reference to the germination problem and the need for frequent transplanting.

For unambiguous evidence of mint in recipes, we have to wait till the 3rd century BC in Greece and soon after that in Rome. A Roman writer on farming, Cato, recommended adding mint, coriander, cumin, fennel and rue to a dish of chopped mixed olives dressed with oil and vinegar. A few centuries later, Apicius's cookbook made frequent mention of mint, both fresh and dried, in sauces and dressings to be served with cooked meats and fish. It is tempting to trace mint sauce back to the Romans, but in none of the fifty or so recipes given by Apicius is mint the sole, or even the dominant, flavouring ingredient, as it is in mint sauce. It is more accurate to say that the practice of moistening hot and cold meats with thin, piquant sauces is at least two thousand years old.

Knowledge of various mints continued into the mediaeval period. In the 9th century AD, the Benedictine monk Walahfrid Strabo, writing about his little garden, stressed that 'I shall never lack a good supply of common mint, in all its many varieties, all its colours, all its virtues'. He would have used mints in both food and medicines. The 14th-century royal recipe collection *The Forme of Cury* called for 'mynts' in a herb custard, in 'salat', green sauce, and in mackerel simmered in 'mynt sawse'. Mint was boiled with meat as a pot-herb, and in Mediterranean countries joined parsley and marjoram in flavouring fish dishes. In Tudor times, the distinctive pennyroyal also had a culinary role that extended across northern Europe. It was the dominant herb in black pudding, a use that continued in northern England into the 20th century, where its alternative name was 'pudding grass'.

By the late 16th century, herbalists could describe four or five garden mints, including two curly-leaved forms. The spearmint is recognisable in their descriptions but we can't be sure which hybrids John Gerard was calling red mint and heart mint. John Parkinson referred to a variegated mint in 1629 and observed that mints were still boiled with mackerel, combined with pennyroyal in puddings and added to pease pottage. As a gardener, he was not enthusiastic about the habits of the mints: 'the rootes runne creeping in the ground, and . . . will hardly be cleared out of a garden, being once therein, in that the smallest peece thereof will growe and encrease apace'.

By the end of the 17th century, a mint with an orange flavour was recommended for use in mixed salads, and for a salad exclusively of mint, dressed with orange juice and sugar. We now know that orange mint is a variety of *M. x piperita*, so it is not surprising that the true peppermint made an appearance at about the same time. The word 'pepper-mint' was used for the first time in a recipe in 1736. Professor Richard Bradley gave instructions for making 'Pepper-Mint Water': six handfuls of peppermint were to be infused in clear spirit, drawn off in a cold still and bottled with a knob of loaf sugar. Bradley's description neatly explains why the words 'pepper' and 'mint', with their contrasting associations of hot and cold, were put together: 'This is an incomparable pleasant Dram, tasting like Ice, or Snow, in the Mouth, but creates a fine warmth in the Stomach, and yields a most refreshing Flavour.' He added that this was a rare form of mint, 'lately cultivated in some Physick Gardens at Mitcham'. Two varieties of Mitcham peppermint are still grown commercially to produce oil.

Mint has been commonly paired with pulses since mediaeval times—at first with dried pea pottages, then with green pea soups in the 17th century, and finally with green peas as a vegetable. Our characteristic mint sauce appears in the mid-18th century and is described thus in a 1756 recipe: 'very young Mint, chopped with Sugar and Vinegar', to be served not with lamb but with 'A Quarter of Pig Lamb Fashion'. The practice of forcing mints into premature growth on hot beds provided fresh shoots for winter salads as well as for mint sauce. Lamb was considered a great delicacy for December meals, but until hot beds were in widespread use it would not have been accompanied by fresh mint sauce. The combination of mint with new potatoes did not become common for another century. Perhaps it was the influential Mrs Beeton's instructions to boil them with a few sprigs of mint which made it a British icon.

Europeans are not the only users of mint in cooking. While Middle Eastern and North African cuisines use their own regional varieties of spearmint, Indians use selections from horsemint in their fresh chutneys. In East Asia, Japanese mint (*hakka*) has been classified as a variety of the cornmint (*M. arvensis* var. *piperascens,* recently reclassified as *M. canadensis*), while one Chinese mint has been assigned its own species (*M. haplocalyx*). The Chinese use its flowers to scent tea. As for the Vietnamese mint, it is not a member of the genus *Mentha* at all, but a type of knotweed, *Polygonum odoratum* (see rau rǎm on page 130).

you stretch your imagination, a tropical fruit scent. Both of these mints have a rather disappointing flavour, though they do make attractive garden subjects and garnishes, and are also more tolerant of dry conditions.

Peppermint (*M. x piperita*) has the highest menthol content of all the mints and is used commercially to make peppermint oil for the food and pharmaceutical industries. We love its flavour in tea but use it sparingly in cooked dishes and salads.

Another mint which is often included in culinary herb gardens is eau-de-Cologne mint (*M. x piperita citrata*). Apart from using a sprig or two to garnish jugs of fruit drink, we think that its best use is in pot-pourri.

We see many different unnamed mints in people's gardens and as potted plants in nurseries and garden centres. Many of these will have potential for kitchen use, as most mints are interchangeable to some degree, though

amounts needed to achieve a similar flavour intensity may vary widely. The only way is to experiment and, once you find one you like, propagate from it and give plants away to lucky friends.

CULTIVATION

Mint's greatest need is adequate moisture. It grows best in free-draining, light but moisture-retentive soil which is kept consistently damp but not soggy. Mint likes to have cool, damp roots but dry foliage. A fresh mulch applied each spring helps to achieve this requirement. At planting time, incorporate plenty of well-rotted compost into the bed.

Mint develops its full flavour potential when sited so that it receives full sun for at least half of each day—preferably morning sun. Providing moisture levels are maintained, it is also happy in all-day sun. Contrary to

Winter mint

Apple Mint

Pineapple mint

Peppermint

popular belief, mint is unhappy in deep shade: it becomes straggly, is prone to rust and lacks scent and flavour.

Siting mint presents a dilemma for the gardening cook. The first priority is the production of plenty of fresh young leaves for the kitchen. The second priority is to stop mint from taking over the garden and smothering other desirable herbs and vegetables. Growing mint in tubs and pots solves the spreading problem but, as it is difficult to maintain adequate moisture levels and thus optimum leaf production, supplies for the kitchen fall behind demand. Our answer is to use large pots but to sink them up to their rims in the kitchen garden. We use 30–35 cm diameter pots, both terracotta and plastic, with a good layer of broken bricks or tiles or irregular shaped stones in the bottom and filled with a standard potting mix plus extra horticultural grit (5:1). Moisture levels are easily maintained with rainfall topped up when needed with routine garden watering. Our mint plants produce adequate harvests for 2 years. After that we find that the roots have become tangled, overcrowded and the odd one has begun to explore greener pastures beyond the pot. We aim to have 2 pots for each mint type so that, alternately, one can be given a maintenance trim while the other continues to supply the kitchen.

In a large garden, mint can be grown as groundcover in a semi-wild area. Mary grows a large patch of winter mint in an area of pasture grass. Once it has flowered, it is cut down with a mower set to cut high from the ground or a line trimmer. Before long new shoots appear and the productive cycle begins again.

It is possible to grow mint directly in the kitchen garden without it taking over, providing it is lifted each spring, divided and replanted. The spreading roots are not too difficult to trace and remove at this stage. Some herb writers suggest having a separate bed for a mint collection.

Mint produces long, horizontal, thick, creamy-white roots, called stolons, as its means of multiplying. The propagation of mint is very easy. Commercial mint fields are planted by simply scattering pieces of stolons on the field and discing them in. In the home garden, mint can be propagated by dividing an established plant, by severing a piece of wandering stolon or by stem cuttings.

When dividing an old, overcrowded mint clump, first chop it into sections with a sharp spade to reduce the weight, then dig out each piece. Select healthy outer shoots with roots attached to pot up or replant immediately.

To propagate mint from a wandering stolon, find a

small new shoot appearing some distance from the parent plant, trace its stolon back and cut it off. Dig up the shoot and attached stolon, trim the stolon to about 8–10 cm long and replant it horizontally, 5 cm deep. Keep it well watered until new feeding roots develop and more shoots appear.

Stem cuttings are also successful. Cut a stem, before it flowers, about 15 cm long. Strip the leaves from the lower two thirds of the stem and place it in water on a window sill. Keep in a warm place, well lit but out of direct sunlight, and if necessary mist to prevent wilting. Roots will appear in 1–2 weeks. Pot up and keep moist. Once the shoot starts growing vigorously, it can be planted outside after hardening off.

Mint is not propagated from seed, as many of the varieties grown are hybrids and thus sterile, while those that do produce viable seed cross so freely that resulting plants are unlikely to be true to type.

All mints are perennials, producing new shoots each spring which develop flowers in summer and then die down. Winter mint continues to produce new shoots through winter while the other mints remain dormant. Once a mint shoot has flowered, its leaves become tough and lose flavour, and have no further use in the kitchen. Mints can be kept in production longer by regularly cutting back the long stems, just before flower production starts, to about 5 cm from the ground. The plant quickly responds by producing succulent, flavoursome new shoots. We cut our mints back at least 3 times each season. Regular harvesting of sprigs encourages bushy growth. In the winter it is wise to cut back and remove all the old foliage to eliminate overwintering sites for pests.

A good yearly mulch with compost normally keeps mint plants productive but, if you are harvesting leaves frequently or restricting the root run, a monthly watering with a liquid fertiliser is beneficial.

Rust is a major mint disease in some areas. We have very little trouble with it and have found that, if it does appear, all that is needed is to cut the affected plant right back, allowing fresh rust-free shoots to grow. Dividing and shifting your mints every 2–3 years is a good preventative measure. Avoid the use of manures near your mint plants as this practice is linked with rust infestation. If you continue to have trouble with rust, grow winter mint rather than spearmint as the latter is prone to the disease. White flies and spider mites are also reported to be troublesome for some gardeners—hosing, or using an insecticidal soap are the best lines of defence.

GROWING IN CONTAINERS

Mint does well in pots providing it receives adequate moisture, sufficient sunshine and has room for its vigorous roots. Plant up in spring in roomy containers filled with a free-draining proprietary mix. Keep moist but not soggy. Position the pots inside or outside where they will receive at least 5 hours of direct sunshine a day (avoid scorching the leaves by putting too close to a window). Cut back the stems frequently, to 10–15 cm, for better-tasting leaves and to prevent the mint from flowering. Feed with liquid house-plant fertiliser, at half strength, every 3–4 weeks. Divide and repot each spring.

HARVESTING

Mint sprigs and leaves can be snipped freely throughout the growing season—in fact, frequent harvesting ensures a continuing supply of young leaves. Once flowers appear, mint stops growing, its aromatic oil content decreases and the leaves become tough. Handle mint gently, as the leaves bruise easily, resulting in flavour loss and darkening of the leaves.

The levels of menthol, mint's aromatic oil, are highest at the beginning of flowering, so this is the best time to harvest for drying. Mint dries reasonably well, and is the preferred form in many Middle Eastern and North African cuisines. Cut the stems down to the level of the first set of leaves just before the flowers open. Stripping the leaves from the stems is not recommended as they are too easily bruised. Handle as gently as possible. Tie the stems upside down and hang in a warm, dark, well-ventilated place. Alternatively, use the microwave or electric oven drying methods described on pages 16–17, in which case snip the leaves carefully as close as possible to the stems. Store in light-proof and airtight containers. If dried well, mint should retain much of its flavour. Use within 6 months.

IN THE KITCHEN

Mint leaves, picked from the stems, and terminal sprigs can be chopped finely or coarsely, or sliced finely into strips (a chiffonade). Chop or slice just before using to minimise discolouring and loss of flavour.

Mint flavour is slowly lost with cooking, so most recipes specify adding it at the last minute.

Sprigs and individual leaves can also be used for garnishing.

The quantity of mint to use depends on what food it is to accompany and what mint variety you are using. Mints vary considerably in their strength of flavour, with peppermint being the strongest but sweetest. Start with a tablespoon of chopped mint, probably the minimum required for a minty taste, and be prepared to add more. If just a hint is required, infuse whole sprigs in hot liquid and then discard them. For example, mint sprigs can be added to a syrup for poaching fruit or to milk or cream for custard or ice-cream.

Mint complements delicate flavours, as in minted peas, steamed new potatoes and cucumber raita or soup. It can also be used to balance spicy, hot foods—for example, some Indian curries and harissa (a fiery North African chilli sauce). Experiment and learn how useful mint is— possibly the cook's most versatile herb!

HOW TO USE MINT

- Finely chopped leaves of spearmint or winter mint give a lift to simple green leafy salads.
- Add chopped mint to cooked vegetables just before serving—especially cabbage, peas, carrots, new potatoes, cucumber, tomatoes.
- Add mint as a flavoursome garnish to hot and cold soups—especially sweet carrot, spicy lentil, pea (both dried and fresh), thick potato, chicken, tomato and chilled cucumber.
- Despite the critics, we continue to enjoy our mother's mint sauce with roast lamb or, even better, hogget. We included her recipe in our first book, *The Cook's Garden*. Here it is again, using wine or cider vinegar instead of malt vinegar, which was all you could buy when we were growing up. Combine 1 tablespoon of finely chopped mint with 1 tablespoon of caster sugar in a small bowl. Add 1 tablespoon of boiling water and stir until the sugar has dissolved. Add 2 tablespoons of wine or cider vinegar and allow to cool.
- Redcurrant mint sauce is a change from plain mint sauce. Spoon 1/3 cup of redcurrant jelly into a small bowl. Add 1 tablespoon of finely chopped mint and the grated rind of half an orange. Stir to mix.
- Mint and gooseberries grow prolifically in our gardens. We make a traditional mint jelly to serve with roast lamb and grilled lamb steaks or chops, or even beef steaks. Stew 1 kg of green gooseberries with 1 cup of water until very soft. Strain through a jelly bag overnight. Measure the gooseberry juice and pour it into a preserving pan. For every cup of juice, add 3/4 cup of sugar, 2 teaspoons of wine vinegar and 2 tablespoons of chopped mint. Heat, stirring constantly, until the sugar has dissolved. Boil until setting point is reached. (To test, put a teaspoon of jelly on a cold saucer placed in an open window or other cool place. Leave to cool for a few minutes. Touch the surface with the tip of a finger: if ready, the surface will lift and show signs of wrinkling.) Remove any froth by skimming with a perforated spoon. Don't worry if you lose mint trapped in the froth, as the jelly will be well flavoured already. Pour into small jars or pots and apply cellophane covers. Other fruits such as apples, crab-apples or redcurrants can replace the gooseberries.
- Make a mint marinade for lamb steaks or chops. For 4 servings, in a non-metal dish combine the juice of 1 lemon, 1 tablespoon of oil, 1 finely chopped clove of garlic, 1 thinly sliced medium-sized red-skinned onion, black pepper and 2 tablespoons of chopped mint. Add the meat and turn each piece over to coat. Marinate for 3–4 hours, turning the meat once during this time. Cook the meat on a hot barbecue along with the onion.
- For a Middle Eastern flavour, add chopped mint, thyme, ground cumin seeds, ground allspice berries, a little honey and wine to a casserole of lamb and cook very slowly. Serve with couscous.
- Drizzle white wine or a liqueur over sliced fruits and sprinkle with a chiffonade of mint.
- Substitute mint for dill in salmon recipes.
- Add chopped spearmint or peppermint (about 1 tablespoon) to your favourite chocolate mousse recipe.
- Make your own minted tea by combining dried peppermint with your usual everyday tea, or a tisane with fresh spearmint or peppermint (see pages 19–20).
- A childhood sandwich filling was equal quantities of

chopped raisins and mint, moistened with hot water to mix. Dates can be used in place of raisins.

- Lightly fry bananas in butter or oil until golden. Sprinkle with chopped mint and serve with grilled pork or lamb chops.
- Add chopped apple mint to apple sauce to serve with roast pork.
- Try a sprig of mint with, or instead of, the usual lemon slice in a gin and tonic.
- Make the classic American mint julep by combining 1 teaspoon of caster sugar and 1 tablespoon of finely chopped mint leaves in a mortar. Crush with a pestle to form a paste. Add 1 tablespoon of water and stir. Half fill a tall glass with crushed ice and add the mint syrup and 1–2 tablespoons of bourbon. Top up the glass with more crushed ice. Decorate with mint sprigs and serve with a straw.
- Mint makes a refreshing addition to coleslaw, especially one containing grated carrot and diced fruit such as apple, kiwifruit, pears or pineapple.
- Dress a simple salad of cooked baby broad beans, chopped tomatoes and spring onions with plenty of mint and a lemon vinaigrette.
- Make an orange and mint salad to serve on a bed of lettuce and/or rocket leaves. Garnish with roasted almonds or sunflower seeds (see page 21) and dress with a vinaigrette flavoured with orange zest.

MINT & CUCUMBER RAITA

Serve with curries and other hot and spicy foods.

1 cup plain yoghurt
2 tablespoon finely chopped mint
1/2 teaspoon cumin seeds, dry roasted and ground
1/2 teaspoon sugar
1/4 teaspoon salt
black pepper
150–200 g piece of cucumber, peeled if necessary, large seeds discarded and flesh cut into 1 cm cubes

In a small bowl, whisk the yoghurt until smooth. Add the remaining ingredients and stir gently to mix. Serve immediately or chill for up to 2 hours.

CABBAGE, TOMATO & MINT SAUTÉ
Serves 2–4

This is really a warm salad—a little like a warm version of an Indian raita. It is a great way to use part of a summer cabbage when everyone is tired of coleslaw.

2 tablespoons oil
1/4 medium-sized cabbage, sliced
1/4 teaspoon salt
black pepper
1/3 cup plain yoghurt
2 tomatoes, cut into bite-sized pieces
6 cm piece of cucumber, peeled if necessary, and cut into bite-sized pieces
6 sprigs of mint, chopped

In a large frying pan, stir-fry the cabbage in oil until tender-crisp but still bright green. Add the remaining ingredients, except the mint. Stir gently to mix. Tip into a serving bowl and sprinkle with the mint. Serve warm or at room temperature.

FRESH MINT CHUTNEY (PODINA CHATNI)
Serves 6

The idea for this curry side dish comes from Charmaine Solomon's *The Complete Asian Cookbook*. In her more recent book, *Charmaine Solomon's Encyclopedia of Asian Food*, a treasure house of information, she explains that this 'chutney' is one of the most popular Indian accompaniments made with mint. If you have a productive mint patch, this fresh chutney can be made in minutes with the help of a food processor or blender.

1 cup packed mint leaves and soft stalks
1 shallot, or 4 spring onions, or half a small red-skinned onion
1–2 fresh green chillies (quantity depends on how hot your chillies are and how hot you want your chutney), deseeded
1 clove garlic, finely chopped
1/2 teaspoon salt
2 teaspoons sugar
1 teaspoon garam masala
1/3 cup lemon juice, or 50/50 lemon juice/orange juice
extra water if needed

Place all the ingredients in a blender or food processor. Blend until smooth. Add about 2 tablespoons of extra water, if needed, to produce a spoonable purée. Cover and store in a refrigerator for up to 2 days.

VIETNAMESE-STYLE BEEF STIR-FRY WITH MINT
Serves 2

This traditional dish is a cross between a warm salad and a stir-fry. Mint is a commonly used herb in Vietnam.

200 g rump steak, cut across the grain into thin slices
1 clove garlic, very finely chopped
1 tablespoon fish sauce
1/2–1 teaspoon curry powder
1 slice fresh ginger, finely chopped

2 small carrots, peeled and cut into matchsticks
150 g piece of cucumber, peeled if skin is tough, flesh cut into matchsticks
1 cup finely sliced lettuce leaves
30 g pea or bean sprouts

75 g rice vermicelli noodles

1 tablespoon cooking oil
2 tablespoons chopped mint
1/3 cup roasted peanuts (see page 21), roughly chopped

Combine the meat, garlic, fish sauce, curry powder and ginger in a small bowl. Cover and refrigerate for 1–3 hours.

Assemble the vegetables, keeping the carrot sticks in a separate pile.

Place the noodles in a bowl and cover with boiling water. Soak for 5 minutes. Drain.

Heat the oil in a wok. Fry the meat until browned and tender. Just before the meat is ready, add the carrots and toss. Cover the wok and continue to cook for 1–2 minutes until the carrot softens slightly.

Remove from the heat and add the other vegetables. Toss. Add the noodles and mix them through using tongs. Sprinkle with the mint and peanuts, and serve immediately.

MEDITERRANEAN-STYLE FISH WITH MINT
Serves 2–3

Serve this simple, quickly cooked fish stew at room temperature with steamed new potatoes or crusty bread and a green vegetable or salad.

500 g firm fleshed fish fillets (groper is ideal), cut into 2–3 cm chunks
1/4 cup flour
1/2 teaspoon salt
black pepper
2 tablespoons oil
1 clove garlic, very finely chopped
1/4 cup white wine vinegar
1/4 cup water
2 tablespoons coarsely chopped mint, plus a little extra for garnishing
1 tablespoon capers

Mix the flour and seasoning together on a plate and use to coat the fish pieces. Heat the oil in a large frying pan over a moderate heat. Lightly fry the fish, turning until golden brown on both sides. Add the garlic, wine vinegar, water, mint and capers. Bring to the boil and simmer very gently until the fish is cooked through but not broken. Remove from the heat and dish up on to a suitable platter. Cover and allow to cool a little or to room temperature. Garnish with extra chopped mint and serve.

MINTED POTATO SALAD
Serves 4–6

The idea of dressing new potatoes with balsamic vinegar, olives and lots of mint comes from the gardening chef Jerry Traunfeld at the Herbfarm Restaurant near Seattle, USA. His book *The Herbfarm Cookbook* is both inspirational and practical.

4 tablespoons balsamic vinegar
1 small red-skinned onion, cut into quarters and then sliced thinly
1 clove garlic, very finely chopped
1/2 teaspoon salt

1 kg small new potatoes, scrubbed or scraped depending on
whether you prefer skins on or off

1 red or yellow capsicum, deseeded and thinly sliced
1/4 cup best quality olive oil
1/4 cup chopped black olives
1/2 cup coarsely chopped mint
1/4 cup coarsely chopped parsley
2 tablespoons finely chopped oregano (Greek if you grow it)
black pepper

In a large bowl, combine the vinegar, onion, garlic and salt. Cover and leave at room temperature for 1–2 hours. This allows the onion to soften and the flavours to develop.

Meanwhile, cook the potatoes, preferably by steaming. Drain and if necessary cut into bite-sized pieces.

Add the capsicum, oil, olives, mint, parsley, oregano and pepper to the vinegar mix. Stir to combine. Lastly, add the still-warm potatoes and stir gently to coat. Serve immediately, still slightly warm, or store in the refrigerator for up to 24 hours.

MANDY'S BEETROOT SAUCE ON PASTA WITH MINT
Serves 2

An unusual, brilliant pink sauce to serve on any shaped pasta you choose.

2 tablespoons oil
1 small red-skinned onion, finely chopped
2 medium-sized raw beetroot, peeled and grated
100 ml dry red wine
1 tablespoon lemon juice
1/4–1/2 teaspoon salt
black pepper

150 g pasta
shavings of Parmesan cheese (use a potato peeler)
plenty of chopped mint

In a small saucepan, sauté the onion in the oil for about 5 minutes or until soft. Add the beetroot and sauté for a further 5 minutes, stirring from time to time. Add the wine, lemon juice and seasoning. Cover the saucepan and simmer for 15–25 minutes or until the beetroot is tender.

Cook the pasta in plenty of boiling, lightly salted water until tender. Drain and stir into the beetroot sauce. Spoon into individual pasta bowls and top each with plenty of Parmesan shavings and chopped mint.

MINTED TREBLE CHOCOLATE MUFFINS
makes 12 medium-sized muffins or 24 mini-muffins

Peppermint is the chocolate-lover's herb! These moist, chocolate-rich muffins are the perfect accompaniment to a cup of coffee. Containing cocoa, chocolate chips and a surprise centre of a dark chocolate melt, they have a rich and full flavour which is enhanced with a hint of peppermint. An optional addition to the chocolate filling is a small spoonful of sour cream, producing an even moister muffin. This works well with medium-sized muffins but is fiddly in mini-muffins. Instead, serve the sour cream as a topping or filling to be added just before eating. Our thanks go to Alison and Simon Holst for their basic chocolate muffin recipe from *More Marvellous Muffins*.

1/2 cup white sugar
2–3 tablespoons roughly chopped peppermint

1 3/4 cups white flour
4 teaspoons baking powder
1/4 cup cocoa
1/2 cup chocolate chips

2 large eggs
75 g butter, melted
3/4 cup milk

Filling
dark chocolate melts
3–4 tablespoons sour cream (optional)

Combine the white sugar and peppermint in a food processor and process until the mint is finely chopped. Tip into a large bowl.

Sift the flour, baking powder and cocoa and add to the minted sugar. Stir in the chocolate chips.

In a small bowl, beat the eggs, melted butter and milk until well mixed.

Pour the liquid ingredients into the dry ingredients and stir together until just combined. Do not over-mix.

Lightly grease 12 medium or 24 small non-stick muffin pans. Using a dessert spoon or teaspoon, one-third fill each muffin pan. Press a chocolate melt into the centre of each. If desired, add a scant teaspoon of sour cream on top of the chocolate melt. Divide the remaining mixture between the muffins, making sure that the filling is covered.

Bake in a hot oven (200°C) for about 8 minutes for mini-muffins and 10–15 minutes for the larger ones. They should be well risen and the centres should spring back when lightly pressed. Leave in the pans for 5 minutes before loosening and removing. Serve warm or at room temperature.

MOROCCAN MINT TEA
Pours 2 standard-sized teacups

According to Robert Carrier in his book *Taste of Morocco*, mint-flavoured tea is the ritual drink of Moroccan hospitality. The sweet tea is made with green tea and a handful of spearmint, and is surprisingly refreshing. It is served from a silver or brass teapot into highly decorated glasses. Spearmint is the authentic mint to use.

1 dessertspoon green tea (we use Gunpowder)
sufficient spearmint sprigs to loosely fill three-quarters
of 500 ml teapot
boiling water
1 tablespoon caster sugar

Heat the teapot with boiling water and drain. Measure the tea into the pot and cover generously with boiling water. Swirl the water around and then immediately pour off to remove any tea dust. Add the mint sprigs and almost fill the pot with boiling water. Add the caster sugar, stir, replace the lid and leave to infuse for 5 minutes. Pour into 2 cups through a strainer.

MINT GREEN SPARKLER
Serves 2–3

Mimosa is a classic brunch drink made with orange juice and champagne. It is likely named after the pretty yellow perfumed flowers of *Acacia dealbata*, an Australian wattle commonly called mimosa. The link is presumably the attractive yellow colour. Our minted version is not yellow but a gorgeous green, so the name mimosa is not appropriate. Instead, we have called it mint green sparkler, for want of a better name.

If serving it for brunch, chill the orange juice and sparkling white wine by placing in a refrigerator the night before.

2 tablespoons finely chopped peppermint
1 tablespoon caster sugar
1/3 cup orange juice
méthode traditionnelle sparkling white wine (brut), chilled

Place the peppermint and caster sugar in a mortar and crush with a pestle until a paste is formed. Add to the orange juice and mix well. Pour through a fine sieve into a small jug. Pour about 2 tablespoons of the minted orange juice into each champagne flute and fill slowly with the wine. Take care, as frothing may be vigorous. Serve immediately.

oregano and marjoram

Most herb gardens include one or more plants of the *Origanum* genus. These are known to the gardener and cook by their common names as marjoram and oregano. With the confusion surrounding these names, many gardening cooks do not realise that there are several different species, all of which have distinct flavours, and some are more desirable for kitchen use than others. The most commonly grown (probably because it is the easiest), *O. vulgare* subsp. *vulgare*, is considered by many food writers to be inferior to other culinary forms. *O. majorana* is reported to have the most delicate and sweet flavour of all but, because it does not survive well in colder climates and needs to be treated as an annual, is only grown by the real enthusiast.

Many gardeners and cooks use 'marjoram' to describe whatever species it is they grow, while others use 'oregano' or 'oreganum' in the same way. In an attempt to unravel the confusion, we have prepared a table matching widely used common names with the botanical ones, and giving each a plant description and likely culinary characteristics. Our table includes only the culinary *Origanum* species which are reasonably easily obtained by home gardeners. It does not include the many subspecies used commercially.

Common names, although sometimes misleading, will continue to be used by gardeners and cooks—a recipe calling for *O. onites* would be strange indeed. To clarify identification when specifying the best oregano or marjoram to use in a recipe, we use the following common names: oregano for the stronger flavoured forms (*O. vulgare* sp. and *O. onites*), best for pizzas, pasta dishes, etc.; and marjoram (*O. majorana*) for the sweeter, delicate flavour desirable in salads, egg dishes, etc.

VARIETIES

See table on page 104. Choose species that are suitable for your climate, and include both *O. majorana* and one of the better-flavoured *O. vulgare* species or *O. onites*.

103

Botanical names	Common names	Description	Culinary characteristics
Origanum vulgare subsp. *vulgare* Note: there are many regional subspecies, seldom available for home gardeners except the following one.	Oregano Wild marjoram	Creeping plant, forming mat throughout year; heart-shaped, dark green leaves; reddish brown stalks bear pinkish purple flowers; 30–45 cm tall.	Flavour varies according to climate and habitat. In warm, dry climates it can be intense. In cooler climates the flavour may be lacking.
Origanum vulgare subsp. *hirtum*	Greek oregano Rigani	Hardy perennial, similar to above.	Desirable intense flavour especially in hot, dry climates.
Origanum vulgare 'Aureum'	Golden oregano or marjoram	Has golden leaves.	Lacking in flavour but decorative in the garden and as a garnish.
Origanum onites	Pot marjoram Turkish oregano French marjoram	Looks like a dainty form of *O. vulgare*, except leaves are lighter green and smaller; flowers are white or pale pink; stems are shorter. Hardy perennial.	Flavour is stronger than *O. vulgare* subsp. *vulgare*. Retains more flavour when cooked.
Origanum majorana	Sweet marjoram Knotted marjoram	Upright evergreen subshrub usually grown as an annual; ovate, grey-green leaves; flowers white or pink, opening from knot-like heads. Half-hardy perennial.	Delicate sweet flavour very different to *O. vulgare* species and *O. onites*. Flavour lost when cooked, so add just before serving.

CULTIVATION

O. vulgare species and *O. onites*

These oregano leaf-producing species have similar site requirements and cultivation techniques, so will be treated together.

Good drainage is the key requirement. Unless your soil is naturally free-draining, build up a suitable bed with the addition of plenty of organic matter and coarse horticultural grit. The pH of the soil should be neutral to slightly acid.

The best flavour is produced if summers are warm and relatively dry. Grow in full sun, except for *O. vulgare* 'Aureum', which needs shade from afternoon sun to prevent scorching of its young, pale gold leaves.

It is possible to produce plants from seed but this is not the method preferred by home gardeners, as variable quality plants can result. Also, the seed is very fine and requires bottom heat to maintain the desired germination temperature of 20°C. The tiny plants should be thinned to allow more room for remaining specimens to develop uncrowded. Prick out into individual pots once they are large enough to handle (see page 11).

The most reliable method of propagation is by division of the roots of older plants in spring or by offsets at any time (see page 13). Pot up until growing well or plant directly. Space plants 30–40 cm apart.

In dry seasons provide a thorough watering in the morning when needed. Avoid watering too frequently or when temperatures are cold. In cold, damp, poorly drained soils, plants are susceptible to rotting diseases. For this reason, it is a good idea to restart plants in a new site every 2–3 years.

If soils are very free-draining, the plants will benefit from a feed of liquid fertiliser every 6 weeks.

For maximum leaf production, trim off the flowering stalks as they start to develop. For beauty and bees, allow some to flower (a continuing supply of young shoots hide under the flower stalks). In autumn (or spring in very frosty areas), prune all flowering stalks off, leaving the underneath mat of fresh growth.

Some species, particularly *O. vulgare*, can be a nuisance by self-seeding too freely. To prevent this, prune off flowering stalks before seed is ripe. Another problem is excessive spreading by thickened roots. These need to be pulled to the surface and cut off to retain the desired spread.

O. MAJORANA

As sweet marjoram is only a half-hardy perennial, it is usually grown as an annual. It will overwinter in mild climates providing soils stay reasonably dry, or it can be grown in a glasshouse, tunnel house or conservatory.

Choose a garden site that is sheltered and receives full sun. Ensure good drainage by building up the bed with plenty of organic matter and well-rotted animal manure. The soil pH should be neutral or slightly acid. As the plants are frost tender, sow seeds indoors 6 weeks before the date after which frosts are unlikely to occur in your area. Sow the seed in punnets or seed boxes filled with good quality seed-raising mix. Don't be tempted to use garden soil, as damping-off diseases can be a problem. Ensure that the mix is evenly dampened but not saturated. As the seed is very fine, it can be helpful to mix it with a little dry sand. Leave the seed uncovered or sieve a little mix to partially cover it. Cover the containers with glass or clear plastic and provide bottom heat if necessary. The ideal temperature of the mix for good germination rates is 15°C (see page 11).

If necessary, thin seedlings to allow adequate growing space for the remainder. As soon as the seedlings are large enough to handle, prick out into individual containers, filled with potting mix. Water as required, but avoid over-watering especially if temperatures are low. Gradually harden off prior to planting outside.

Space plants 20–25 cm apart. Keep well weeded and apply water only as necessary. Cold temperatures and wet soil can be fatal at this early stage. Have covers available should late frosts threaten.

Keep plants well picked for a bushy shape and to prevent seed from setting. Apply a dilute liquid fertiliser every 6 weeks, and following a major harvest, to encourage new growth.

Plants can be divided in autumn and replanted in pots to overwinter under cover. Replant into the garden in late spring.

GROWING IN CONTAINERS

O. majorana grows well in pots indoors or on a sheltered patio in summer. It needs plenty of sun. Plant well-grown seedlings into pots filled with a free-draining potting mix. Add horticultural grit to lighten if necessary. Keep adequately but not excessively watered and feed with liquid fertiliser, diluted to half the recommended strength, at monthly intervals. Keep well picked for bushy plants.

Other origanums make attractive, easy-care pot subjects. Ensure that the potting mix drains well and be careful not to overwater. Keep plants shapely by frequent picking. Apply diluted liquid fertiliser monthly.

HARVESTING

Similar methods are used for all the culinary species. Avoid picking from young plants until they are well established and growing well, at about 10–15 cm tall. It is important to pinch back *O. majorana* plants at this early stage to encourage a bushy shape.

The best flavour develops after flower buds form, so this is the ideal time to harvest stems for drying. For *O. majorana* cut the branches about 5 cm off the ground, just above a 2-leaf bud, to encourage new growth. Other species can be cut back to the mat of short shoots.

Dry stems by tying in bunches and hanging in a warm, dry, airy, darkish place. Alternatively, place stems loosely in large brown paper bags and hang these. Leaves and small sprigs can also be dried in a microwave or electric oven or in a dehydrator (see pages 16–17).

IN THE KITCHEN

Pick as required for optimum flavour. Washing is necessary only if leaves are dusty. Leaves are usually chopped finely just before adding to a dish. If stalks have become woody, pick leaves off and discard stalks before chopping. Add chopped leaves of marjoram just before serving, as the

Oregano (*Origanum vulgare* subsp. *vulgare*)

Greek marjoram (*Origanum vulgare* subsp. *hirtum*)

Golden oregano (*Origanum vulgare* 'Aureum')

Sweet marjoram (*Origanum majorana*)

OREGANO AND SWEET MARJORAM
(*Origanum* spp.)

Though we may not realise it, the herb oregano has been undergoing a revolutionary change in status. From being an ingredient identified with particular regional cuisines, it has turned into a global superstar. The revolution began in the United States with the rise of fast-food outlets selling Italian pizza or Mexican fajitas, both of which are flavoured with oregano. Since the opening of the first Pizza Hut in 1958, American imports of oregano have increased sixfold, and oregano is now commonly known as the 'pizza herb'. By 1995 enough of it was brought into America each year to flavour six billion slices of pizza. Reliance on the herb in chilli dishes, spaghetti sauces and pizzas has even spread to East Asia, as commercialised ethnic foods go global.

Until the late 1950s, 20 or more of the 46 different sorts of plants belonging to the genus *Origanum* provided herbs for strictly localised cooking traditions around the Mediterranean. In Crete, *O. onites* (also known as Turkish oregano or pot marjoram) was one of the wild origanums used under the name *rhigani*, while Lebanese cooks gathered 'white oregano' (*O. syriacum*) as their *rigani* or *za'atar*. Greeks harvested several wild sorts of *rigani*, but especially *O. vulgare* subsp. *hirtum*. We know this as Greek oregano—to the people of north-west Turkey it is 'black oregano'. As their *origano*, Italian cooks gathered two subspecies of *O. vulgare*—subsp. *hirtum* and *viridulum*—as well as the Mediterranean island species *O. heracleoticum*. But they also grew *maggiorana* (*O. majorana*), which English speakers call sweet or knotted marjoram.

The only perennial origanum which can cope with the cold of Continental Europe is *O. vulgare* subsp. *vulgare*. Unfortunately, it lacks the powerful spicy aroma of the Mediterranean origanums. As a result, cooks in Germany and England became more interested in the distinctly sweet-flavoured knotted marjoram, which they could grow as an annual, and dry the leaves and flower stalks for use as a traditional 'sweet herb'. Thus in England the general term for origanum became marjoram, with three forms distinguished: sweet or knotted (*O. majorana*), pot (*O. onites*, quite closely related to the sweet marjoram), and wild (*O. vulgare* subsp. *vulgare*, which became naturalised on the chalk downlands).

In the United States, edible members of the *Origanum* genus are usually called oregano, which is borrowed from the original Spanish name, applied in Spain to *O. vulgare* subsp. *virens*. However, in America, the name has been extended to quite unrelated plants such as *Lippia graveolens* (known as Mexican oregano) which have a similar composition of essential oils and comparable taste. Nowadays, 'oregano' is treated more as a term for a characteristic flavour than as a name for particular species and subspecies of *Origanum*. The 6000 tonnes imported into the United States each year between 1990 and 1995 consisted of both Mexican oregano and a variety of true origanums. Before export, Turkey, the largest supplier, blends the various wild species gathered in the mountains to match international standard specifications for oil content and other qualities. The resulting product is consistent, but the pizza-eater in New York, Sydney or Tokyo has no idea what species of plant are flavouring his 'napolitana', nor their country of origin.

Regaining control over your origanum sources by growing your own requires some research into the best varieties and a readiness to taste and experiment. Gardeners in temperate climates seeking the true oregano flavour will need to choose a variety or subspecies of *O. vulgare* with a moderate to high oil content, such as the subspecies *hirtum* (also sold as 'Greek oregano'). A similar aromatic flavour can be obtained from *O. onites* (pot marjoram) and *O. heracleoticum*. These types produce an essential oil mix rich in carvacrol and thymol, necessary for the true oregano taste. Because oil content is affected by season, hours of daylight, soil type and water supply, gardeners in temperate areas should experiment with their harvesting times and try to provide the tough Mediterranean conditions that enhance flavour. The Albanians have a saying likening their *rigoni* to a stoic and brave person—'he stands like the oregano at the top of a rock'—which can act as a guide to the best habitat. Unfortunately, the wild marjoram of central and north-western Europe, now also naturalised in parts of the United States and New Zealand, cannot match the Mediterranean types for aroma and oil quantity.

From the very beginning of history, writers have been aware of this great diversity of qualities in the origanum family. Close to the original homeland of the genus, the ancient Greeks spoke of several sorts of *origanon*, distinguishing varieties from particular locations. But they seem to have been more interested in *amárakon* (probably sweet marjoram), which was used for wreaths, and in perfumed ointments and waters. They also wrote about *dictamnon*, the Cretan origanum or true dittany, a plant renowned for its medicinal values.

The Romans incorporated *origanum* in sauces to accompany game animals and birds, fish and pulses. These typically combined origanum with pepper, lovage and onion. The herb was also a common ingredient of stuffings, along with brains and eggs. According to Pliny, origanum and savory were never used in the same dish, a reflection perhaps of their similar chemical composition.

There is surprisingly little evidence for the culinary use of any origanum in Western Europe during mediaeval times, and it was not until the 15th century that sweet marjoram was named as a recipe ingredient. For Thomas Tusser in 1580, 'knotted Majerom' was a herb to strew on floors, while contemporary French farmers were advised to grow it as a sweet herb to dry for the cooking pot in winter, and as a perfumed addition to the flower garden in summer. John Gerard (1597) listed four sorts of 'Marjerome' and another four of 'wilde Marjerome and Organie', but it is difficult to match these to modern variety names.

Through the 17th century, sweet marjoram consolidated its position in Western Europe as a scented plant, raised in pots or the flower garden, to be cut for nosegays and perfumed powders. Flower fanciers became particularly interested in the variegated and golden 'marieromes'. In the kitchen, however, winter or pot marjoram supplied the leaves for soups and stuffings. Cookbooks of the 18th century seldom specified the individual components of the 'sweet herbs' called for in these dishes, but we can guess they included the aromatic origanum, thyme and savory. In this relatively insignificant role, the origanum family persisted in the English tradition of cooking until the mid-20th century, when Elizabeth David's writings about Mediterranean cuisines sparked our interest in exotic flavours. For American cooks, however, it was the discovery of Mexican and Italian fast foods that propelled this herb family to stardom.

---

delicate flavour is lost with cooking. Oregano, especially *O. onites*, retains its flavour so can be added early to dishes requiring long, slow cooking. We like to add a few extra, freshly chopped leaves to the finished dish.

The quantity to use depends on the flavour of the particular plants and the current growing season and weather. In general, use larger quantities of *O. majorana* and *O. vulgare* subsp. *vulgare* where it is grown in damp and cooler seasons and climates. Start with one tablespoon of chopped leaves and add more if the desired flavour is not present.

HOW TO USE OREGANO (*O. onites* and *O. vulgare* sp.)

- Oregano is an essential herb for Mediterranean-style cooking, where it is often used dried as well as fresh.
- Oregano flavour is also important in many Mexican dishes (see pages 110 and 111).
- Like basil, oregano has a natural affinity for tomatoes. Use it in well-flavoured tomato-based pasta sauces.
- Long, slow cooking develops the flavour of oregano. Use in casseroles, especially lamb, chicken and vegetable.
- Make oregano-flavoured red wine or cider vinegar (see page 17).

- Add to stuffings for turkey and pot roasts, or add sprigs to the pan when roasting hogget.
- Combine with sage, nutmeg and savory in home-made sausages (see page 148).
- As a change from the ever-popular basil flavour for pizzas, use oregano, especially if your topping includes salami, sliced sausages, ham or bacon.
- Tiny sprigs of *O. vulgare* 'Aureum' are attractive additions in leafy salads.
- Add to vegetable dishes, especially zucchini, potatoes, pumpkin and oxalis yams.
- Grow oregano near the barbecue and pick small sprigs to add to the sizzling meats. Also use chopped leaves in marinades for steak.

HOW TO USE MARJORAM (*O. majorana*)

- Marjoram is the species to use when a delicate flavour is important.
- *O. majorana* and *O. vulgare* 'Aureum' are the only *Origanum* species we use in salads. Add small quantities of whole leaves (picked off the stems) or chopped young shoots.
- Marjoram enhances rather than overpowers the flavour of many vegetables, particularly carrots, mushrooms,

beetroot, globe artichokes and broccoli.

- Add to omelettes (see pages 46–47), scrambled eggs and baked egg dishes. It is often combined with parsley.
- Add to soups at the last minute, or use as a garnish.
- Combine with other herbs, such as parsley and chives, in dressings for salads.
- Marjoram adds flavour to young cheeses, for example mozzarella, and also combines with other herbs in cottage cheese, potted cheese and most cheese dishes. Next time you make that old favourite, macaroni cheese, add one tablespoon of finely chopped marjoram as a garnish for a real flavour boost.
- Make flavoured butter for baked potatoes or kumara (sweet potato). See page 19 for a general herb butter recipe.
- Our favourite roast chicken stuffing: sauté 1 finely chopped small onion in a little butter until soft, add 2 cups of soft breadcrumbs, 2 tablespoons of chopped parsley, 3 tablespoons of chopped marjoram, 1 teaspoon of chopped lemon thyme, 1/2 teaspoon of salt, black pepper, and one egg, lightly beaten, to bind.
- Add to marinades for chicken or pork.
- Make a marjoram-flavoured white wine vinegar to use in salad dressings or marinades (see page 17).

CARROT & MARJORAM SOUP
Serves 4–6

The natural sweetness of carrots and the subtle spiciness of marjoram blend well together. The cashew nuts or almonds in this soup provide interest, flavour and body. If using almonds, you may prefer to blanch them and then remove their skins. Bought skinned almonds lose their freshness rapidly, and so we always buy whole almonds still in their skins. When time is short, we leave them unskinned—and in this soup the little dark flecks of skin are hardly noticeable. The flavour is not affected.

2 tablespoons cooking oil
2 cloves garlic, chopped
1 large onion, chopped
1/4 cup chopped cashews or almonds, plus a few extra for garnishing
700 g carrots, peeled and sliced
1 medium-sized potato, peeled and sliced
3 cups chicken stock
black pepper
salt to taste
1 cup canned evaporated milk
1 teaspoon honey
2–3 tablespoons finely chopped marjoram

Garnish
yoghurt, or whipped cream, or sour cream
toasted nuts, roughly chopped

In a large saucepan, sauté the garlic, onion and nuts until golden but not brown (don't hurry this step). Add the carrots and potato. Sauté for a few minutes more. Add the stock and seasoning. Bring to the boil and simmer for 30–45 minutes or until the carrots are very tender. Purée in batches in a blender or food processor, or put through a mouli or sieve.

Add the evaporated milk and honey. Reheat very gently (do not boil). Add the marjoram and serve with the selected garnishes.

BLACK BEAN SOUP
Serves 4–6

Black beans are a staple food throughout the Caribbean, Central and South America and Mexico. They are tender, and have a sweet flavour and intriguing colour. Mary's soup recipe has developed over the years to show both Mexican and Brazilian influences. It uses the Mexican flavours of ground cumin and coriander seeds, and lots of oregano, as well as the orange juice, rind and segments found in many Brazilian dishes. If you grow the Mexican herb epazote, add 2–4 sprigs during the last 15 minutes of cooking. Discard with the bay leaves.

2 cups dry black beans, rinsed thoroughly and soaked overnight in plenty of cold water

2 tablespoons cooking oil
2 rashers trimmed, lean bacon, cut into small pieces
2 medium-sized onions, chopped
3 cloves garlic, very finely chopped
2 medium-sized carrots, peeled and finely chopped
2 stalks celery, finely chopped
1 teaspoon cumin seeds, dry roasted and freshly ground
1 teaspoon coriander seeds, dry roasted and freshly ground
1/2 teaspoon chilli powder (or to taste)
black pepper
3 cups chicken stock
2–3 tablespoons chopped oregano
1 bay leaf

grated rind 1 orange
juice 2 oranges
2 tablespoons dry sherry
salt to taste

Garnish
plain thick yoghurt or sour cream
orange segments, cut into small pieces
chopped oregano

Drain the beans, place in them in a large saucepan and cover with plenty of cold water. Bring to the boil, cover and cook for about 45–60 minutes until the beans are tender. Drain and put aside.

Sauté the bacon, onions and garlic in oil for 5 minutes.

Add the carrots and celery and sauté for a further 5 minutes. Add the spices and sauté for another 2 minutes. Add the stock, oregano and bay leaf. Simmer for 20–30 minutes or until the carrots are tender. Remove the bay leaf.

Add the beans, orange rind, juice, sherry, and salt if needed. Reheat.

Garnish each serving with a dollop of yoghurt, a few pieces of orange segment and a sprinkling of oregano.

BARLEY & MUSHROOM RISOTTO
Serves 3–4

This oven-cooked risotto is quick to prepare and requires no attention while cooking. Use intense-flavoured brown mushrooms and plenty of chopped fresh marjoram or oregano to complement the nutty flavour of pearl barley.

200 g pearl barley, soaked overnight in plenty of cold water

3 tablespoons cooking oil
1 small onion, finely chopped
2 cloves garlic, very finely chopped
2 small sticks celery, cut lengthwise into quarters, then finely sliced

200 g brown mushrooms, chopped
1 cup hot chicken stock

1 tablespoon chopped oregano, or marjoram
black pepper
salt to taste

extra herbs, chopped for garnishing

Preheat the oven to 180°C.

In a heavy-based, metal casserole dish, sauté the onion, garlic and celery in the oil until soft (about 5 minutes). Add the mushrooms and sauté for a further 5 minutes.

Drain the barley and rinse thoroughly. Drain again. Add to the casserole and stir to coat the grains with the oil. Add the hot stock and chopped oregano or marjoram. Season to taste. Cover tightly and place in the preheated oven for 40–45 minutes or until all the liquid has been absorbed and the barley is tender.

Garnish with the extra herbs and serve immediately.

VEGETABLE CHILLI
Serves 4–6

Oregano has a natural affinity with chilli and cumin in this Mexican-style bean casserole. Serve with flour tortillas, either as a base under the vegetable chilli with salad ingredients piled on top, or with the filling ingredients rolled inside and eaten with fingers. Though not essential, the Mexican theme is further developed by serving a salsa (see page 60) in a separate bowl. Grated cheese and/or yoghurt can also be offered as optional extras. Large, soft, baked potatoes can take the place of the tortillas. We have specified carrots, parsnip and pumpkin as the main vegetables, but use whatever is available, making a total weight of prepared vegetables of about 1 kg including the onions. This recipe can be cooked in an oven or a crockpot or slow-cooker.

2 cups dried kidney beans, rinsed and soaked overnight in plenty of cold water

2 tablespoons cooking oil
2 small onions, chopped
2 cloves garlic, finely chopped
2 small carrots, peeled and thinly sliced
1 small parsnip, peeled, quartered lengthwise and then thinly sliced, crosswise
200 g pumpkin, weighed after removing seeds and skin and then thinly sliced
1 green capsicum, seeds discarded and flesh cut into chunks
1 teaspoon cumin seeds, freshly roasted and ground
1/2–1 teaspoon chilli powder
1 tablespoon finely chopped oregano
1/2 teaspoon salt or to taste
black pepper
400 g can peeled tomatoes in juice
3 dessertspoons tomato paste
1/2 cup red wine

Drain the soaked beans, rinse, place in a large saucepan and cover with plenty of water. Bring to the boil, cover with a lid and cook for about an hour until the beans are tender. Drain and put aside.

Preheat the oven to 180°C. Sauté the onions and garlic in the oil in a large metal casserole until soft. Add the prepared vegetables. Sauté for a further 5 minutes, stirring frequently. Add the spices, oregano and seasonings and stir to mix well. Break up the tomatoes and combine with the tomato paste and wine in a small bowl. Pour into the casserole along with the beans. Stir to mix and then cover with a tight-fitting lid. Transfer to the oven and bake for 1 1/2 hours, or cook on high in a crockpot or slow-cooker for 4–5 hours. Serve hot or warm.

GREEK-STYLE SALAD
Serves 4

4 medium-sized ripe tomatoes, cut into small chunks
1 small red-skinned onion or large shallot, thinly sliced
1 small cucumber (about 300 g), peeled if thick skinned, flesh cut into small cubes
1/2 cup black olives, stoned and cut in half
150 g feta-style cheese, cut into small cubes
1 tablespoon finely chopped fresh oregano, or 2 tablespoons chopped marjoram

Dressing
6 tablespoons good quality extra virgin olive oil
2 tablespoons red wine vinegar, or lemon juice
1 clove garlic, very finely chopped
1/2 teaspoon sugar
black pepper
salt to taste (omit if cheese is salty)

Combine all the salad ingredients in a large bowl. Combine the dressing ingredients and pour over the salad and mix gently. Spoon into a serving bowl.

MIDDLE EASTERN-STYLE MEAT PATTIES IN PITTA BREAD
Serves 3–6

Oregano, lemon, cinnamon and tomato flavours characterise Greek cuisine. Here they are used to provide a variation on 'hamburgers'. Serve them in warm pitta breads with the yoghurt sauce and a salad featuring tomatoes (rocket leaves, sliced tomatoes and cucumber are a delicious combination).

Yoghurt dressing
1/2 cup plain yoghurt
1 tablespoon chopped mint
1 tablespoon chopped coriander
1/4 teaspoon garlic salt
1 teaspoon lemon juice

Patties
400 g lean mince
3 slices bread, crumbled
1 small onion, finely chopped
small handful of parsley, chopped
2–3 tablespoons chopped oregano
3 sprigs lemon thyme, chopped
grated rind and juice of 1 lemon
1/4 teaspoon salt
black pepper
1/4 teaspoon cinnamon
1/4 teaspoon ground cloves

Combine all the dressing ingredients in a small bowl and allow to stand at room temperature while you make the patties.

Combine all the patty ingredients thoroughly and shape into suitable-sized patties for the pitta bread. Fry in a minimum of hot oil in a non-stick pan.

After warming the pitta breads by toasting lightly, or placing in a moderate oven for a few minutes, split them open with a sharp knife. Place a patty in each, top with salad ingredients and a good dollop of yoghurt dressing. Close and serve immediately.

JAMBALAYA
Serves 4–5

Jambalaya is a well-known example of Creole cooking from Louisiana. A blend of Spanish, French, American-Indian, Anglo-Saxon and African Negro influences are combined to form a unique crossroads cuisine. The dish is derived from the Spanish paella but uses whatever local ingredients are available. Many variations exist but all show a superb balance of seasonings where not one spice or herb dominates. We thank our Dunedin friend and well-known food writer, Joan Bishop, for the basis of this recipe.

1 1/2 cups raw long-grain rice, cooked ahead to produce about 3 cups

4 boneless, skinless single chicken breasts cut into 1 cm strips
1 tablespoon cooking oil
1 medium-sized onion, finely chopped
2 cloves garlic, very finely chopped
400 g can peeled tomatoes in juice, roughly chopped
2 tablespoons tomato paste
2–3 tablespoons finely chopped fresh oregano
1–2 tablespoons finely chopped parsley
3 sage leaves, finely sliced
1 fresh bay leaf, left whole
3 fresh thyme sprigs, left whole
1/8 teaspoon cayenne pepper
3/4 cup white wine
1/2 cup chicken stock
1 green capsicum, deseeded and cut into fine strips
300 g smoked chicken breast, cut across the grain into strips, or similar weight of ham, cooked bacon or cooked and peeled prawns or large shrimps
salt to taste (quantity will depend on saltiness of other ingredients)

In a large pan, fry the chicken in the oil until the pink colour has gone and the pieces have just started to brown (about 3–5 minutes). Remove from the pan. Lower the heat and add extra oil if needed. Sauté the onion and garlic until soft. Add the tomatoes and juice, tomato paste, herbs and cayenne, white wine, stock and capsicum. Bring to the boil and cook rapidly for about 5 minutes to concentrate the sauce. Remove the bay leaf and thyme stalks. Lower the heat and add the rice, cooked chicken and smoked chicken or alternatives. Stir gently to mix. Taste, and add salt if necessary. Cover and heat through gently.

FAJITAS
Serves 4

Fajita (pronounced fah-*hee*-ta) has become a well-known fast food in the USA. It originated in Texas in the kitchens of Mexican immigrants. The original version was made with skirt steak, a cheap cut. To make it more palatable, it was marinated with traditional Mexican flavourings, grilled, sliced into strips and then eaten burrito-style in warm flour tortillas, accompanied with a variety of garnishes, including salad greens, salsa, guacamole, refried beans, etc. The word *fajita* comes from the Spanish for skirt steak. Nowadays, many different foods are substituted for the skirt steak, including rump steak, pork or chicken, and we have even seen a vegetarian version.

500 g skirt steak

Marinade
1 small onion, thinly sliced
1 clove garlic, finely chopped
1 teaspoon cumin seeds, dry roasted and freshly ground
1/2 teaspoon chopped fresh chilli, or more to taste
1 tablespoon chopped oregano
3 tablespoons lemon juice
1 tablespoon cooking oil

Salsa
400 g ripe tomatoes, chopped
2 tablespoons chopped, pickled Jalapeno chillies, or
1/2–1 teaspoon commercially prepared minced chilli
1 small red-skinned onion, or shallot, finely chopped
2 tablespoons chopped coriander leaves
1 tablespoon chopped mint
juice 1/2 lemon or 1 lime
1/4 teaspoon garlic salt

1 tablespoon cooking oil
8 flour tortillas

Extras (optional)
shredded salad greens
diced cucumber
diced coloured capsicums
guacamole or diced avocado
sautéed onions
sour cream

Peel any fatty membrane from the skirt steak with a very sharp knife. Place in a pottery or glass baking dish.

Combine all the marinade ingredients together and spoon over the steak. Cover and leave in a refrigerator for at least 4 hours but preferably for 8 hours, turning the steak over once.

Make the salsa by combining all the ingredients together in a small bowl. Chill until required.

Prepare any extra ingredients required.

Preheat a grill or barbecue until hot. Brush the meat with the oil and place under or over the heat source. Use a fairly high heat to achieve a well-browned exterior but a medium-rare interior (or cooked to your preference). Remove the meat to a cutting board and leave to stand for 5 minutes before slicing across the grain into 5 mm thick strips. Place in a warmed serving dish. Warm the tortillas under the grill or on the barbecue.

To serve: each person makes their own fajita by taking a warmed tortilla, spooning some of the meat into the centre, topping with a little salsa and adding a selection of the extras. Roll up and eat with fingers.

parsley

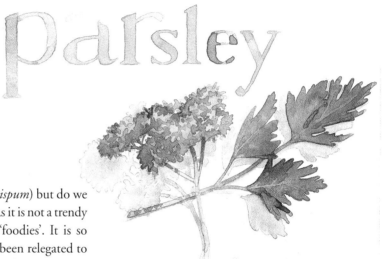

We all know parsley (*Petroselinum crispum*) but do we fully appreciate its value and versatility? As it is not a trendy herb, it has been rather neglected by 'foodies'. It is so familiar that it seems plain! Parsley has been relegated to the role of a garnishing herb on steaks, fish and chips, often abandoned on the side of the plate at the end of the meal. Most of us are generous in our use of basil in Italian-style dishes, but how many of us know that garlic, olive oil and parsley form the basis of many soups, pasta sauces and vegetable recipes from Italy?

In the last few years gardening cooks have begun to seek more kitchen uses for their attractive parsley borders or filled patio pots. Its flavour should not be underestimated. Parsley can star in a recipe or it can support other savoury herbs. It blends with delicate herbs, such as tarragon, chives and chervil, without overpowering them, but when combined with strong-tasting herbs like rosemary and sage it is able to tone them down. The parsley garnish does nothing to promote its fresh and sweet flavour—it is time to chop it and use it as a foundation herb.

Parsley is a biennial herb. It grows tasty leaves in its first year, puts its energies into flowering in the second year, and then dies. Leaves are tougher and a little bitter in the second year, so cooks treat parsley as an annual. For a continuous supply in all but the hottest climates, sow or plant seedlings twice each year, once in early spring and again in late summer. In hot areas it may have to be treated as a cool-season crop only.

Parsley has the reputation of being hard to grow. With knowledge of its habits and site requirements, it flourishes in most climates, providing beauty in the garden, an essential herb for the kitchen and, if allowed to run to seed, a haven for beneficial insects and a source of material for floral arrangements.

VARIETIES

The herb parsley has 2 forms: the more common curly-leaved type and the flat- or broad-leaved one, sometimes known as Italian parsley. Another parsley, called Hamburg, is grown for its roots and treated as a vegetable. Its leaves are tough and lack flavour.

Food writers are divided as to which of the herb parsleys has the better flavour and texture. Some say that the flat-leaved one has a stronger, sweeter taste and is preferred by chefs, while others favour the curly parsley. While agreeing that the flat-leaved form is slightly sweeter, we think they can be substituted for each other and that perceived differences may be caused by soil type, climate and age of the leaves. What is more important is that parsley leaves should be young and freshly picked. When there is a choice, we select flat-leaved parsley to add to salads as the individual leaves can be left whole or torn. The curly parsley is easier to chop finely.

The flat-leaved form is slightly hardier for winter crops, as it does not collect rain or snow in its leaves as the curly one does. However, Mary has harvested curly parsley after a frost, with leaves still frozen, and has found that it could be chopped for a winter soup with no apparent ill effects.

There are several named cultivars of parsley seed available. In the curly category we have grown 'Moss Curled' and 'Triple Curled' (which as the name suggests has the tightest curls). Recently we trialled 'Green Rivers' and were impressed. Named seedlings are seldom available at garden centres, though specialist nurseries may stock a limited selection. Of the flat-leaved parsleys we enjoy a particularly vigorous and tasty one called 'Gigante Italian'. As it is difficult to buy flat-leaved parsley as a seedling, the gardening cook may need to start with seed.

CULTIVATION

Parsley is hardy in temperate climates, though in areas which experience hard frosts it does better during winter if covered. Full sun is important for winter crops. In hot climates it grows better during cooler months and afternoon shade is beneficial.

The soil should be on the heavy side, moisture retentive, nutrient rich and deeply dug. Parsley does not like light sandy soils. If necessary, fork in plenty of coarse organic matter. Crown rot can be a problem if the soil becomes waterlogged, particularly in winter. Provide built-up beds to ensure good drainage.

Parsley is a hungry herb, requiring additional compost and/or well-rotted manure to improve soil fertility. Applications of liquid fertiliser while seedlings are becoming established and after harvesting are also beneficial.

Parsley is best grown as an annual to obtain the best textured and flavoured leaves, although you can take advantage of its biennial life cycle to provide continuity of kitchen supplies while waiting for the new season's crop to be ready for harvesting. We sow seed for our first crop as early in spring as soil conditions permit, or we plant out seedlings in mid-spring. These grow quickly and are usually large enough to pick from just as the old plants,

sown the year before, begin to run to seed. Most years, space permitting, we sow a second crop in late summer. This ensures good harvests the following spring. Six plants will cope with frequent harvesting by the average household.

Flat-leaf parsley

Two new curly-leaf parsley cultivars—'Petra' in the foreground and 'Favorit' at the back.

PARSLEY

(*Petroselinum crispum*)

The common parsley 'is so well knowne, that it is almost needlesse to describe it', observed John Parkinson in 1629. Nearly 350 years later Tom Stobart wrote: 'Parsley is such a common herb and has proved so adaptable to almost all climates that it almost needs no description'. They were not, however, referring to the same parsley. Parkinson had in mind a parsley with flat leaves, while the parsley visualised by English-speaking writers in the 20th century has tightly curled leaves giving the appearance of moss. It is a pity that there aren't better descriptions of parsley in the historical literature, because they might help us unravel the confused history of the plant (and its close cousin celery) over the past three millennia.

Take the English word 'parsley', for example: apart from the cultivated parsley which we are supposed to know so well, there is corn parsley, cow parsley, the poisonous fool's parsley, hedge parsley and stone parsley. Over two thousand years ago, in Greece, the plant family referred to as *sélinon* had nearly as many variants. There was *hippo-* (horse-), *oreo-* (mountain-), *eleo-* (marsh-) and *petro-sélinon* (rock-*sélinon*). The last of these became *petroselinum* in Latin and ultimately supplied the genus name for our parsley. But was *petrosélinon* parsley?

Translators of ancient Greek texts often refer to *sélinon* as celery. This cannot possibly be the celery we are familiar with, which did not develop until the 15th–16th century AD in Italy, but it might have been a cultivated but still primitive form of the ancestor of celery known as smallage (*Apium graveolens*). According to Theophrastus, the cultivated *sélinon* came in two forms: one was close and curly with rough leaves; the other was of more open, flatter growth, with larger stalks. This variation sounds more like parsley than primitive celery. Roman writers like Columella borrowed from Theophrastus' work, including the advice that you could change the broad-leaved type into the curly by pounding its seed with a softwood pestle, or by rolling the plot after sowing! Both Columella and Pliny used the word *apium* for the plant in question and, confusingly, this is sometimes translated as 'parsley', sometimes as 'celery'.

The natural distribution of the wild ancestors of smallage and parsley encompasses southern Europe and the eastern Mediterranean, so we can't use that to narrow down the identities of *apium* and *sélinon*. Archaeological evidence exists of smallage leaves (which look like flat-leaved parsley) in one of the pectoral garlands adorning Tutankhamun's mummy. However, the ancient Egyptian word for this plant, *matet*, is thought to apply also to parsley. Only medicinal uses are described in the papyri, including treatment of urinary problems—the family's diuretic properties are still well recognised. About 1300 BC, Mycenaeans were using seeds from what they called *se-ri-no*, and by the time of Homer *sélinon* was used to make crowns of victory for games, as well as to feed horses. The first food usage is recorded much later, about the time an improved kind of *petrosélinon* arrived from Macedonia. Apicius's Roman cookery book sometimes included both *petroselinum* and *apium* in sauces for meat and fish, in some cases specifying the aromatic seeds, occasionally the green leaves. But there were six times as many recipes calling for the herb lovage as there were for *petroselinum*.

Mediaeval cooks and physicians were more enthusiastic users of this plant complex, which they called *petrosello*, *petersilie*, *percil* and *parsel*. It was included in green sauces, joined mint and marjoram in flavouring many Mediterranean fish dishes, and was added to chicken stuffings and herb custards. The famous 15th-century 'salat' from *The Forme of Cury* begins with the instruction 'Take parsel, sawge, garlec . . .'. Institutional records from the 14th century show purchases of large quantities of parsley seed, sufficient for sowing half an acre (2000 square metres) or more. Illustrations in manuscript herbals all show what appears to be the flat-leaved parsley.

By the late 16th century, there are clear descriptions of the two sorts of garden parsley, flat-leaved and curled, along with warnings about slow germination and their dislike of transplanting. Smallage was still being grown, but was considered a medicinal plant. An improved form was by now present in Italy. In 1629 John Parkinson described a plant seen in the Venetian Ambassador's garden in London which looked like smallage but was much sweeter. He reported that the Venetians usually blanched it, then ate it raw with a pepper and oil dressing. Significantly, he could not decide whether to call this plant 'sweete parsley' or 'sweete smallage'. It was probably an early celery selection, though we cannot rule out the thick-stalked, celery-leaved Neapolitan parsley.

John Parkinson drew attention to the versatility of parsley, writing that it 'is much used in all sortes of meates, both boyled, roasted, fryed, stewed, &c. and being greene it serveth to lay upon sundry meates . . .'. This was the first explicit mention of parsley as a garnish, a role which would have a profound effect on its subsequent development. Meanwhile, celery became a very fashionable vegetable, squeezing the unimproved smallage out of the garden. Parsley retained its popularity as a herb and garnish. John Worlidge described it in 1688 as 'the most universally used in the Kitchin of all *Garden* Herbs'. While the English valued it for eliminating the 'rank' smell of garlic and onions from dishes, the French saw it as an alternative to '*Pepper* and *spice*'.

In mid-18th-century England, the plain-leaved parsley began to face some discrimination. The influential Philip Miller of the Chelsea Physic Garden made a statement in his *Gardeners Dictionary* (1768) which seems to have sparked a public health scare: 'There are some persons who are afraid to use Parsley in their kitchens, lest they should suffer by having the lesser Hemlock mixed with it, whose leaves are so like Parsley . . . to prevent this, I have for many years cultivated the sort with curled leaves'. His advice was repeated in the 19th century by John Claudius Loudon, and elaborated in William Robinson's edition of the great Vilmorin-Andrieux catalogue (1885). Only the plain parsley was likely to be mistaken for the 'virulently poisonous' fool's parsley, as the lesser hemlock (*Aethusa cynapium*) had been renamed. 'The leaves of the two plants are so much alike', warned Robinson, 'that even a practical gardener cannot distinguish one from the other with certainty unless he tests them by taste and smell'. In his opinion, gardeners should make it 'a rule never to grow any kind except the Curled-leaved or Fern-leaved varieties, which are quite as good for flavouring as the Common Parsley, and much better for garnishing'. The fact that the seed of the former was more expensive was 'hardly worth mentioning'! Self-interest by the suppliers of the new double-curled, triple-curled and moss-curled parsley varieties clearly encouraged these scare tactics, as more recent herb writers have described fool's parsley as having a noticeably unpleasant scent when cut, and a burning taste.

Another factor was important in this trend towards the curled varieties: garnishing was becoming the prime use for parsley among English-speaking cooks. The plant was in demand all year round and appeared in the Victorian dining room in table decorations as well as garnishes, both raw and deep-fried. Only the tightly curled varieties were suited to these ornamental roles. Inevitably, this treatment of parsley attracted criticism. In 1980, Waverley Root, noting that the plain-leaved form had almost disappeared from American markets, declared that 'prettiness seems to be preferred to tastefulness', while Tom Stobart observed in 1977 that 'the plain-leaved parsley is not so pretty as a garnish, but this is no drawback in countries where parsley is added as a flavouring rather than planted like trees in a garden of cold meat'. Not unexpectedly, opinion is divided as to the flavour of the curled-leaved parsleys, with supporters of Continental cuisines arguing their inferiority and pro-English cooks asserting that any difference is based on soil and climatic variations.

As with many herbs, breeding and selection programmes during the second half of the 20th century have put the needs of the food industry and market producers paramount. To provide a year-round supply, frost hardiness was an important criterion, while resistance to wilting meant a longer shelf life. Appearance has also been important, with dark green foliage that looks bushy in supermarket packs considered the ideal. There is even a new 'convenience' parsley, whose inward- rather than outward-curling leaves are considered easier to clean. Home gardeners whose prime concern is flavour may need to seek out heirloom and Continental flat-leaved varieties.

Parsley is known as being difficult to germinate—it can take over a month. Our experience has taught us that the most important single factor for success is moisture. The seedbed or containers must never be allowed to dry out.

According to Vicki Mattern, a senior editor of *Organic Gardening* (November 1993 issue), parsley is known to have a lower viability percentage (60%) than most other seeds. Bearing this in mind, we sow a few extra seeds to compensate. Parsley seeds are relatively large and easy to handle.

Providing we sow our parsley seeds in spring, when soil moisture levels are still adequate and the weather is kind with regular showers of rain or misty days, we have no difficulties in obtaining a good strike within 2–4 weeks. We have found that the flat-leaved varieties germinate faster.

A late summer sowing is more difficult. Water the drill

thoroughly (about a litre for every metre of row) before sowing the seed, and use a gentle sprinkler or watering can with a fine rose to keep the bed moist. Some writers recommend soaking the seed in warm water, but we have found no advantage in doing this. Also, wet seeds stick together, making them difficult to sow evenly.

Sow parsley seed 1–2 cm deep and thin the seedlings before they touch, initially to 15 cm and finally to 30 cm spacing.

Some gardeners prefer to raise parsley seedlings under cover, as this gives them more control over the germinating environment. In wet springs it enables an earlier start to be made with seed sowing. Parsley should be raised in individual containers and transplanted to the garden while still small, before the taproot develops. Use a moist, standard potting mix with 3–4 seeds per pot. Cover the seeds with 1 cm depth of mix. Keep the soil damp and dark by covering with wet newspaper and black plastic, and mist if the surface starts to dry out. With bottom heat in a propagator, and a soil temperature of 20–23°C, germination will be much quicker than the 3–8 weeks it can take outdoors. Thin to the strongest seedlings and grow on with plenty of light. Start hardening off a week or so before planting into the garden at 30 cm spacing.

When purchasing parsley plants from a garden centre, select only small seedlings, preferably in individual containers or cells, and check that they are not rootbound. Reject any with yellow leaves. Unfortunately, transplanted parsley has a tendency to run to seed prematurely and may do so in the same season as it is planted.

Young parsley plants require constant moisture. Without regular rainfall this will have to be supplied with a hose or watering can. Once soil temperatures have warmed, a mulch of compost is beneficial. Monthly light feedings with a liquid fertiliser will encourage good leaf development, starting when the plants are about 10 cm tall.

Remove any flower stalks that develop. From time to time, clear the ground under parsley bushes to remove any yellow or decaying leaves, which may harbour disease. We have lost the odd large parsley plant during a wet winter due to crown rot. It is important to rotate parsley sites to avoid a build-up of these types of disease.

In the second year, once a new crop of parsley has reached harvesting size, the old plants, which will be beginning to flower, should be dug out and composted. If you have room, leave one or two to attract beneficial insects and to collect seed from.

GROWING IN CONTAINERS

Parsley grows well on a well-lit kitchen window sill as long as it is kept watered, fed and cut. It also makes a pretty edging to a large patio pot of nasturtiums, though the serious cook will want other parsley supplies so as not to spoil the effect with constant picking.

Use a deep 20 cm diameter pot filled with ordinary potting mix. Either pot up 2 or 3 seedling-sized purchased plants or sow 6–8 seeds in small trenches. To encourage germination, moisten the mix by setting the pot in luke-warm water until damp right through. Allow to drain. Cover the pot with damp newspaper and black plastic. Leave in a warm place and watch for signs of germination—this is likely to be quicker than outdoor sowings. Thin to 3–4 plants and allow to grow on.

Container-grown parsley should receive a minimum of 5 hours of direct sunshine each day—avoid scorching in a sunny window. As parsley prefers cooler temperatures, don't attempt to grow it in a hot conservatory.

HARVESTING

Harvesting can start when the plants are about 15 cm tall. Cut conservatively to start with, so that they will recover. A minimum of 6 plants is needed to allow large enough pickings at this early stage.

Use scissors to cut the long stems off about 2 cm above the ground, cutting the outer stems first. The flavour of the leaves is best during their first year.

As it is a year-round herb and fresh supplies are available in supermarkets, there is no advantage in drying parsley. Dried parsley loses its fresh flavour and smells like grass.

IN THE KITCHEN

Avoid washing parsley unless it is dusty. If you have to, swish the stems in a bowl of water and then lift into a colander to drain. Spin in a salad spinner or pat dry with paper towels or a clean tea-towel.

To chop, hold the parsley by the stems and use scissors

to snip off the sprigs from the stems onto a board. Gather the sprigs together with your fingers into a compact bunch and, using a sharp cook's knife, chop finely in one direction. Then, holding the point of the knife down on the board with your other hand, use a chopping motion across the parsley, stopping from time to time to gather it back into a pile, until the desired degree of fineness is achieved. Some food writers claim that chopping parsley in a food processor bruises the leaves and causes a loss of flavour. Others claim that it is the best method. We use a knife to chop small quantities, and the processor for larger amounts.

Parsley loses some colour and flavour when cooked, so it is best added just before serving. Retain a little to sprinkle fresh over the finished dish.

Parsley as a garnish should be small enough, fresh looking and appealing to eat. Individual leaves of flat-leaved parsley make an attractive garnish. Curly parsley is probably best chopped coarsely and sprinkled over a dish.

Discarded stalks have a more intense flavour than the leaves and can be used in soups, stocks and marinades. If they are tied in bundles they are easy to remove.

HOW TO USE PARSLEY

- Parsley is appropriate in nearly anything savoury, so get into the habit of using it more frequently. Tom Stobart said, 'Many continental cooks add small quantities of chopped parsley to food as instinctively as they add salt.'
- Parsley blends so well with other herbs that it makes an excellent filler when you want a large quantity of herbs but not a strong flavour. It can fill out a herb mixture, for example in herb muffins, herb bread, herb butter and herb dumplings.
- Parsley is the main herb in the classic blend of fines herbes (see page 180).
- Make parsley butter to top grilled fillet steaks, lamb chops, fish fillets or baked potatoes. Toss with cooked vegetables, use in sandwiches and on savoury scones. See the general recipe on page 19.
- Combine chopped parsley with grated cheese to fill an omelette. A basic omelette recipe is given under chervil on pages 46–47.
- Parsley is as good with new potatoes as the traditional mint. Mix chopped parsley, garlic, grated lemon rind, seasoning and olive oil. Stir into steamed new potatoes and serve hot.
- Fond childhood food memories include fricassées with chopped parsley. Our live-in grandmother often made these with chicken or rabbit. Simmer the meat gently in well-seasoned milk and water until tender. Remove the meat and keep warm. Make a white sauce using a 50/50 mix of milk and strained cooking liquor. Season well and stir in chopped parsley. Place the chicken or rabbit pieces in a shallow serving dish and cover with the sauce. Garnish with extra very finely chopped parsley and paprika.
- One of our favourite salads from *The Cook's Garden* is made with layers of cooked kumara (sweet potato), slices of peeled orange, sliced spring onions or chives and coarsely chopped parsley. The salad is dressed with a simple vinaigrette of 4 parts of salad oil to 1 part of cider vinegar, salt and pepper. We have tried other herbs but we still prefer the mild, fresh flavour and colour of parsley.
- Chopped parsley is usually readily available to add to cooked vegetables just before serving. In particular, we enjoy parsley with potatoes, parsnips, leeks, asparagus, cauliflower, beans, Brussels sprouts and swedes.
- Parsley cheese toast makes an interesting accompaniment to a soup meal. Bake 1 cm thick slices of baguette or other bread until crisp and golden. Rub both sides with a cut clove of garlic. Combine grated mozzarella cheese and chopped parsley and sprinkle over the pieces of toast. Grill until the cheese is melted and bubbly.

TABBOULEH
Serves 6 in large soft pitta breads

Burghul is made from wholewheat grains that have been cracked by boiling before being dried and then coarsely ground. Tabbouleh, a Middle Eastern salad which has become popular in the West, depends on generous amounts of freshly gathered young parsley leaves plus a smaller quantity of mint. Other additions include tomatoes, mild-flavoured onion and sometimes cucumber and olives. It is dressed with lemon juice and extra virgin olive oil.

1 cup burghul
1 cup finely chopped parsley leaves
1/4 cup finely chopped mint
1 small red-skinned onion, finely chopped, or equivalent amount of shallots or sliced spring onions
250 g ripe but firm tomatoes, chopped
1/4 cup lemon juice
1/4 cup extra virgin olive oil
pinch chilli powder
1/2 teaspoon salt

Pour plenty of boiling water over the burghul and leave to soak for 30–60 minutes. Drain thoroughly in a sieve, pressing firmly to extract as much water as possible. Tip into a large bowl. Add the herbs, onion and tomatoes and stir gently to mix. Whisk together the lemon juice, oil, chilli powder and salt. Pour over the tabbouleh and mix through. Spoon into a serving bowl, cover and chill for at least 1 hour but no longer than 24 hours before serving with large, warm pitta breads to be split open and filled. Alternatively, serve tabbouleh as an accompanying salad.

HUMMUS WITH PARSLEY

This Middle Eastern pâté or dip is now well known in the West. The supermarket versions often lack flavour so we prefer to make it quickly and easily at home. Start with dry chick-peas and remember to soak them overnight, or use a can of cooked chick-peas. The addition of parsley improves the appearance and, as this herb is widely used in the Middle East, the added flavour blends well.

1/2 cup chick-peas, soaked overnight in plenty of cold water

3 tablespoons tahini
2 cloves garlic, crushed
3 tablespoons lemon juice
1/2 teaspoon cumin seeds, dry roasted and freshly ground
1/4–1/2 teaspoon salt
black pepper
1/2 cup packed parsley leaves
1 tablespoon olive oil

Garnish
olive oil
paprika
flat-leaved parsley or chopped curly parsley

Drain the soaked chick-peas and rinse. Tip into a saucepan, cover with fresh cold water and bring to the boil. Simmer gently with the lid in place for 60–90 minutes or until very tender. Drain, reserving a little of the cooking liquor.

Tip the cooked chick-peas into the bowl of a food processor and add all the remaining ingredients. Process until smooth, adding a little of the cooking liquor to obtain the desired consistency. Taste, and adjust the seasoning if necessary.

Spoon into a bowl, cover and chill for at least an hour to allow the flavours to blend. Before serving with warmed pitta bread wedges, decorate the surface of the hummus with a little drizzled olive oil, a dusting of paprika and finely chopped curly parsley or small leaves of flat-leaved parsley.

GREEN SAUCE

The French make various pounded mixtures with fresh green herbs. Pistou (see page 30) is made with basil, garlic and olive oil and is similar to Italian pesto. Persillade combines parsley and garlic, while others include grated lemon rind or nuts. These are most likely direct descendants of the mediaeval green sauces. The principle of combining finely chopped fresh green herbs with small quantities of flavour-balancing ingredients, and possibly a thickener or carrier, can be used to create modern variations. What they all have in common is their brilliant green colour.

Our recipe and its variation have wide uses. Add zest and colour excitement to a simple, thick and creamy pumpkin soup (see following recipe). They also complement poultry, seafood, salads and vegetables.

3 cups parsley leaves (about 100 g)
3 cloves garlic, peeled and crushed with the flat side of a knife
1/4 teaspoon salt
1/2 cup extra virgin olive oil (avoid strong-tasting ones)

Purée all the ingredients together in a processor or blender until smooth. You may need at intervals to scrape the ingredients down from the sides. Spoon into a small bowl. Cover and store in a refrigerator for up to 4 days.

Variation

This version of green sauce, with the addition of capers and lemon juice, has a slight tartness which combines well with a simple potato salad and fish dishes.

Add 1 tablespoon of drained capers and 3 tablespoons of lemon juice to the ingredients of the previous recipe, and process the same way. As the capers may be salty, omit the 1/4 teaspoon of salt if desired.

PUMPKIN SOUP WITH GREEN SAUCE
Serves 2–3

2 tablespoons oil
1 medium-sized onion, chopped
1 clove garlic, finely chopped
500 g prepared pumpkin (deseeded, peeled,
cut into small chunks)
500 ml chicken stock
2 bay leaves
black pepper
freshly grated nutmeg

Heat the oil in a saucepan. Sauté the onion and garlic until soft but not brown. Add the pumpkin, stock, bay leaves and seasoning. Simmer with the lid in place until the pumpkin is very tender. Discard the bay leaves. Put through a blender, processor or fine sieve. Return to saucepan and reheat. Ladle into bowls. Add a heaped teaspoon of green sauce to each bowl and swirl with a spoon.

PARSLEY, CORN & CHEESE BREAD

Made in a breadmaker, this light-textured bread speckled with green and gold is extra tasty and attractive.

2 teaspoons Surebake yeast, or 1 1/2 teaspoons instant dried
yeast
320 g white bread flour
40 g polenta
1 teaspoon sugar
1/4 teaspoon salt
1 tablespoon oil
1/4 cup freshly grated Parmesan cheese
3/4 cup whole kernel corn from can, drained
1 cup parsley leaves, finely chopped
170 ml warm water

Measure the ingredients into the pan of the breadmaker in the order given, or follow the manufacturer's recommendations. Select the white cycle and appropriate size setting, if available. After 5 minutes of the initial kneading, lift the lid and check the dough consistency. It should be soft and still slightly sticky. Add extra water or flour if required.

PARSLEY SOUP
Serves 4 as a first course

Although this soup is made from humble ingredients, it has such a beautiful colour and appetising taste that we include it in dinner party menus.

2 tablespoons oil
1 medium-sized onion, chopped
2 cloves garlic, chopped
130 g (about) parsley—weigh both stalks and leaves
1 stick celery, sliced
300 g potatoes, peeled and sliced
500 ml chicken stock
white pepper
1 1/2 cups canned evaporated milk

Optional toppings
flat-leaved parsley leaves
freshly grated Parmesan cheese
grated lemon rind or thin slices of lemon
scissored chives
dollops of whipped cream, or yoghurt, or pouring cream, swirled into the soup

In a large saucepan, heat the oil and sauté the onion and garlic until soft but not brown. Snip the leaves from the parsley stalks and put aside. Roughly slice the stalks and add to the saucepan with the celery and potatoes. Sauté gently, stirring occasionally, for about 10 minutes. Add the chicken stock and pepper. Simmer with the lid on until the vegetables are very tender. Remove from the heat and stir in the parsley leaves. Purée the soup in a blender or food processor. Return to the saucepan, stir in the evaporated milk and check seasoning. Reheat gently—do not allow to boil. Ladle into bowls and garnish with chosen topping.

TUNA, RED CAPSICUM & PARSLEY PASTA SAUCE
Serves 3–4

This simple pasta sauce is a good example of the everyday Italian use of the classic combination of parsley, garlic and olive oil. It can be made in the time it takes to cook the pasta and the result is superb.

1 egg
425 g can tuna, drained
1 clove garlic, very finely chopped
3 tablespoons coarsely chopped parsley (use flat-leaved if available, retaining a few whole leaves for garnishing)
2 tablespoons extra virgin olive oil
3/4 cup cream, or canned evaporated milk, or 50/50 combination
1/2 cup finely grated Parmesan cheese
1 red capsicum, deseeded and diced
black pepper
salt to taste

300 g dry pasta (a hollow shape will soak up the sauce nicely)

In a medium-sized bowl, lightly beat the egg and then add all the remaining ingredients, except the pasta. Stir to combine and break up large lumps of tuna. Set aside while you cook the pasta. Once cooked, drain thoroughly in a colander. Tip the sauce ingredients into the hot saucepan and add the pasta. Toss lightly to mix. Serve immediately, topped with a few parsley leaves or finely chopped parsley.

perilla

Perilla (*Perilla frutescens*), also known as 'shiso' (Japanese), is a commonly used food plant in Japan, Korea and Vietnam, but is a relative newcomer to Western kitchens. The Japanese produce it in bulk and use it in many ways. For example, the green-leaved form is used as a vegetable in sushi to wrap around or be layered with rice and fish. It is a popular tempura ingredient: whole leaves are dipped in batter and fried in oil until feather light and crisp. Other

Green Perilla

PERILLA
(*Perilla frutescens*)

It is hard to believe that Shirley Hibberd was talking about perilla when he wrote in 1871: 'Though the popularity of this plant has greatly declined within the past few years, it cannot be dispensed with, for its solemn bronzy-purple colour gives it a most distinctive character, of great value to the colourist'. Since the mid-19th century, Victorian gardeners had been using this purple-foliaged half-hardy annual in bedding-out schemes. When these came under attack, the perilla was singled out for its 'funereal' aspect—the epitome of bad taste. What is fascinating to us now is that Victorians grew but never actually tasted this edible plant. Nearly a century was to pass before perilla was re-introduced to Britain as a food item.

In contrast, a long history of medicinal and culinary use can be documented in East and South-east Asia. Today, however, perilla is particularly associated with Korean and Japanese cuisine. The Koreans use the foliage (*kkaennip namul*) as well as the oil pressed from the seeds. In Japan, many varieties have been developed for different purposes. Green-leaved forms (*ao-shiso*) are treated as a vegetable and the leaves serve as wrappers for rice cakes, are cooked in tempura batter, and are added to salads and soups. Seedlings of the red-leaved perilla (*aka shiso*) are a common garnish for raw fish (*sashimi*) and tofu. Its flower spikes, produced as day length declines in late summer (or is mimicked with artificial lighting), are popular fried in tempura batter and added to soups. Both leaves and seeds may be salted and used as a condiment, while the seeds are an ingredient of the famous seven spice mixture (*shichimi*). Many Western consumers first encounter red perilla when they order sushi at a Japanese restaurant—it imparts the pink colour to the pickled sliced ginger that accompanies this dish. Red perilla also colours the famous Japanese pickled 'plums' (*umeboshi*).

As a member of the mint family, it is not surprising that perilla is aromatic. Like the mints that Western cooks are familiar with, it comes in a number of flavours which we characterise by comparison with Western flavours such as peppermint, cinnamon, cumin or lemon. Variation in leaf colour, from bright green through speckled red to deep purple, is matched by variation in leaf form, with some cultivars having curled leaves with ruffled edges, others with creped leaf surfaces, and still others with large smooth leaves. Perilla's attractive appearance, range of flavours and versatility should make it a welcome addition to the 21st-century herb garden and kitchen.

vegetables, such as pumpkin, green beans, capsicums, mushrooms, and sometimes sliced fish or large shrimps, are treated in the same way. The combination of foods is served on a platter with a dipping sauce and finely grated daikon and ginger as condiments. The Vietnamese serve the young leaves in salads and use larger leaves to wrap around grilled meats.

Red perilla is grown commercially, in large quantities, for the food-processing industry, as its deep red colour is a valuable colouring agent in many pickles. It can make an attractive addition to home-made pickles, turning pale-coloured vinegar a delicate shade of pink.

Perilla is also grown commercially as a seedling crop, to be used raw as a seasoning and for garnishing. Flowers are also produced to be purchased as a popular garnish.

With its intriguing and unique flavour, and attractively shaped and coloured leaves, it deserves a place in the cook's herb garden. Unfortunately for those of us living in cooler climates and where growing basil outside is difficult some years, the cultivation of perilla presents a challenge. However, by following the traditional Japanese methods of seedling production, useful harvests can be obtained.

VARIETIES

Both the green-leaved and red-leaved forms are available as seed. The cultivar 'Crispa' reportedly has attractive, extra-crinkled leaves.

CULTIVATION
To produce mature plants

Perilla is a tender, bushy annual growing best at temperatures above 18°C. It prefers well-drained, slightly acid soil, long daylight hours and adequate moisture. In cooler climates, choose a sunny and sheltered corner and be prepared to provide cover. Partial shade is satisfactory during summer months in warmer areas. Garden beds should be raised, by adding additional organic matter, and well cultivated before planting out or sowing perilla *in situ*.

Germination can be a problem, as the seeds have a limited storage life. Purchase fresh seed each year and store it carefully in a cool place.

In cooler climates, raise seedlings indoors in late spring ready to plant out in early summer when frosts are unlikely and the soil temperature is warm. Earlier crops should be possible in warmer climates. The ideal germinating temperature for seed-sowing mix is 18–24°C. A horticultural heating pad may be necessary to achieve this temperature.

Outdoor sowings can be made in early summer as long as soil temperatures are adequate. In changeable weather, have small plastic or glass cloches available to protect the seedbed.

Perilla seed is very small and requires light for germination, so sow on the surface of fine seed-sowing mix. The mix should be well dampened but not saturated. Press the seeds lightly into the mix and cover the container with a sheet of glass or plastic. Keep moist until seeds germinate (see page 11).

Prick out the seedlings at the 3–5 leaf stage, either into individual pots or larger containers with plenty of space between plants. Use a good quality potting mix. Continue to grow indoors until the weather and outdoor soil temperatures are suitable. Harden the seedlings off gradually over 10 days.

Plant the seedlings out into final positions with a spacing of 30 cm. Keep well watered and encourage a bushy growth habit by nipping back the growing tips.

For outdoor sowings, ensure that the soil in the drill is fine enough by sieving, and moist by watering the bottom of the drill if necessary. Barely cover the seed with the lightest layer of sieved soil or sand (see page 12). Be vigilant in keeping the seedbed damp. Thin seedlings progressively to a final spacing of 30 cm—use them in the kitchen.

If desired, allow several plants to produce flowers. Allow a little extra space between plants and keep growth constant by applying a liquid fertiliser at fortnightly intervals. The plants will begin to produce flower shoots when day lengths decrease in early autumn.

To produce seedling crops

For outdoor summer crops, prepare a raised bed incorporating plenty of compost and working the surface to a fine tilth. For glasshouse or tunnel house crops, prepare seedbeds in a similar way or fill containers with free-draining potting mix (see page 11). Ensure that the seedbeds or containers are evenly moist. Sow seed by broadcasting evenly over a wide row or sow in shallow drills about 7–10 cm apart. Aim to scatter the seed about 50–100 mm apart. Either cover the seed very lightly with sieved damp seed-sowing mix or sand, or just press the seed lightly into the surface with a flat board. Do not compact the soil. For outdoor crops, cover the bed with plastic or glass unless temperatures are very warm. Keep the surface of the bed moist at all times until germination occurs.

Encourage rapid leaf growth by providing adequate moisture and fortnightly watering with a liquid fertiliser, and, if the crop is under cover, allow for good daytime ventilation.

GROWING IN CONTAINERS

Seedling crops do well when grown in punnets or larger seed-sowing trays. Ensure adequate moisture and for indoor crops provide good daytime ventilation.

Large perilla plants are decorative and undemanding when grown in pots, provided moisture levels are maintained. Pinch out the growing tips to encourage shapely plants—use the tips in the kitchen. Provide liquid fertiliser at regular intervals.

HARVESTING

Pick individual leaves and growing tips from well-established plants.

Harvest seedlings progressively by cutting with scissors, first at an early stage, just as the first true leaves are forming, and then continuously as the leaves get larger.

Harvest flower shoots when 5–6 flowers have opened.

IN THE KITCHEN

Gently wash leaves or seedlings and dry in a salad spinner or with paper towels. Large leaves can be used whole as wrappers or for garnishing. Shred leaves coarsely for soups, stir-fries and salads. Seedlings can be left whole or sliced.

HOW TO USE PERILLA
• Use leaves, shoots or seedlings in traditional Japanese dishes such as sushi, tempura, with noodles and in soups.

Red Perilla

- Use sliced leaves or seedlings in both Asian-style and Western mixed leaf salads.
- Add red leaves to vinegar (pickling white, white wine or cider) to colour it a pretty pink.
- Both red and green perilla leaves, whole or sliced, or seedlings make an eye-catching garnish for many dishes, not just Asian ones.
- Make Asian-style meat patties and serve them in hamburger buns, panini or pitta breads with a selection of salad ingredients including red or green perilla leaves.
- Add shredded leaves or seedlings to coleslaw. Toss with an Asian-style dressing made with 1 tablespoon of Chinese rice vinegar, 2 teaspoons of light-flavoured soy sauce, 1 clove of garlic (very finely chopped), 1 teaspoon of Asian sesame oil, 2 tablespoons of salad oil, 1/2 teaspoon of salt, black pepper and 1/2 teaspoon of sugar.
- Make traditional Vietnamese fresh spring rolls (see recipe on page 134).

KIWIFRUIT, CUCUMBER, RADISH & PERILLA SALAD
Serves 2–3

Perilla adds an intriguing flavour and colourful garnish to this pretty salad.

torn lettuce leaves to line a platter
3 kiwifruit (green or gold), peeled
100–150 g radishes, sliced
100 g piece of cucumber, peeled and sliced
2 tablespoons finely sliced perilla leaves (use both red and green, if available)
1 chive flower head (optional)—snip off the florets

Dressing
3 tablespoons mild-flavoured oil
1/2 teaspoon Asian sesame oil
1 tablespoon Japanese rice vinegar (contains added salt and sweetening), or 1 tablespoon Chinese rice vinegar plus 1/2 teaspoon sugar and pinch of salt
1/2 teaspoon light-flavoured soy sauce
1 tablespoon lemon juice

Make a bed of torn lettuce. Layer the kiwifruit, radishes and cucumber on top. Sprinkle with the perilla and the chive florets.

Whisk the dressing ingredients together and drizzle over the salad. Serve immediately

CUCUMBER, TOMATO, AVOCADO & PERILLA SALAD
Serves 3–4 as a side salad

Perilla is equally at home flavouring and garnishing this typical Western side salad.

2 young cucumbers (approximately 300–400 g total), peeled and diced
1 ripe avocado, peeled and diced
1 cup halved cherry tomatoes or diced larger ones
1/3 cup lightly packed, finely sliced perilla (use both red and green, if available)
2 tablespoons finely sliced chives

Dressing
3 tablespoons extra virgin olive oil
4 tablespoons lemon juice
1/4 teaspoon salt
black pepper

bed of torn lettuce (optional)

Less than an hour before serving, combine the cucumber, avocado, tomatoes, perilla and chives in a small bowl.

Whisk together the dressing ingredients and pour over the salad. Toss gently to coat.

Cover the base of a serving platter with the lettuce and spoon the salad over the top. Serve immediately.

CHICKEN AND NOODLE SALAD WITH PERILLA & RAU RAM
Serves 2–3

Pasta salads are popular and have become standard fare for buffets, picnics and lunches. We enjoy the many varieties of Asian noodles now available, especially those which require minimum cooking. To complement the noodles and the Asian herbs, we coat this salad with an appropriate dressing. The result is a refreshingly light meal which, conveniently, is best made a few hours ahead to allow the flavours to mingle.

2 small chicken breasts (approximately 300 g total)

Poaching liquid
500 ml water
thick slice lemon, or thick end of stalk of lemon grass, peeled and bruised
1 shallot, or similar-sized piece of onion, chopped
1 slice fresh ginger
2 rau răm leaves

Simmer the chicken gently in the poaching liquid until tender (about 10 minutes). Remove with a slotted spoon and allow to cool. Slice thinly across the grain. Use the slotted spoon to remove and discard the solid pieces from the stock. Return the stock to the pan and put aside.

Dressing
1/4 cup Japanese rice vinegar, (or Chinese rice vinegar plus 1 teaspoon sugar)
1 tablespoon fish sauce
1 slice fresh ginger (about 3 cm diameter), peeled and very finely chopped
half small shallot, finely chopped, or 2 spring onions, sliced
2 rau răm leaves, finely sliced
1–2 tablespoons finely sliced green perilla

200 g dried noodles

70 g snow peas, julienne sliced
2 tablespoons roughly chopped freshly roasted peanuts (see page 21)
extra red or green perilla, finely sliced, for garnishing

Combine the dressing ingredients together in a large bowl.

Cook the noodles according to the manufacturer's instructions. Drain and refresh with plenty of cold water. Drain thoroughly. Tip into the dressing and, using tongs, toss to coat.

Blanch the julienned snow peas in the retained chicken stock for 1 minute. Drain and refresh. Pat dry with paper towels. Add to the noodles with the chicken and toss gently to mix thoroughly.

Chill in a refrigerator for 1–4 hours before serving. Sprinkle the top with peanuts and extra perilla.

JAPANESE-STYLE SOUP
Serves 4

Use green or red perilla leaves or mitsuba leaves to garnish this Western version of a traditional Japanese noodle soup.

300g udon (thick wheat noodles) or any favourite noodle type
4 cups homemade or a good quality purchased chicken stock
1/4 cup dry sherry
1/4 cup light soy sauce (we use a low salt one)
1 chicken breast, skin discarded, flesh sliced thinly
100g button mushrooms, sliced
1 small carrot, cut into matchsticks
1 small celery stick, cut into matchsticks
1 small daikon or 150g of a large daikon, cut
into matchsticks

Garnish
2 spring onions, sliced
perilla or mitsuba leaves, roughly shredded or chopped

Cook the noodles in plenty of boiling, lightly salted water. Drain and cover with cold water until required. In a large saucepan bring the stock, sherry and soy sauce to boiling point. Add the chicken and vegetables. Simmer for 5–10 minutes until the chicken is tender and the vegetables are tender-crisp. Add the noodles and heat through.

Serve in bowls or in traditional Japanese bowls with lids. Sprinkle each serving with spring onions and garnish with perilla or mitsuba.

Joy Larkcom, in her book Oriental Vegetables, describes the use of red perilla in the making of Japanese pickles to colour the vinegar pink. Mary makes a mixed vegetable sweet-sour pickle to take advantage of a crop of daikon (Japanese radish). These and other vegetables are cut into matchstick shapes, blanched and pickled with rice wine vinegar flavoured with ginger. The addition of red perilla leaves adds colour and a subtle spiciness.

ASIAN-STYLE MIXED
VEGETABLE PICKLE
Fills three 500 ml preserving jars

1 kg prepared vegetables (cut into similar-sized matchstick shapes): carrots, scrubbed; daikon, peeled; cucumber, peeled and large seeds removed; celery trimmed; red and green peppers, seeds removed; green beans, topped and tailed; small onions, cut into quarters and divided into layers.

300 ml white wine vinegar
300 ml white rice wine vinegar (preferably a non-sweetened type—reduce the sugar if using a sweetened sushi vinegar)
5 cm piece of fresh ginger, peeled and cut into thin slices
red perilla leaves, shredded (quantity according to colour and flavour desired)
1 teaspoon salt
1 cup sugar
1 teaspoon peppercorns
1 fresh green or red chilli, seeds removed and flesh sliced

Blanch the vegetables all together in a large saucepan of boiling water. As soon as boiling point is regained, allow 30 seconds blanching time. Tip the vegetables into a colander and refresh them under cold running water. Drain and dry thoroughly with paper towels.

Bring the vinegars, ginger, perilla, salt, sugar, and peppercorns to boiling point. Allow to cool slightly.

Pack the vegetables into sterilised jars. Add a few slices of chilli to each jar. Pour the vinegar mixture over the vegetables, making sure that they are covered. Seal. Cool. Store in a refrigerator. Do not use for at least a week.

rau răm

Finding a new herb is an exciting occasion for any serious cook, and it is doubly exciting for the gardening cook! In May 1995 Mary returned home from a New Zealand Guild of Food Writers conference in Auckland with a small sprig of rau răm or Vietnamese mint (*Polygonum odoratum*), carefully wrapped in a damp tissue and plastic bag. How would this reportedly tropical herb survive south of the 45th parallel? For 3 years it was cosseted in a glasshouse, surviving the winters, but miserable in summer sharing the dry heat so enjoyed by the tomatoes. After nearly killing it on several occasions by forgetting to provide water, Mary decided to plant it outside. The result was a much more vigorous and lush plant. Rooted cuttings were taken and potted up before the first hard frosts, and again it was given shelter in the glasshouse. The parent plant was forgotten over the winter, being left with its extensive mound of dead shoots covering the roots. Spring arrived and the rau răm burst into life again. It had survived several −10°C frosts. Since that time it has been a full-time outdoor herb.

The next question was what to do with rau răm in the kitchen? Our first experiments, using the leaves from a stressed plant in salads, were a failure. Its aroma was reminiscent of coriander but its flavour was far too pungent. Even in soups it was overpowering. Now that we grow it in better conditions we find that the tender young leaves provide a fascinating mix of flavours: coriander, basil and mint, with lemon and pepper after-tastes. Rau răm was a great discovery. It is well worth seeking out.

Fortunately, it is a very easy herb to grow. Its only problem, in warmer areas, is a tendency to spread out of control. Gardeners should be cautious about dumping the prunings on waste ground or trying to compost it, in case it becomes another 'wandering willy'. In cooler climates it is a manageable, creeping perennial which dies back in winter and can reach 1 m high in one season. In warmer climates it is available all year round.

Rau răm has pretty, long leaves with distinctive dark markings up the centres of some, and purple-tinged stems.

RAU RAM
(*Polygonum odoratum*)

Many herb writers refer to this plant as Vietnamese mint. We are reluctant to use this English name because in the United States 'Vietnamese mint' is actually a sweet spearmint of the *Mentha* genus. Americans call *Polygonum odoratum* 'Vietnamese coriander'! In Australia, this close relative of the knotweed is referred to as either 'hot mint' or 'Vietnamese mint', and it is being trialled there as a source of kesom, an essential oil with reputedly the highest concentration of citrus flavour compounds of any vegetable crop. In Singapore the plant is known as *laksa*, in Malaysia *daun kesom*, in Thailand *phak phai*, and in Vietnam *rau răm*. *Rau* is a generic term for 'vegetable, greens'. Since the Vietnamese domesticated this plant and made it a significant ingredient of their cuisine, it would be an excellent idea if Western cooks adopted the traditional name *rau răm*, instead of needlessly confusing the identity and uses of the plant with the already complicated mints and corianders.

Rau răm first came to the attention of the West in 1790, when the flora of the region then called Cochin China was described by the Portuguese botanist de Loureiro. He reported that it was cultivated throughout the country, and was regularly eaten with both meat and fish dishes. It took nearly two centuries more before it began to appear in Western kitchens. Its introduction has been linked by various writers to the arrival of Vietnamese refugees and migrants in Pacific rim countries such as Australia, New Zealand and the United States, at the end of the Vietnam conflict.

Westerners found the taste of rau răm quite assertive: descriptions range from 'hot and peppery' to 'as hot as mild chilli, piquant as onion and fragrant as mint'. As one might guess from the species' name *odoratum*, the plant has a characteristic odour described as both 'intense' and 'refreshing'. In California, as recently as 1988, rau răm was considered an acquired taste and Robert Bond reported that it was 'never cooked in restaurants' but 'served as a garnish' and 'rarely offered to westerners'. Ten years later in Australia, it was acquiring gourmet status, especially in cosmopolitan cities with large numbers of cafés and restaurants featuring South-east Asian and Pacific rim or 'fusion' cuisines.

For rau răm to gain popularity, cooks will need to learn to use it young and rapidly grown.

CULTIVATION

Rau răm grows most vigorously in warm or tropical climates, but will also survive in colder areas providing its root area is protected during winter. This can be done by leaving the considerable pile of dead shoots as a mulch or, for appearances, cutting it back in late autumn, tidying and then covering the roots with a pile of straw. If frosts are likely to be colder than −10°C, a safeguard would be to pot up some rooted side shoots to shift under cover. These can then be replanted in the garden in late spring.

Rau răm's requirements are very similar to those of mint. It prefers fertile, moist but well-drained soil and dappled shade during the hotter part of the day. In cooler climates it thrives in full sun, providing it is kept moist.

Rau răm is a very easy plant to propagate. Its stems conveniently root where they touch the ground, making it easy to obtain a new plant by detaching a newly rooted section from the parent and replanting in the garden, or potting up to protect during winter. One plant, even in a cool garden, seems to supply sufficient for a small household.

If you cannot obtain a plant from a fellow gardener or local garden centre, then purchase it as a fresh herb from an Asian food store and place some trimmed stems in water. It does not take too long to sprout roots. Plant out

Rau răm

into a permanent site in the garden or pot up into a large container. We have not seen rau răm listed in seed catalogues.

Rau răm's spreading habit is reported to be a nuisance in warmer climates. Growing it in sunken containers, as we suggested for mint, or replanting each spring are possible solutions. Dividing and replanting every 2–3 years keeps your plant vigorous and productive.

To encourage lots of fresh young growth, cut back several times a season. Fertilise occasionally during spring and summer.

GROWING IN CONTAINERS

Rau răm makes an attractive and productive pot plant. Choose a large pot or several smaller ones and fill with a good potting mix. Plant in spring. Be prepared to water on a daily basis during hot periods and to provide the occasional boost with a liquid fertiliser at the appropriate strength. Site in a cool place with dappled sun during summer—it is not happy in a dry, hot conservatory. During winter, if rau răm is placed in a cool but frost-free site under cover, it may die back and watering frequency should be reduced. In a warmer site, it will continue to grow and require regular water and fertiliser. Rau răm should be repotted each year.

In frosty climates leave last season's dead stems to protect the new growth.

HARVESTING

Pick individual leaves or sprigs as required. Rau răm does not retain its flavour when dried, so is not used in that form. Choose young leaves, near the top of the shoots, when picking for a salad or when using as a finely sliced

Rau răm is a vigorous plant reaching to a metre or more in one short season.

garnish. When picking a sprig, use scissors and snip just above a small side-shoot.

IN THE KITCHEN

Pick the leaves from the stems. Whole leaves of rau răm are used as flavouring in soups and stock. They are discarded before serving. Finely sliced leaves are added to salads and sprinkled over cooked dishes as a garnish. As the centre veins tend to be tough, they should be torn out before the leaves are sliced. Use the method described for lemon verbena (see page 89).

HOW TO USE RAU RAM

- Rau răm provides a refreshing, slightly sour flavour in soups. See page 134 for our version of the famous laksa.
- In southern Vietnam, rau răm is commonly included as part of a selection of green leaves that are dipped into hot soups using chop sticks and then eaten along with the broth.
- Add finely sliced rau răm to Asian-style stir-fries (see recipe on page 133).
- Rau răm makes a tangy addition to leafy salads, especially those containing Asian greens such as mizuna, pak choi, Chinese cabbage and mustards, though we often substitute cos lettuce, spinach or European cabbage. Other ingredients can include seed sprouts, cucumber, roasted peanuts or cashews, radishes, and spring onions. Use 2–4 tablespoons of finely shredded rau răm in a salad to serve 4–6. Start with the smaller amount, as rau răm tends to be an acquired taste. Make an Asian-style dressing with 1/4 of a cup of lemon or lime juice, 1 teaspoon of fish sauce, a stalk of finely sliced lemon grass, a finely sliced small shallot, and 1/2 teaspoon of commercially prepared chilli or fresh chilli.

WARM GREEN BEAN, MUSHROOM & RAU RAM SALAD
Serves 2–3

This is a great side salad to serve with grilled or barbecued meats, fish or poultry. The Asian flavours of the peanut dressing complement the rau răm.

Dressing
2 tablespoons freshly roasted peanuts, coarsely ground
1 teaspoon sweet chilli sauce
1 tablespoon fish sauce
1 tablespoon rice vinegar
1 tablespoon lemon juice

Salad
200 g green beans, cut into 3–4 cm chunks
1 tablespoon peanut oil
100 g mushrooms, sliced
3 garlic chives, sliced into 1 cm pieces, or 1–2 spring onions, finely sliced
3–4 rau răm leaves, finely sliced

Combine all the dressing ingredients. This is easily done in a food processor: process the peanuts first and then add the remaining ingredients.

Blanch the beans for 3 minutes. Drain and refresh. In a wok or pan, heat the oil and, when hot, briefly stir-fry the mushrooms for about 1 minute. Add the beans and garlic chives and stir-fry for 1 minute further. Remove from the heat.

Spoon the stir-fry ingredients into a serving bowl and add the dressing. Mix gently to coat. Sprinkle with the rau răm and serve warm or at room temperature.

FRIED RICE & RAU RAM
Serves 2

It is worth cooking extra rice for a previous meal to have some on hand for this quickly prepared, spicy light meal. Our recipe is for the basic version, good enough to eat on its own, but for a more substantial meal add cooked seafoods, sliced cooked meats or vegetables.

2 cups cooked long-grain rice (start with 2/3 cup raw rice)
2 teaspoons peanut oil
1 shallot, finely chopped
1 clove garlic, very finely chopped
2 teaspoons finely sliced lemon grass
1 teaspoon ground turmeric
1/2 teaspoon commercially prepared chilli, or 1/2 small red chilli, deseeded and very finely chopped
2 teaspoons fish sauce
black pepper
2 tablespoons freshly roasted peanuts (see page 21)
1–2 tablespoons finely sliced rau răm plus a little extra for garnishing

As soon as the rice is cooked and cooled, spread it out on a plate and store, covered with a paper towel, in a refrigerator overnight to dry. Rice cooked in a rice cooker will be dry enough, so place it in a small bowl, cover and refrigerate.

Heat the oil in a wok or pan. Stir-fry the shallot, garlic and lemon grass until softened. Add the turmeric and chilli. Stir-fry for a further minute. Add the rice, fish sauce, black pepper and peanuts. Stir-fry until heated through. Just before serving, add the rau răm and stir through. Spoon into bowls and sprinkle with a little extra rau răm.

VIETNAMESE-STYLE CHICKEN WITH PINEAPPLE & CASHEWS
Serves 3–4

This typical stir-fry combination includes chicken marinated with rau răm, fish sauces, ginger and rice vinegar. Pineapple, cashews and an assortment of available vegetables complete the dish. We have listed snow peas and red capsicum, but beans, or asparagus and carrots, could be substituted. Serve in deep bowls over steaming rice.

Marinade
1/2 teaspoon sugar
1 clove garlic, finely chopped
1 slice fresh ginger, finely chopped
1 tablespoon finely chopped rau răm
1 spring onion, finely sliced
2 tablespoons fish sauce
2 tablespoons oyster sauce
2 teaspoons rice vinegar

300–400 g chicken breasts, skinned, and flesh cut across grain into thin slices

1 tablespoon peanut oil, plus extra if necessary
1 green chilli, deseeded and finely chopped
100–150 g snow peas, trimmed and cut into 2–3cm pieces
1 small red capsicum, deseeded and cut into strips
50 g roasted whole cashews (see page 21)
225 g can unsweetened pineapple pieces, or 3/4 cup fresh pineapple chunks
1 spring onion, sliced
2–4 rau răm leaves, thinly sliced

Combine the marinade ingredients and mix with the chicken in a small bowl. Cover and leave to marinate in a refrigerator for at least 2 hours or up to 8 hours.

Heat the peanut oil in a wok until hot. Add the chicken mixture and chilli and stir-fry until the chicken is tender. Transfer from the wok back into the small bowl.

If necessary, add a little extra oil and stir-fry the snow peas and capsicum for about 1 minute. Add a tablespoon of water and cover the wok. Steam over a high heat for a few minutes or until the vegetables are tender-crisp.

Return the chicken to the wok. Add the cashews, pineapple and spring onion, and reheat. Spoon over rice in individual bowls and sprinkle with the rau răm shreds.

LAKSA

Serves 4 for a main meal

Rau răm is so closely associated with the famous Malaysian and Singaporean noodle dish, laksa, that it is known locally as *daun laksa* (laksa leaf). The name is related to Sanskrit for 'hundred thousand', and probably refers to the many ingredients in this dish.

There are many versions of laksa and, like many Westerners returning home after holidaying in Singapore, we had to create a version to make in our own kitchens. We have specified fish balls and prawns but any cooked fish products or chicken can be substituted. Don't be put off by the long list of ingredients: when broken down into its component parts, laksa is really very simple to make and well worth the effort.

Paste
1 teaspoon commercially prepared chilli
1 tablespoon chopped fresh ginger
2 tablespoons chopped fresh lemon grass
2 teaspoons dried shrimp paste (it doesn't taste like its smell)
3 cloves garlic, chopped
1 teaspoon ground turmeric
1 tablespoon whole coriander seeds, freshly ground
3 tablespoons cashew nuts
1 tablespoon peanut oil

Broth
1 tablespoon peanut oil
3 shallots, finely chopped
400 g can coconut cream (use a low-fat brand if preferred)
2 cups fish stock (we use a 375 ml Tetrapac plus 1/2 cup water)
juice 1/2 lemon
1 teaspoon sugar
2 whole rau răm leaves

Extras
250 g dried rice noodles or 500 g fresh egg noodles, cooked or softened according to manufacturer's instructions
100 g long bean sprouts, blanched in boiling water for 1 minute, drained and refreshed
1 small cucumber (about 150 g), peeled and cut into matchsticks

300 g fish balls
200 g raw peeled prawns
2 tablespoons finely sliced rau răm

Measure all the paste ingredients into a food processor and process until finely ground.

In a large saucepan, heat the oil and sauté the shallots without browning until soft. Add the paste from the food processor and cook for 1–2 minutes, stirring constantly. Add the coconut cream and stir until well mixed. Add the stock, lemon juice, sugar and whole rau răm leaves. Simmer the broth gently for 10 minutes.

Meanwhile, divide the drained noodles, bean sprouts and cucumber evenly between 4 deep bowls.

Just before serving, add the fish balls and prawns to the broth and simmer gently for 2 minutes. Ladle the broth into the bowls, dividing the fish balls and prawns equally. Sprinkle with the rau răm. Serve with chopsticks and spoons.

FRESH SPRING ROLLS WITH SALAD

The Vietnamese serve this type of salad roll with most sit-down meals. It usually consists of rice-paper wrappers, lettuce leaves (whole or finely shredded) and a selection of whole-leaf fresh herbs, such as mint, rau răm and perilla. Each person softens a rice-paper wrapper by dipping it briefly into warm water and shaking off the excess moisture. It is then topped with the lettuce and herbs and securely wrapped. As a snack at any time of the day, the rolls can include portions of grilled meats, seafood or omelette. The rolls are served with a dipping sauce.

Dipping sauce
For 4 servings
1/2 teaspoon sugar
2 tablespoons fish sauce
1 tablespoon lemon or lime juice
1/2–1 teaspoon commercially prepared chilli

rosemary

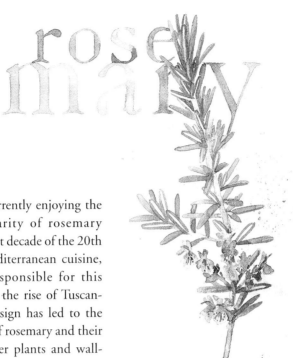

Cooks and gardeners alike are currently enjoying the unprecedented climb in popularity of rosemary (*Rosmarinus officinalis*) during the last decade of the 20th century. A growing interest in Mediterranean cuisine, especially Italian, is probably responsible for this phenomenon in the kitchen, while the rise of Tuscan-style architecture and landscape design has led to the production of several new varieties of rosemary and their fashionable use as hedges, container plants and wall-trailers. Their easy-care cultivation, delightful perfume, colour and flowering season in winter/early spring and beyond may partly explain their high status in the garden. In the kitchen, rosemary's availability all year round is a bonus, but some care needs to be taken not to overdo its use. As one of the most aromatic of all culinary herbs, it can easily overpower a dish, so start cautiously, adding just a hint and increase the amount as desired.

VARIETIES

Rosemary is an evergreen shrub, either bushy and growing up to 1.5–2 m high, or low growing with a weeping or cascading habit. All varieties seem to have a similar flavour. The best types to grow for an abundance of tender shoots for the kitchen are the more vigorous, hardy ones. The upright species, *R. officinalis*, and some of the readily available cultivars are prolific in their growth habit. The named cultivars have the added advantage of producing larger flowers in a variety of colours, including white, pink and various shades and intensities of blue. Some cultivars are lower growing or cascading and some are ideal for hedges. Read the plant labels and choose the ones best suited to your proposed garden site. The creeping form, *R. o.* 'Prostratus', is said to be less hardy than the others but has the longest flowering season, almost continuous in some gardens. Two cultivars which we enjoy are 'Tuscan Blue', with its darker blue flowers, wider leaves and vigorous tall habit, and 'Blue Lagoon', with its very bright blue flowers, narrow leaves and shorter, bushy habit.

CULTIVATION

With ideal growing conditions, rosemary is a trouble-free herb. The most important requirement is good drainage, if root rot is to be prevented. Its natural environment is a limy and stony soil, so for heavy soils incorporate coarse grit and if acid, add 200 g of dolomite lime per square metre. Full sun is preferred, but rosemary will tolerate partial shade.

The ideal climate is warm and relatively dry, with most rain falling in the winter. It is tolerant of wind and salt, so is a valuable shrub by the sea. In frost-prone areas,

ROSEMARY
(*Rosmarinus officinalis*)

It is customary to quote Shakespeare when introducing rosemary in cookbooks, and the usual selection is from Ophelia's speech, 'There's rosemary, that's for remembrance'. This is a curious choice, because it refers to the use of sprigs of rosemary in a funeral ceremony. Shakespeare mentioned this plant seven times in his plays: three in this sombre role, twice in association with weddings, and once as a strewing herb. Only one reference was connected with rosemary as a culinary herb: the chaste heroine in *Pericles* is likened to a roast dressed with the typical Elizabethan garnish of rosemary branches and bay leaves! Shakespeare fairly reflects the significance of rosemary at the end of the 16th century—compared with its ceremonial roles, its kitchen uses were relatively minor.

Looking back to the ancient civilisations of Greece and Rome, there is even less evidence that rosemary was employed in cooking. Even though Apicius's Roman recipe book called for many different herbs and spices, rosemary was not one of them. Pliny the Elder stated that the plant which the Romans knew as *ros marinum* was called *libanotis* by the Greeks because of the similarity of its smell to frankincense (*libanos*). The Greek writer Theophrastus had earlier described two forms of *libanotis*, one with leaves larger than the marsh celery, the other with leaves like wild lettuce. Neither fits the picture of our rosemary, with its needle-like leaves. However, Roman descriptions of the properties of *ros marinum* are much closer to our rosemary: they said it was particularly attractive to bees, it grew as low shrubs on gravelly hills, and it could cope with maritime conditions. In fact Pliny's nephew (Pliny the Younger) used it at his seaside villa, wherever the salt spray had killed off the box hedging. Its popular Latin name is usually translated as 'dew of the sea'. The Romans also grew it in tomb gardens, and both they and the Greeks wove it into wreaths. Since the natural distribution of the plant is in dry scrub (*maquis*) in the Mediterranean region, stretching from the Azores in the east to Crimea in the west, and from Crete and Malta in the south to as far north as Switzerland, it did not need to become a garden plant to play a significant role. There was plenty to be gathered from the wild. But its commonness and funerary associations may have made kitchen use less likely.

In the early mediaeval period, medicinal uses may have been more significant than the culinary ones, for rosemary was included in the physic garden of the idealised monastery plan for St Gall (9th century AD) rather than in the kitchen garden. By late mediaeval times, however, rosemary had acquired some culinary status. A 15th-century English recipe for 'Salat' included 'rosemarye', and it was an ingredient in the stuffing of capons, along with parsley, sage, hyssop and thyme. A contemporary Italian book recommended that sardines should be stuffed with a mixture of marjoram, rosemary and sage, together with saffron and good spices; a sprig of rosemary was advocated as a brush for spreading marinade on spit-roasting sea bass and kid. It was added to wine as one of the Tudor 'herbes for the cuppe'.

Rosemary did not reach northern European gardens until the 14th century. In 1338 the Countess of Hainault sent instructions on how to grow it to her daughter Queen Philippa of England. The plants arrived in England about 1340. English gardeners discovered that rosemary could withstand white frost and snow (unless it lay too heavily on the branches) but not the black desiccating frosts associated with winds from the north to eastern quarter.

Rosemary was now closely linked with Christian ritual and belief. It was said to grow no taller than the height Christ had reached at the time of His crucifixion, thereafter growing outwards. The flower was believed to have acquired its blue colouring from having Mary's cloak draped over it while she rested. Above all, the English spelling of *rosmarin* underwent a transformation to rosemary, 'the rose of [the Virgin] Mary', despite the fact that for the Romans its name had no link to either the rose or the Virgin. This religious association strengthened belief in its medicinal powers. According to John Gerard, a conserve made of rosemary flowers and sugar 'restoreth speech unto them that are possessed with the dumbe palsie' (stroke?), while the candied flowers comforted the heart and boosted the spirits. In 1629 John Parkinson made the telling comment that rosemary was 'in every womans garden', noting its usage in medicine and ceremony but not in connection with food. In Elizabethan times it was sometimes trained into the shape of carts or peacocks. It was also a popular herb for bowers and arbours for its 'wondrous sweet and pleasant' smell.

By the 17th century, the popularity of rosemary with English country women led to comments that it was one of 'the most Vulgar, yet most useful and necessary' evergreens. One of these uses was as an ingredient in the bunches of 'sweet herbes' added to the liquor in which joints of meat, poultry or fish were boiled. Another interesting use was an infusion of rosemary flowers in the wine vinegar intended for salad dressing. This practice was probably derived from the habit of serving wine with sprigs of rosemary to flavour it. Italian cooks knew that olive oil could be similarly treated. However, it was not rosemary as an infusing herb that attracted Elizabeth David's attention when she wrote about aromatics in 1970, but what she considered gross overuse of the herb by the Italians in stuffing joints of lamb and pork: 'The meat is drowned in the acrid taste of the herb and the spiky little leaves get stuck between your teeth'. We shouldn't forget that, when she wrote this, English cooks had not used rosemary to any extent for two centuries or more. It had disappeared from English recipe books for most of the 18th and 19th centuries. Despite her disapproval, rosemary went on to become a fashionable herb in Western cuisines during the 1990s.

So what is rosemary's role to be in the 21st century? The ceremonial uses have vanished, although herb growers still use it in lotions and shampoos. Does it deserve its current popularity in the kitchen? The camphor which constitutes up to 25% of rosemary's essential oil provides a good reason for caution. Learning from the past, we should concentrate on culinary uses that transfuse the complex flavour into marinades, wines, vinegars and oils. Knowing that bread ovens in Provence were once heated with rosemary wood should encourage us to sprinkle leaves on the charcoal in our barbecues, or to place sprigs under bread dough before it is cooked. For the herb of remembrance, it would be a pity to forget its wide-ranging historical roles.

especially where late-season frosts are common, some tips may get burnt, so choose a warm, sheltered place (against a sunny house wall is ideal) and protect young plants until they grow taller. Where frosts get below −10°C, rosemary is best grown in containers so that they may be moved indoors in winter. Although rosemary is described as a drought-tolerant shrub, softer, more succulent shoots are produced when water is provided regularly. The general rule is: don't over-water or under-water.

Low-growing rosemary

Good named cultivars are available from specialist nurseries and most garden centres. The best way to produce your own plants is by semi-hardwood cuttings taken from non-flowering shoots in summer to early autumn (see page 14). Layering can be used for prostrate forms (see page 13). Seed sowing is slow and unreliable, as seedlings will not necessarily remain true to type.

Position plants as specimen shrubs or as groups. We suggest a minimum of 2 to cope with frequent picking for the kitchen. If growing as a hedge, plant 50 cm apart. Choose positions carefully, as rosemary is taprooted and resents being moved.

Occasional watering with liquid fertiliser is beneficial, though not essential.

Some cultivars of rosemary tend to be floppy and sprawl, so benefit from light pruning. Rosemary flowers on old growth in late winter, so wait until flowering is complete before pruning. Prune lightly or just the tips, and never cut back into leafless wood: it will not resprout. If a bush is regularly picked for kitchen use, then pruning is not normally required. Rosemary hedges should be trimmed and shaped immediately after flowering.

GROWING IN CONTAINERS
Rosemary, especially the lower-growing and prostrate forms, does well in pots, providing good drainage is assured. Use porous pots and a coarse mix with lots of grit or perlite, or use a proprietary cactus mix. Feed with

a weak liquid fertiliser once a month. Remember not to overwater or underwater. Position pots outdoors in full sun or partial shade. In very cold areas, pots should be brought inside for the winter. Ensure that they receive a minimum of 2 hours sunshine each day. Providing rosemary is fed regularly and watered when required, it does not mind having crowded roots and this may even encourage flowering.

HARVESTING

Pick shoots continually throughout the year, though be careful not to weaken plants by excessive picking — especially container-grown shrubs. Plant 2 or more if demand is heavy. As the flavour of rosemary is best when fresh, pick just before required. Bees love rosemary, so be careful when picking while shrubs are in flower. Pick individual small flowers to use as a pretty garnish. The flowers have a milder flavour than the leaves.

IN THE KITCHEN

Rosemary leaves are leathery, and tough and spiky to chew. Whole sprigs or small branches may be used to flavour roast meats but, as some leaves may drop off, you may need to strain the juices before making a gravy or sauce. To incorporate leaves into a dish or baked product, use only tender leaves and chop or scissor them very finely. If the stems are woody or tough, strip the leaves before chopping.

Rosemary has both strong and subtle flavours, so discretion should be used when combining it with food and other herbs. This highly aromatic herb is capable of lifting the plainest food, but there is a fine line between adding a sweet, elusive flavour to overpowering with a bitter taste reminiscent of camphor and pine.

HOW TO USE ROSEMARY

- Roast a leg or other cut of lamb or hogget in the Mediterranean way with rosemary and garlic. Trim the excess fat from the meat. Use the point of a sharp knife to cut about 12 incisions evenly over the upper surface. Insert 1/2 clove of garlic into each incision. Place the meat in a roasting pan which has been brushed with olive oil. Brush the surface of the meat with oil and sprinkle with freshly ground black pepper and salt. Lay 3 large sprigs of rosemary in the pan and roast the meat for the appropriate time according to weight. Baste frequently. Allow the meat to rest at room temperature for 30 minutes before carving. If you prefer to serve roast meat hot with gravy, then omit the resting time and pour off any fat from the juices and strain to remove sharp rosemary leaves before making gravy.

- Rosemary enhances many vegetables, especially aubergines, beans, cabbage, cauliflower, potatoes, pumpkin, silverbeet, kumara (sweet potatoes) and tomatoes.

- It combines well with thyme, bay, garlic and red wine in marinades.

- Make rosemary sugar by placing a couple of sprigs in a jar of white sugar. Use the flavoured sugar in baking and to sprinkle over tart fresh fruit.

- Add a little finely chopped rosemary to a mild-flavoured clover honey. It tastes wonderful on fresh crusty brown bread.

- Add a sprig of rosemary to the water when boiling pickled pork.

- Add a little finely chopped rosemary to robust stews, casseroles and soups.

- Two sprigs of rosemary added to mulled wine when heating gives a spirited lift.

- To flavour milk- or cream-based desserts, add a sprig of rosemary to the milk or cream and heat gently to boiling point. Remove from the heat and leave to infuse for 1–2 hours. Strain the leaves out before using.

- Rosemary-flavoured bread goes well with cheeses. For one loaf or batch of rolls, add a tablespoon of very finely chopped leaves to the dough.

- Enhance the natural sweetness of fruit in unsweetened fruit salads by adding a pinch of very finely chopped rosemary leaves.

- Rosemary adds to the atmosphere of a barbecue. Place several sprigs or branches on the hot coals to permeate the air with a delicious smell. Soak the end of a rosemary branch in oil and use it to baste barbecuing meat or vegetables. Straight branches, stripped of their leaves, can be used as skewers when barbecuing meat or vegetables.

- Enhance your favourite potato or pumpkin soup with the addition of 1 teaspoon of finely chopped rosemary. Add to the soup after it has been puréed.

- A quarter of a teaspoon of finely chopped rosemary adds a subtle but intriguing flavour to shortbread and other baked products.
- Pick tiny rosemary flowers to garnish desserts and salads.
- Make rosemary vinegar to add to marinades (see page 17).
- Rosemary leaves make a popular tea which is best served with honey as a sweetener. The flowers produce a more delicate brew (see pages 19–20).
- Rosemary enhances desserts based on oranges and apples. Add rosemary flowers to fruit crumbles, reserving a few for garnishing.
- Add a little finely chopped rosemary to shepherd's pie, either to the minced lamb or to the mashed potato topping.

TRUE ITALIAN PIZZA
Makes 2 (approximately 20 cm diameter)

Although we enjoyed New Zealand pizzas, piled high with toppings, we knew that the true Italian ones were very different. When Mary and her husband travelled to Italy in May 2000, they soon became addicted to the original, much simpler versions. Cooked in brick ovens, they are very thin and crisp and are often left unadorned, dressed only with olive oil and salt and sometimes sprinkled with garlic and herbs—rosemary being a favourite. Other toppings, such as cheese, tomatoes, globe artichokes, olives, and so on, are also used, but singly, with the focus always on the bread. We still enjoy our main meal-sized New Zealand pizzas but frequently make the Italian ones to serve as snacks and with pre-dinner drinks by the barbecue.

 Our cooking method simulates the traditional brick oven by using a set of unglazed quarry tiles set on an oven rack and preheated with the oven for at least 30 minutes. A heavy oven slide or pizza stone are acceptable alternatives. The dough is quickly prepared in a bread machine or with a little more effort by hand.

3 teaspoons Surebake yeast, or 1 1/2 teaspoons instant yeast
480 g bread-making flour
1 teaspoon sugar
1/2 teaspoon salt
2 tablespoons olive oil (not extra virgin)
300 ml (about) warm water (blood heat)

Topping
2 tablespoon olive oil (not extra virgin)
1 tablespoon finely chopped rosemary
6 cloves garlic, very finely chopped
salt to taste

To prepare the dough
If using a breadmaker, place all the ingredients in the pan in the order recommended by the manufacturer. Select the white dough setting and start the machine. After a few minutes into the first kneading cycle, lift the lid and check the consistency of the dough. It should be smooth, soft and slightly sticky. If not, add a little extra flour or water.

 If preparing by hand, combine 1 cup of the weighed flour with the yeast, sugar and salt in a large bowl. Add 150 ml of cold water, followed immediately with 150 ml of boiling water. Beat vigorously until a smooth batter is formed. Leave to rest for 3 minutes. Add another cup of the weighed flour and the oil, and stir to form a sticky dough. Add sufficient extra flour to form a soft dough. Turn onto a floured board and knead for 5–10 minutes or until elastic. Leave to rest, covered, for 15 minutes.

To make the pizzas
Place the quarry tiles or alternative on a rack in the middle of the oven. Preheat for at least 30 minutes to 250°C.

 Prepare the topping by combining the oil with the rosemary and garlic. Allow to stand for the flavours to combine.

 Shape the dough by dividing in half and rolling each piece out on a well-floured board to approximately 20 cm diameter. Leave on the boards, brush the surface with a little of the flavoured oil, cover lightly with plastic film and leave to rest for 20 minutes.

 Remove the film, dimple the surface with your fingers and brush with the remaining flavoured oil. Sprinkle with the salt. Working quickly, use a thin baking sheet to transfer the pizzas directly to the hot quarry tiles or alternative. Bake for 8–10 minutes or until golden brown. Slide onto racks to cool a little before serving.

THICK PEA SOUP WITH ROSEMARY
Serves 6–8

Soup made from dried peas can taste rather bland and stodgy. In this recipe the humble pea soup is lifted to new heights.

500 g split green peas (use fresh supplies as flavour deteriorates with age)
100 g bacon, trimmed and cut into small pieces
1 small onion, diced
3 cloves garlic, finely chopped
2 medium-sized carrots, peeled and finely diced
3 stalks celery, finely diced
2 tablespoons cooking oil
1 bay leaf
1–2 tablespoons finely chopped rosemary
1/2–1 teaspoon salt (depending on how salty the bacon is)
black pepper

Place the peas in a large bowl. Cover with cold water 5 cm deeper than the peas and leave to soak overnight or for a minimum of 4 hours.

In a large, heavy-based saucepan, sauté the bacon and vegetables in the oil until soft. Add the peas and soaking water, the herbs and seasoning. Bring to the boil and simmer for 1 1/2–2 hours. Add sufficient extra water to achieve the desired consistency.

ROSEMARY AND GARLIC FLAVOURED BEAN PÂTÉ

1 cup dry haricot beans, soaked overnight in plenty of cold water
3 tablespoons mild-flavoured olive oil
3 cloves garlic, very finely chopped
1 teaspoon very finely chopped rosemary
1 tablespoon lemon juice
black pepper
salt

Drain the soaked beans and place in a large saucepan. Cover with fresh water and bring to the boil. Cover and simmer gently for about 1 hour or until the beans are very tender. Drain, retaining a few spoonfuls of cooking liquid.

In a small saucepan, gently sauté the garlic and rosemary in the oil for 5 minutes or until the garlic is lightly coloured. Add the cooked beans and cook a further 5–10 minutes, adding a little of the reserved liquid if the mixture becomes too dry. Stir frequently. Season with lemon juice, salt and pepper and beat with a wooden spoon or mash to produce a coarse purée. Spoon into a small bowl. Allow to cool and store in a refrigerator. Will keep for 2–3 days.

To serve: spread thickly on bruschetta and top with a sprinkling of finely diced tomatoes and freshly ground black pepper. Bruschetta are thick slices of bread, toasted or grilled, rubbed with garlic and drizzled with olive oil.

MEDITERRANEAN-STYLE BEEF STEW WITH ROSEMARY & JUNIPER BERRIES
Serves 4

The combination of rosemary, juniper berries, bay, bacon, garlic and wine gives this stew a rich, full taste, even though the meat is not pre-browned—a great saving in time and mess!

800 g stewing beef, cut into 3 cm chunks
1/4 cup flour
black pepper
1/4 teaspoon salt
100 g bacon, trimmed and cut into small pieces
1/2 cup red wine
400 g can tomatoes in juice, roughly chopped
2 cloves garlic, finely chopped
1 medium-sized onion, chopped
2 teaspoons finely chopped rosemary leaves
1 bay leaf
10 juniper berries, roughly crushed

Place the beef, flour, pepper and salt in a plastic bag and shake to coat the meat thoroughly. Tip into a heavy casserole and add the remaining ingredients. Stir to mix. Cover tightly by lining the lid with a piece of aluminium foil. Bake at 150°C for 4 hours.

ROSEMARY HEMPHILL'S
ROSEMARY SCONES
Makes 8 scones

The Penguin Book of Herbs and Spices (1966) by the famous Australian herb writer, Rosemary Hemphill, was Mary's first book about culinary herbs. It was first published as *Fragrance and Flavour* and *Spice and Savour* by Angus & Robertson in 1959 and 1965. These books played a major part in the resurgence of interest in herb gardening and cooking, and are still worth having today.

Rosemary Hemphill introduces her rosemary scone recipe by saying: 'I have often served these scones to people who are interested in the unique flavour that herbs give to everyday food. As there could be nothing more everyday than scones, and as the recipe has been so popular, here it is.' And here is our slightly modified version.

2 cups self-raising flour
pinch salt
1 tablespoon sugar
2 tablespoons (30 g) cold butter, coarsely grated
1 tablespoon finely chopped rosemary
200 ml (about) milk

Preheat the oven to 225°C with a shelf just above the middle.

In a large bowl, combine the flour, salt, sugar, grated butter and rosemary. Stir to mix thoroughly. Gradually add sufficient of the milk (or a little more) to make a soft dough—it should still be slightly sticky. Tip onto a floured board and gently knead 12 times. Roll out to a circle about 2 cm thick. With a sharp, floured knife cut into 8 wedges. Reassemble the circle on an oven tray, leaving about 1 cm between the segments. Bake in the oven for 10–15 minutes or until well risen and golden brown on top and underneath.

Best eaten fresh with butter. Left-overs can be frozen. They are also good toasted and served with a topping of cream cheese.

ROSEMARY ICE-CREAM

Make in an ice-cream machine for the smoothest texture.

The subtle hint of rosemary combined with the sweetness of a late-harvest dessert wine produces a truly memorable ice-cream. Serve scoops in small glass or china bowls and decorate with rosemary flowers.

375 ml can evaporated milk
3/4 cup sugar
1 teaspoon very finely chopped rosemary leaves
2 eggs
3/4 cup cream
1/2 cup dessert wine
1 teaspoon natural vanilla essence, or use whole vanilla pod
rosemary flowers for garnishing

Combine the milk, sugar and rosemary, and vanilla pod if available, in a small saucepan. Heat gently to just reach boiling point. Remove from the heat. Remove the vanilla pod if used. While the milk is heating, beat the eggs and cream together in a large bowl, to combine thoroughly. Pour the hot milk mixture into the eggs and cream and continue beating for a few seconds to mix well. Return the vanilla pod, if using, to the bowl. Cover the bowl and allow to cool to room temperature. Remove the vanilla pod (wash well, dry and store for future use).

When cool, add the wine, and vanilla essence if a pod has not been used. Stir to mix. Cover again and place in a refrigerator for at least 2 hours or overnight.

To make, follow your ice-cream machine manufacturer's instructions. Alternatively, to make by hand: pour the mixture into a freezer container and freeze as quickly as possible to a mushy stage. Remove from the freezer and beat thoroughly. Return to the freezer until frozen.

Serve the ice-cream fresh and softly frozen, or store in a freezer for up to a week. If too hard, allow to warm a little before serving. Garnish with rosemary flowers.

Sage

How many old packets of dried sage languish in kitchen cupboards? If they are more than 6 months old, their tired and musty flavour makes a dismal comparison with highly aromatic garden-fresh leaves. We suspect that those who dislike sage may have sampled only the dried form. Also, the heavy-handed addition of dried sage to commercial herb mixes for use in store-baked breads does nothing to promote fresh sage with its wonderful depth of flavour, reminiscent of rosemary and pine with a hint of mint, lemon and warm spices.

Sage (*Salvia officinalis*) is a sub-shrubby, evergreen perennial which grows into an attractive

mound, making an easy-care subject for the front of the border. With a plant in the garden, or a pot or two of sage on a patio, the cook can throw out that tired old packet. Sage is a particularly valuable herb as it is available year round. It can be picked in winter, when fresh herbs tend to be scarce. If you are a gardening cook whose sage bushes invariably die, then take heart, as the usual cause of failure is poor drainage and that can be fixed, as we discuss later.

To those cooks who avoid sage, we suggest that you take another look at it. Try the Italian method of cooking it in butter or oil before sprinkling over vegetable, meat or pasta dishes. Treated this way, sage becomes more mellow and a sweet flavour replaces any astringency—even whole leaves are a delight to eat!

VARIETIES
There is a large number of different sage varieties available, but many can be regarded as more decorative than culinary. For the gardening cook, the choice is between 2 types of green-leaved sage, gold/green variegated forms, a popular purple one and the fascinating cultivar 'Tricolor', which bears grey-green leaves, zoned cream and pink to purple.

Common or garden sage (*S. officinalis*) has oblong leaves of the well-known sage green colour and pretty lilac blue flowers in summer. There are also broad-leaved forms of green sage which have been selected for culinary purposes. These are vigorous plants which produce larger, round leaves but they normally don't flower, putting their energies into leaf production instead.

Purple sage (*S. officinalis* 'Purpurascens'), with its beautiful deep, plum-coloured new growth, is a popular

SAGE
(*Salvia officinalis*)

In its long history, sage has become the subject of some curious sayings and beliefs, which personal experience unfortunately refutes. 'He who would live for aye must eat sage in May' and 'Why should a man die whilst sage grows in his garden?' are just two of them. These somewhat undeserved tributes to sage's ability to procure immortality can be traced right back to the Middle Ages. Waverley Root quoted another European belief that your sage 'will not flourish if your money affairs are in bad order'. The healthy sage bush at one of the flats I occupied as a student proved that one wrong too. But rather than laugh at the naivety of our ancestors, it is more interesting to ask what this body of superstition tells us about the history of sage.

There is no doubt that sage has been a medicinal herb for over two thousand years, a status reinforced by its Latin name, *salvia*. When Romans greeted each other with the word '*Salve!*' they meant more than 'Hello!' or 'Good day!' but 'Be in good health!' *Salvia* became the herb that brought you to or kept you in good health. Its reputation increased as it was transferred from its original homelands in the western and central Mediterranean to colder regions of Europe, for it was one of the few evergreens in the mediaeval physic or kitchen garden. Evergreen plants were seen as symbols of everlasting life. The monk Walahfrid Strabo wrote a poem about the plants in his garden early in the 9th century AD in which he praised sage with the words:

> *It deserves to grow green for ever, enjoying perpetual youth;*
> *For it is rich in virtue and good to mix in a potion,*
> *Of proven use for many a human ailment.*

Unfortunately, the new growth in Walahfrid's sage bushes had a tendency to smother and kill the old wood, and had to be pruned back vigorously.

In mediaeval thought, there was no sharp division between food and medicine. With sage's medicinal virtues so well known, it is not surprising that it became increasingly common as an ingredient in recipes. As a culinary herb it had been little used in Roman kitchens until the final stages of the Roman empire; so its rise to fame in mediaeval Europe was very rapid. It never quite achieved the popularity of parsley and mint, but it appears with them in green sauces, with fried onions and apples as a flavouring for cooked broad beans, in herb omelettes, with green peas, with hard-boiled eggs and vinegar as a typical mediaeval sauce for cold cooked pork, in salads, in simmered chickens, and most significantly

in the stuffing of geese. 'Take sawge, parsel [parsley], ysope [hyssop], and savory; quinces and peers, garlek and Grapes, and fylle the gees therwith.', begins the 14th-century recipe for 'Gees with Sawse Madame'.

By the 17th century, sage was commonly used in sauces and stuffings, especially for veal and pork. It was boiled with calf's head and added to the minced brains as a sauce. With currants it served as a sauce for roasted pig's brains. The American writer Euell Gibbons has argued that sage was first added to food to counteract the indigestible qualities of rich foods. Not having tried roasted pig's brains, with or without sage, we cannot confirm his hypothesis. Certainly, herb writers for the past four centuries have been conscious of sage's potency. According to John Parkinson in 1629, 'It is in small quantity (in regard of the strong taste thereof) put among other fasting herbes, to serve as sawce for peeces of Veale, when they are farsed or stuffed therewith, and rosted, which they call Ollives'—clearly an early version of beef olives. As a health-giving herb, sage was the chief ingredient of sage ale, which continued to be made as late as the 19th century.

Several sorts of sage were grown in English gardens from the 16th century on, but the botanists couldn't agree on how these were related. There was a tendency to separate the culinary sages according to leaf size, and a general consensus that the narrow-leaved form had the better flavour. However, the discovery by John Tradescant of a tricoloured 'painted' sage, with leaves 'diversly marked and spotted with white and red among the greene', even more attractive in plant collectors' eyes than the green and white variegated form, diverted attention from the plain green and red sages. The painted sages were moved out of the kitchen garden into the 'Garden of pleasant Flowers', as the 17th-century flower garden was known. For much of the 18th century, only the red (which we call purple) sage was left in the kitchen garden.

As a salad ingredient, sage was in favour in England only during the 17th century. Perhaps the 'almost imperceptible *Insects*' (thrips?) and 'Venomous Slime' (spittlebug excreta?) which defiled John Evelyn's sage bushes at the end of the 17th century were a deterrent. However, sage tea became a popular 18th-century beverage, persisting well into the 19th century. Eighteenth-century recipe books also included instructions for making sage cheeses. We think of these as marbled green, which was indeed their original colour, but in the 18th century so little green sage was grown that spinach juice had to be added to the purplish sage to achieve the desired effect.

As with so many herbs, the 19th century saw a contraction in the use of sage by English-speaking cooks, back to the traditional stuffing role in roast pork, goose and sausages. In the United States, sage became mandatory in the stuffing of Thanksgiving Day turkeys, but neither the Americans nor the British shared the Continental enthusiasm for sage with other dishes. Even sage cheeses became rare by the early 19th century. Of course, tastes change and the obsession for 'dainty dishes' which prevailed in Victorian and early 20th century English-speaking households led to the perception that sage was crude and old-fashioned. In the words of Louise Beebe Wilder (1932):

As a flavouring Sage is easily over-done. In stuffings of duck and goose the tiniest smitch only is admissible, more spoils the dish. Our forefathers relished Sage cheese and were dosed with Sage tea, but endurance is not what it was.

In the last three decades we have had to relearn the value of sage from other European cuisines. The French pickle the leaves, use them to flavour marinades, thread them through and around different sorts of roasts, and make sage vinegar with them. Germans and Italians add them to eel dishes, to liver and to veal. American cooks have come up with cream cheese and chopped pineapple sage (*S. rutilans*) as a cracker spread. Sage tea has been revived and the powerfully antiseptic sage oil is an important commercial product. There are even researchers examining sage extracts for dementia therapy. What was that saying again? 'Eat sage in May and you'll live for aye!'

plant for the front of the border, with the bonus of being valuable to the cook. Its flowers are purple blue. The other coloured culinary forms are all attractive compact sages, but they lack vigour and need renewing more frequently.

Pineapple sage is a different species (*S. rutilans*). It is a tender perennial with limited culinary uses, mainly as a garnish on punches and fruit salads. Its aroma, strongly reminiscent of pineapple sweets, is better than its taste. See page 179 for information on its cultivation.

CULTIVATION

The biggest threat to a healthy sage bush is wet roots. If you notice that a whole branch suddenly wilts and dies, or worse still the whole bush succumbs, then fungal root disease is the likely diagnosis, resulting from poor drainage. Sage requires very free-draining, sandy or gritty soils with a neutral or slightly alkaline pH. It does not cope with heavy clay soils. If necessary, construct a built-up bed, incorporating coarse organic matter, horticultural grit and

Variegated sage looks attractive but may lack vigour.

Common sage

a handful of dolomite lime. The alternative is to grow your sage plants in large clay pots.

Green sage bushes are very hardy. They will withstand heavy frosts, only dropping a few leaves, before a full recovery in spring.

Sage plants need full sun and should be positioned where there is good air circulation, as overcrowding encourages mildew. They cope well with drought conditions, though occasional waterings ensure continuing production of young leaves for the kitchen.

Green sage can be propagated from seed but, as germination tends to be erratic and it takes 2 years to produce good-sized plants, this method is not popular. If you want a challenge or the potential for a large number of plants, we suggest that you first test the viability of the relatively large seeds by placing a few on a damp paper towel in a closed container in a warm place. Check each day for signs of germination. The viable seed can be used for sowing. Start seed indoors in early spring in small pots filled with a seed-sowing mix. Cover the seed with perlite and place on a heating pad. The ideal temperature for germination is 15–21°C, which should take 2–3 weeks (see page 11).

An easier method of producing sage plants is by

Sage flowers have a milder flavour than the leaves and additional sweetness.

layering. Peg down side branches with wire hoops and cover the pegged portions with 1 cm of soil. Wait until roots form, when the new plant can be severed from the parent and transplanted (see page 13). We have found that layering often occurs naturally, so be on the lookout.

Sage plants can also be produced from 10–15 cm long softwood or semi-hardwood cuttings taken in late spring or early summer from strong new growth (see pages 13–14).

Some writers suggest dividing old-established plants to obtain fresh rooted pieces. As sage is a woody shrub, this is not very easy to do but worth trying.

By far the simplest method is to purchase plants from a garden centre or specialist nursery. We suggest that keen cooks have at least 2 green sages: one common sage, so that flowers can be harvested in addition to leaves, and the other a broad-leaved type to ensure generous year-round leaf supplies. If space permits, include some coloured sages, especially the purple one.

Sage bushes should be given plenty of space to grow and spread. Allow a minimum of 50 cm between green sage bushes (even more for broad-leaved types) and 30 cm for the less vigorous coloured forms.

Purple sage

Sage bushes benefit from the application of a liquid fertiliser in spring and again after cutting back. During periods of drought, provide a deep soaking once a week.

To keep sage plants bushy, prune them lightly in spring to encourage young shoots. Sage bushes that have flowered should also be cut back as the flowers fade in late summer. Aim to cut stems back by about half to a third of their length but never into woody branches, as these will not produce new growth. In cold climates, avoid pruning in autumn as soft growth is more susceptible to frost damage.

If mildew becomes a problem, use a baking soda spray (1 teaspoon of baking soda and 1 teaspoon of cooking oil in a litre of water).

Sage bushes eventually become woody and straggly, so aim to replace every 4–5 years.

GROWING IN CONTAINERS

Sage bushes make excellent outdoor pot subjects, giving the gardener control over moisture and drainage. They are not happy inside, being too prone to mildew. Select large terracotta pots, place a layer of broken tiles or irregular stones in the bottom and fill with a potting mix containing extra horticultural grit (5:1). Plant in the spring and water well until established. Later allow the soil to partially dry out between waterings. Trim back the growing shoots by harvesting regularly to encourage a good shape. Prune after flowering (if this occurs) and apply a liquid fertiliser. Sage plants will need fairly frequent replacing, possibly every 1–2 years.

HARVESTING

Use kitchen scissors or secateurs to snip whole sage sprigs just above a pair of leaves. This method, rather than plucking individual leaves, promotes the development of new shoots. Young shoots have the best flavour. As they get older, they become stronger and often bitter in taste.

Harvest flowers by grasping the petals between a thumb and forefinger and gently pulling to leave the calyx behind.

Dried sage retains quite a lot of flavour, providing it is done well. However, we cannot see the point of taking the time to dry sage when you have a bush in the garden—fresh sage is definitely superior. Lay leaves for drying on paper towels or racks in a warm, darkish and airy place, or dry in a slow oven, dehydrator or microwave (see pages 16–17). Being leathery, the leaves are slow to dry, tending to remain leathery rather than crisp. If drying takes too long, they develop a musty scent and taste mouldy.

IN THE KITCHEN

Trim sage leaves from their stalks. As sage has a very assertive flavour when raw, use it cautiously and avoid adding it to delicate-tasting foods. Sage is best cooked. It responds well to frying, roasting, stewing and grilling or barbecuing, with its flavour being enhanced rather than lost. To use sage in a briefly cooked dish, it should be either finely chopped or cooked first (see below). Treated this way, even whole leaves can be eaten and enjoyed. Their flavour becomes gentle and sweet rather than astringent and biting, as may be the case with whole raw leaves.

Use flowers in salads—they taste mildly of the leaves but have an additional sweetness.

HOW TO USE SAGE
- Cook whole leaves in a little hot butter or oil for a few seconds until crunchy, and drain on a paper towel. They can be used as a delicate and delicious garnish on salads, pasta dishes and vegetables.
- The Italians use sage to perfection, including it in meat dishes (particularly with veal and liver: see page 148), with pasta, polenta, potato dishes and focaccia. It goes wonderfully with Parmesan cheese.
- Sage is the traditional sausage herb (see page 148). Use it also in meat balls, rissoles, meat loaves, hamburger patties, pâtés or terrines.
- Small slivers of sage can be inserted into slits cut on the top of meat for roasting. Place several leaves in the cavity of chicken for roasting. Add sage to stews and marinades and include in stuffings.
- Use sage, preferably fried, with vegetables. It goes particularly well with asparagus, beans, globe and Jerusalem artichokes, leeks, tomatoes and broad beans.
- Sage matches strongly flavoured cheeses. It is traditionally used in potted cheese with a mature Cheddar (see page 184).
- Make slow-cooked baked beans with savory and sage for a treat on a winter's weekend (see recipe page 156).

- Sage need not be restricted to savoury dishes, as the recipe for upside-down apple and sage cake demonstrates (see page 149). Use whole sage leaves to infuse in syrups for combining with fresh fruits, such as cherries, blueberries, orange slices, blackberries, or with cooked baked apples or poached pears (use a 10 cm sprig in a syrup made with 1/2 cup of sugar).
- Add chopped sage leaves to garlic bread to serve with robust soups.
- Add whole sage leaves along with a bouquet garni (see page 180) to lentil, bean or other strongly flavoured soups or casseroles.
- Marinate thick slices of a fresh-tasting mild cheese in extra virgin olive oil with slices of garlic, lots of young sage leaves and crushed whole peppercorns. Leave for 24 hours before using.
- Make a sage-flavoured tisane, either on its own or combined with other herbs (see pages 19–20 for recipes).

SAGE & ORANGE WEDGE POTATOES
Serves 2–3

The mellowness of cooked sage is used to advantage, along with orange zest, in these golden and crusty wedges. Potatoes cooked this way are very popular with chip-lovers who need to restrict their fat intake—a mere tablespoon of oil for 3 servings is minimal.

2–3 large baking potatoes, scrubbed and each cut into
8 wedges
1 tablespoon cooking oil
3 sage leaves, roughly chopped
grated rind 1 orange
black pepper
1/4 teaspoon salt (optional)

Preheat the oven and baking pan to 220°C. Remove the pan from the oven and add the oil, sage, orange rind and pepper. Stir to mix. Add the wedges and toss around to coat. Bake for 35–50 minutes, turning the wedges once. When cooked they should be crisp, golden and tender.

PUMPKIN & POTATO CHOWDER WITH SAGE AND BAY
Serves 4–5

Sage adds a hearty and warming character to this creamy chowder. To make more substantial, add crisp bacon or pieces of cooked sausage or saveloy just before serving, or pass them round separately. Use a food processor to speed preparation, or chop vegetables by hand and allow a longer cooking time.

2 tablespoons cooking oil
1 onion, finely chopped
1 large potato, scrubbed and chopped
500 g pumpkin (weighed after skin and seeds are removed),
finely chopped
1–1 1/2 cups chicken stock
2 bay leaves
1–2 teaspoons finely chopped sage
black pepper
freshly grated nutmeg

1 1/2 cups canned evaporated milk (full milk or low fat), or
fresh milk, or milk plus cream
salt to taste

Garnish
finely grated Parmesan cheese
at least 1 small fried sage leaf per serving

In a large saucepan, sauté the onion in the oil until soft. Add the potato and pumpkin. Cook for 2–3 minutes, stirring frequently. Add the chicken stock, herbs and seasoning, except salt, and bring to the boil. Cover and simmer gently for 30 minutes (longer if vegetable pieces are larger). Stir occasionally and add extra stock or water, if required.

When vegetables are very tender, add the evaporated milk and reheat gently. Don't allow the soup to boil. Check seasoning and add salt if desired. Ladle into bowls and garnish each serving with the cheese and a fried sage leaf.

HOME-MADE CRUMBED SAGE & PORT SAUSAGES
Makes approximately 12 short, fat sausages

Home-made sausages are amazingly easy to produce and far superior to purchased varieties. You have control over how much fat is in them and you can vary the seasonings to create your own unique brand. The only equipment required is a food processor. Our favourite meat for this recipe is a piece of lamb or hogget cut from the leg, but beef and pork cuts are also suitable. Ensure that the dry breadcrumbs for coating are fresh: we prefer to make our own from left-over bread. Cut bread into cubes and bake in a slow oven (160°C) for 30–40 minutes or until crisp and golden. Turn into crumbs in a food processor. Other herbs (winter or summer savory, or oregano) may be added or substituted.

600 g meat
200 g fresh soft bread
1/2 teaspoon salt
lots of black pepper
1 tablespoon coriander seeds, freshly ground
1/2 nutmeg, freshly grated
2 tablespoons roughly chopped sage
1/4 cup port wine
dry breadcrumbs for coating

Cut the meat and bread into cubes. Don't trim away all the fat, as a little keeps the sausages moist during cooking. Place in a food processor with all the other ingredients, except the dry breadcrumbs. You may have to process in 2 batches depending on the size of your machine. Process until very finely chopped and the mixture forms a ball. Shape into sausages with wet hands and roll in the dry breadcrumbs until well coated.

To cook, preheat the oven and a baking dish to 210°C. Remove the hot pan and spread with a tablespoon of oil. Add the sausages and turn to coat. Bake for 20–25 minutes or until browned, turning several times.

TUSCAN-STYLE LIVER WITH SAGE
Serves 2

Liver cooked this way is very different from the leathery casseroles many of our generation endured as children. Even liver-hating family members came to enjoy this tender, moist and scrumptious dish. Calf's liver is the authentic choice but fresh lamb's liver is equally tender and delicately flavoured. We discovered this recipe in a favourite herb book, *Herbs in the Kitchen* by Carolyn Dille and Susan Belsinger.

2 tablespoons butter or oil
4–8 young sage leaves
1 clove garlic, finely chopped
300 g calf's or lamb's liver, trimmed and cut into 8 mm slices
grated rind and juice of 1 lemon (plus 2 thin slices for garnishing)
pinch salt
black pepper

Heat the butter or oil in a large, heavy-based pan. When hot, add the sage leaves and garlic. Stir-fry for 1–2 minutes until the garlic just starts to colour. Add the liver in a single layer. Fry for 3–4 minutes, turning the slices over to brown lightly on both sides. Combine the lemon juice, rind, salt and pepper and pour over the barely cooked liver. (Any residual pinkness will be gone by the time the liver is served.) Cook for a further 30 seconds. Serve immediately, garnished with the lemon slices.

RAINBOW CAPSICUMS WITH SAGE PASTA SAUCE
Serves 2–3

Coarsely chopped sage leaves are transformed by stir-frying in oil to give this colourful sauce a rich flavour typical of the Italian use of this herb. Use a mixture of coloured capsicums—red, green, yellow and purple.

2 tablespoons oil
2–4 tablespoons roughly chopped sage leaves (plus 4–8 small whole sage leaves for garnish)
1 large red-skinned onion, chopped

4 cloves garlic, finely chopped
pinch chilli powder
1/2 teaspoon paprika
3–4 capsicums, depending on size, deseeded and cut into
2–3 cm pieces
1/3 cup white wine
1/4 teaspoon salt
1/2 teaspoon sugar
2 tablespoons chopped parsley
freshly grated Parmesan cheese

In a large pan, heat the oil and when hot stir-fry the chopped sage and whole leaves until crisp. Remove the whole leaves from the pan and set aside on a paper towel. Add the onion and garlic to the pan and sauté for about 5 minutes, until softened and golden but not brown. Add the chilli and paprika and cook for a further minute. Add the capsicums, stir, cover the pan and steam for 3 minutes. Add the wine and seasoning and continue cooking until the capsicums are tender-crisp. Just before serving, stir in the parsley. Serve over cooked pasta in deep bowls, topped with a sprinkling of Parmesan and the whole fried sage leaves.

UPSIDE-DOWN APPLE & SAGE CAKE

This dessert or coffee-time cake is moist with no raw sage flavour, only a rich mellowness which gives the impression of many spices. For dessert, serve it with thickened yoghurt or whipped cream. A major ingredient is the sage-flavoured apple and honey sauce, made in a microwave. Only a cup is required in the recipe but any left-overs make a delicious muesli topping. We often double the sauce recipe for this purpose. The idea for this recipe comes from *Herbs in the Kitchen* by Carolyn Dille and Susan Belsinger.

Sage and honey apple sauce
500 g new season's eating apples, plus 1 extra for cake topping
2 tablespoons clover honey
2 sage leaves
1 tablespoon lemon juice

Cut the apples into quarters and remove the cores (no need to peel). Chop roughly. Combine all the ingredients in a glass bowl or similar container. Cover and microwave on high for 3 minutes. Stir and microwave for a further 3 minutes. Stir again and, if not very soft, microwave a little longer. Allow to cool. Discard the sage leaves and purée the sauce in a food processor until smooth.

Cake
180 g butter, softened (plus 2 tablespoons extra for topping)
1 cup packed dark muscovado sugar (plus 3 tablespoons extra for topping)
1 tablespoon lemon juice
2 large eggs
1 cup sage and honey apple sauce
1 tablespoon finely chopped sage leaves
2 cups white flour
1 teaspoon baking powder
1 teaspoon baking soda
1/2 teaspoon ground cinnamon
1/4 teaspoon freshly grated nutmeg

Preheat the oven to 180°C. Prepare a 21–23 cm diameter round cake pan by fitting a piece of baking paper to cover the base. Melt the 2 tablespoons of extra butter and brush the sides and paper liberally. Sprinkle the 3 tablespoons of extra muscovado sugar uniformly over the base. Cut the extra apple into quarters and remove the core. Slice each piece evenly and finely. Dip the slices in the lemon juice and arrange attractively over the base of the pan.

Cream the butter and muscovado sugar together until light coloured and smooth. Beat in the eggs, one at a time, until the mixture is fluffy. Beat in the apple sauce along with the chopped sage.

Sift the flour, baking powder, soda and cinnamon into a bowl. Stir in the nutmeg. Fold the dry ingredients into the creamed mixture until thoroughly blended. Spoon carefully into the pan. Bake for 50–60 minutes or until the top springs back when lightly pressed with the tip of a finger. Leave in the pan on a cake rack until cool enough to handle. Loosen the sides with a knife and invert onto a cake plate to serve.

The cook who grows both summer savory (*Satureja hortensis*) and winter savory (*S. montana*) has a year-round supply of one of the most useful, but sadly often forgotten, herbs. Both savories have a peppery flavour, reminiscent of a medley of other herbs, particularly thyme and marjoram. Summer savory has the softer texture and milder flavour of the two, and is slightly sweet tasting. As a result, it is the favourite with cooks. Winter savory, however, is the easier of the two to grow: as an evergreen perennial it may be harvested all year round. Summer savory, a half-hardy annual, must be grown from seed each spring and dies in late autumn.

If you don't grow savory, start now and you will soon appreciate its many advantages to the cook. It is one of the most versatile herbs we know; it has a natural affinity with other herbs, seeming to enhance their flavours; it is one of the few herbs that dries well; and is easy to grow.

VARIETIES

Summer and winter savory are the two main species commonly grown as culinary herbs. In the kitchen they can be used interchangeably, but in the garden they have different life cycles and horticultural requirements.

Less well known are the creeping savories, such as *S. spicigera*. These are sometimes labelled as winter savory, as they have similar horticultural requirements and culinary uses. We have also grown and enjoyed the perennial lemon savory, *S. biflora*, which has a pleasant, distinctly lemon flavour.

CULTIVATION

SUMMER SAVORY

Summer savory is a half-hardy annual which needs to be grown from seed each spring, once soil temperatures warm sufficiently. Seedling plants are occasionally available from garden centres or specialist nurseries.

It has a wispy appearance in the garden, with distinctive pink-tinged stems in summer and tiny mauve flowers, much loved by bees. It can reach a height of 50 cm. A short row of 6 plants will provide generous pickings for the kitchen.

As a herb originating in Mediterranean regions, it prefers warmth and full sun. The soil should be moderately fertile and free draining. A light dressing of lime, 6 weeks before planting, will improve an acid soil. As summer savory has rather shallow roots and tends to become top heavy, protection from strong winds is desirable.

WINTER AND SUMMER SAVORY
(*Satureja montana* and *S. hortensis*)

There is a fanciful belief that the Latin word for savory, *satureia* (from which the botanical genus name *Satureja* is derived), comes from the Greek *satyr*, a mythological creature with a strong sexual appetite. Etymologically this is much less likely than the explanation that it comes from a region of the same name in Appulia in Italy, or from the Arabic term *sattar*, applied to the mint family, of which it is a member. During the Middle Ages, the English called it 'saetherie', then 'saverey', which became 'savorie' by the end of the reign of Elizabeth I. Its modern spelling and pronunciation reflect convergence with the unrelated word 'savoury', meaning tasty.

The false link with satyrs has led to some colourful claims, such as that the Greeks used it 'as a stimulant during their sexual orgies'. It is true that the Roman poet Ovid described it as a noxious aphrodisiac; however, most Romans regarded it as a useful culinary herb, both fresh and dried. Apicius's cookbook called for savory to be added to sauces served with truffles, rissoles of porpoise, boiled ostrich, roast venison, hare and various fish. It was also an important ingredient of Lucanian sausages and of the Roman equivalent of bouquets garnis added to barley soup, simmered chicken and mussels. Columella and Virgil praised the honey made from its flowers, ranking it only behind thyme and marjoram as a valuable bee plant.

We are not certain how many types of *Satureja* the Romans used, for several species of this aromatic genus grow wild in Mediterranean countries. We are familiar with the one most tolerant of colder conditions, the perennial winter savory (*S. montana*), and the quick-growing annual summer savory (*S. hortensis*), but the Romans may also have used the species *S. thymbra*, employed today in herbal teas and as a substitute for oregano in eastern Mediterranean countries like Crete.

The species vary in the composition of their essential oils. Of the two commonly grown today, summer savory has the highest proportion of the phenol thymol, and is the most acceptable as a fresh herb. Winter savory has more carvacrol than thymol, so the sweet aroma of the thymol is suppressed by the carvacrol's more minty odour, slightly reminiscent of disinfectant.

A plan for an ideal monastery, including an infirmary garden and a kitchen garden, which was drawn up about 820 AD, called for savory to be planted in both enclosures.

It is possible that winter savory was intended for the former, in view of its medicinal properties, and summer savory for the latter, to flavour food. In either case, the old reputation as an aphrodisiac seems to have vanished. Mediaeval cooks used savory as one of a group of flavouring herbs dominated by parsley and sage. These were used in broth in which capons and chickens were simmered, mixed into the meat fillings of pies, added to sauces and herb custards, and incorporated into the stuffings of geese (along with quinces, pears, garlic and grapes). There is no evidence that savory was used on its own.

Savory retained some of its mediaeval uses well into the 17th century. In his book on the country housewife's garden in 1626, William Lawson described savory as 'good for my Housewifes pot and pye'. Towards the end of the 16th century, writers began to distinguish the two types, summer and winter. The influential John Gerard wrote in 1597 that summer savory 'doth marvellously prevaile against winde: therefore it is with good successe boiled and eaten with beanes, peason [peas], and other windie pulses'. John Parkinson's comments in 1629 suggest that these anti-flatulent properties were better known in Europe:

The Summer Savorie is used in other Countryes much more then [than] with us in their ordinary diets, as condiment or sawce to their meates, sometimes of it selfe, and sometimes with other herbes, and sometimes strewed or layde upon the dishes as we doe Parsley, as also with beanes and pease, rise [rice] and wheate; and sometimes the dryed herbe boyled among pease to make pottage.

Since an alternative German name for savory is *bohnenkraut* (bean herb), and since the French regard summer savory as the correct accompaniment to broad beans, we may guess that Parkinson was referring to the cooking of both France and Germany. He also spoke of winter savory as a 'farcing' herb, an old word meaning stuffing, and described the (new?) practice of mixing dried, powdered winter savory with breadcrumbs 'to breade their meate, be it fish or flesh, to give it the quicker rellish'. We call this 'crumbing'.

By the 1730s, both savory species were falling out of favour in Britain, except for medicinal purposes. Garden manuals mentioned them in lists of sweet herbs, but in 18th-century recipe books, if they appeared at all, they were specified either for old-fashioned dishes such as hodgepodge, a descendant of the mediaeval hoggepot, or in recipes obviously imported from the Continent. For Mrs Beeton and other 19th-century cookbook writers, the savories were insignificant herbs. It has been suggested that their decline was a consequence of the increasing availability and lower costs of the East Indian spices which took over their role as strongly aromatic flavourings. Chronologically this is plausible, but the fact that the savories were not replaced by spices in French and German cookery weakens this explanation.

Renewed interest in herbs in America and Britain from the 1930s involved searching the old herbals and recipe books for uses that might be revived, as well as some genuine innovations. In 1940 Eleanour Sinclair Rohde advocated the use of winter savory in flavoured butter, spiced pepper, spiced salt, herb vinegars, tomato juice cocktails and potted cheese. Later, in 1970, Elizabeth David made the valuable suggestion that summer savory makes a good condiment for people on a salt-free diet. Though it is unlikely that we would want to return to the wide range of Roman uses of savories, their long history in Western kitchens should provide us with many ideas for extending our experience with these herbs. The developing interest in Mediterranean cuisines should help to restore them to a more fitting place in our kitchens and gardens.

Sow in seed-raising mix in containers, 4–6 weeks before the desired planting-out date. Seeds should be either left uncovered or only very thinly covered as light is required for germination, which will take about 10–15 days with a soil temperature of about 18°C. When large enough to handle, prick out into potting mix in small individual containers (see page 11). Plant out in late spring, spacing about 20–25 cm apart. Alternatively, sow directly into the garden once soil temperatures allow and the danger of frosts has passed. Thin plants progressively to 20–25 cm spacing (see page xxx). Take advantage of the delicate flavour of the thinnings to enhance spring salads.

Keep plants growing well with regular watering if necessary, and side applications of liquid fertiliser every 2–3 weeks. Pinch back regularly to encourage bushy plants. The soil can be mounded around the base as a way of preventing any tendency to topple over.

GROWING SUMMER SAVORY IN CONTAINERS
Grow summer savory in a large enough container to support 3–4 plants. Alternatively, grow 3 or 4 plants in smaller individual pots. As they are shallow rooting, pot depth is not a problem. Use a very free-draining mix (see

Summer savoury

Tiny mauve flowers of summer savory.

page 15). Successive sowings will provide a long harvesting season.

Be prepared to maintain soil moisture and provide liquid fertiliser, at pot-plant strength, every 2 weeks. Position pots out of draughts and where full sun is available. Keep plants well picked to encourage plenty of new growth.

WINTER SAVORY

Winter savory makes an attractive edging plant. Trim from time to time to maintain its neat appearance. In late summer it is covered with white flowers, giving it a heath-like appearance. Our plants have always had white flowers, but some herb writers mention pale purple, bluish purple or pink forms.

One well-grown plant produces sufficient leaves for most households, but as it is slow growing and relatively short lived, it is best to start with 2 or 3 and then, once fully grown, start one new plant each year. Don't expect to pick more than just a few short stems from each plant in the first season.

As a native of warm, stony hillsides, winter savory, particularly the creeping form, makes a good candidate for a rockery. With full sun, good drainage and less rich soil than is best for summer savory, plants will flourish. They prefer a neutral to slightly alkaline soil.

To prevent root rot when soils are heavy clay and poorly drained, build up the bed with coarse organic matter and horticultural grit before planting.

Winter savory can be grown from seed or cuttings, but is more easily propagated from root divisions. Each plant section has its own root system, so it is easy to carefully dig out a small piece with its own roots from the side of an established plant. If you dig up a whole large healthy plant, you will be able to divide it into many individual plants (see page 13). The creeping forms tend to layer naturally, and it is often possible to find small rooted pieces beside a parent plant. Pot them up into containers and, once they have established and grown new leaves, they can be planted out into a permanent position. Allow at least 30 cm space from neighbouring plants.

Although winter savory is tolerant of dry conditions, its production of tender stems will be more rapid when watered regularly. Avoid watering during the colder

Winter savory

Winter savory in flower.

months of the year.

Trim frequently to promote new growth. In late spring, remove any dead wood and trim all stems to maintain a compact plant.

It is good practice to divide and shift winter savory every 3–4 years to reduce the risk of root rot. To ensure a continuing supply of stems for the kitchen, we aim to start a new plant each spring.

GROWING WINTER SAVORY IN CONTAINERS

The spreading forms look very attractive trailing down the sides of a pot. Plant in very free-draining mix (see page 15). Allow the soil around winter savories to become moderately dry between waterings and reduce frequency in winter. Trim for kitchen use only sparingly in winter because the rate of recovery after pruning is slow.

HARVESTING

SUMMER SAVORY

Start harvesting when plants are 15 cm high. Keep snipping the tops off the branches to extend the harvesting season. For the best flavour, pick fresh as required and before plants flower. Once flowering, leaves can still be used but the flavour tends to be stronger.

For drying, either cut stems before flowers appear or cut whole flowering plants. See page 16 for general drying instructions. Once dry, strip leaves from stems and store in light-proof and airtight jars in a cool place.

WINTER SAVORY

Sprigs can be picked all year round, though regrowth is slower in winter. The best texture and flavour occur just prior to flowering in summer.

The stems and leaves can be dried, but with year-round availability of fresh leaves this task seems unnecessary. Winter savory is slow to dry owing to the resinous nature of its leaves. Once dry, strip the leaves from the stalks and store in the same way as summer savory.

IN THE KITCHEN

Recipes seldom specify whether the savory listed in the ingredients should be the summer or winter species. Mostly it doesn't matter, as they are generally inter-changeable. As winter savory has the more dominant flavour, we prefer to use it in smaller quantities. We suggest that you start with 1 *tablespoon* of chopped summer savory or 1 *teaspoon* of chopped winter savory as a guide for most dishes.2

Both savories can be used whole as sprigs added to foods during cooking and then removed prior to serving. They can also be used chopped. Both the stems and leaves of summer savory can be coarsely chopped or scissored

but, as the stems of winter savory tend to be woody, the leaves are best stripped off before chopping finely.

HOW TO USE SUMMER SAVORY

- Use in herb blends such as a bouquet garni, or when a mixture of herbs is specified. Summer savory enhances and brings the various flavours together.
- Summer savory is known as the 'bean herb' because of its traditional use with both green and broad beans. Add 2 or 3 sprigs to cooking water as you would mint for peas.
- Place 2 or 3 sprigs on top of vegetables being steamed.
- A few young sprigs, picked before flowering, may be added sparingly to green salads, chicken and other meat-based salads.
- Cook 2 or 3 sprigs with vegetables for creamy soups.
- Add with parsley and chives to egg dishes.
- Make savory vinegar (see page 17).

HOW TO USE WINTER SAVORY

- Add with other herbs, such as bay, thyme and marjoram, to meat stews, casseroles, game dishes and terrines.
- One or 2 sprigs added to the cooking water will lessen the odour of vegetables, such as cabbage, Brussels sprouts, turnips and cauliflower.

ADDITIONAL WAYS TO USE BOTH SAVORIES

- Savory makes a delightful addition to other herbs, such as parsley, marjoram and thyme, in bread stuffings for chicken or other meats.
- Add savory to home-made sausages (see page 148 for recipe).
- Add sprigs to dried beans or lentils when boiling, and add extra chopped leaves to bean and lentil casseroles.
- Savory brings out the flavour of many vegetables, in particular onions, zucchini, carrots, capsicums, cabbage, oxalis yams, aubergines.
- Savory is a traditional herb in the vegetable dishes of Provence, such as ratatouille and tian (a gratin dish).
- The robust flavour of savory is retained in herb breads. It is a good herb to use on focaccia (see page 184).
- Use in vegetable quiches, tarts and savoury pies. Sprinkle on pizzas either before or after baking.

SUMMER SAVORY & GREEN BEAN SALAD
Serves 2

250 g fresh green beans (either French or runner)
3 sprigs summer savory

Dressing
3 tablespoons olive oil
1 tablespoon lemon juice
1/4 teaspoon dried mustard
1/4 teaspoon sugar
1 clove garlic, crushed
salt and black pepper to taste

Garnish
1 teaspoon scissored parsley
1 teaspoon scissored summer savory
1/2 shallot, sliced into rings, or 2 spring onions, sliced
2 tablespoons almonds, toasted (see page 21) and then cut into slivers

Trim the green beans and steam until tender-crisp with the sprigs of savory. Refresh in cold water. Discard the savory. Place the beans on paper towels to dry.

Combine all the dressing ingredients together in a small bowl and whisk.

Place the beans on a serving platter and pour the dressing evenly over. Sprinkle with the scissored herbs, shallot or spring onion, and almonds. Serve immediately at room temperature or chill for a few hours.

SALAD OF SAVORY WITH DRIED BEANS
Serves 2–4

Use whatever type of dried beans are on hand, e.g. pinto, red kidney or haricot.

200 g dried beans, washed and soaked overnight
1 small onion or shallot, peeled but left whole
1 carrot, cut into large chunks
1 stick of celery, cut into large chunks
bouquet garni (see page 180), plus 2 sprigs of summer or winter savory

Dressing
3 tablespoons olive oil
1 tablespoon red wine vinegar
1 clove garlic, crushed
salt and black pepper to taste
1 shallot or 2 spring onions, sliced
2 tablespoons scissored summer savory, or 1 teaspoon finely chopped leaves winter savory
2 tablespoons scissored or chopped parsley

Garnish
cherry tomatoes or pieces of coloured capsicums and/or olives
extra scissored summer savory (optional)

Drain the soaked beans and rinse thoroughly. Place in a large saucepan and cover with water. Add the vegetables and herbs. Bring to the boil, cover and cook for at least 30 minutes or until the beans are tender. Drain and allow to cool. Discard the vegetables and herbs. Place the beans in a bowl.

While the beans are cooking, make the dressing. Combine all the ingredients and whisk to mix thoroughly.

Pour the dressing over the beans and toss gently. Serve immediately at room temperature, or chill in a refrigerator until required. Place the dressed beans in a serving bowl and garnish with cherry tomatoes or capsicum and/or olives. Sprinkle with a little extra scissored fresh summer savory if desired.

GERMAN-STYLE GREEN BEANS WITH SUMMER SAVORY
Serves 4

A simple hot bean side dish with excellent flavour.

1 shallot or 1/2 small onion
1 tablespoon butter or mild-flavoured oil
salt and black pepper
1 tablespoon scissored summer savory
1 tablespoon flour
500 g green beans, cut into 5 cm lengths

In a covered saucepan, sauté the shallot or onion in the butter or oil until soft but not brown. Add the seasoning, savory and flour. Cook over a low heat for a further 2 minutes, stirring constantly. Remove from the heat.

Steam or boil the beans in a separate saucepan until just tender. Drain the beans, saving the cooking water.

Return the onion mixture to the heat and slowly add 1/2 cup of the bean water, stirring constantly, until the mixture thickens and boils. Add extra bean water if necessary to make a thin sauce. Immediately add the cooked beans and stir to coat with the sauce. Pour into a bowl and serve.

BAKED BEANS WITH SAVORY & SAGE
Serves 2–3

This is the ideal recipe to make on a wet winter's weekend. The long cooking time is essential but actual hands-on preparation is minimal. The traditional Boston baked beans, but without the pork and with less sweetening, forms the basis for this recipe. Instead of the pork flavouring, we have added the herbs used in European-style baked bean dishes.

2 cups haricot or black-eyed beans, rinsed and soaked overnight
1 sprig savory (winter or summer)
1 medium-sized onion, finely chopped
1 clove garlic, finely chopped
2 tablespoons extra virgin olive oil
6 sage leaves
1 bay leaf
1 tablespoon chopped summer savory, or 1/2 tablespoon chopped winter savory
2 teaspoons Dijon-style mustard
2 tablespoons treacle
1/2 teaspoon salt
black pepper
pinch cayenne pepper
400 g can skinned tomatoes in purée
grated Cheddar cheese

Drain and rinse the soaked beans. Place in a large saucepan and cover well with water. Add the savory sprig. Bring to the boil, cover and cook until tender but not mushy (45–90 minutes). Drain, saving the cooking water. Discard the savory sprig.

Preheat the oven to 160°C. In a large frying pan, gently sauté the onion and garlic in the oil until soft but not brown. Remove from the heat. Add the herbs, mustard, treacle, seasoning and tomatoes. Use a spoon to roughly chop the tomatoes. Add the beans and 1/2 cup of the bean liquid. Stir to mix well. Spoon into a heavy casserole dish. Cover with a piece of foil and the lid. Bake for 3–3 1/2 hours. Check after 2 hours, adding extra bean liquid if necessary. The beans are cooked when most of the liquid is absorbed and the top starts to brown. Serve on toast or with fresh crusty bread. Sprinkle each serving with a little grated cheese.

RISI E BISI
Serves 2–3

There are many recipes for this famous Venetian dish. A cross between a soup and a risotto, it consists of rice, young peas and Parmesan cheese. It is simpler to make than a risotto, as constant stirring is not required. Additions may include celery and ham. Savory is a favourite flavouring. We prefer to cook the peas separately to ensure that they are cooked to perfection, especially if they are home-grown treasures. Although it is not authentic, we sometimes enjoy young beans as a substitute for the peas. Serve with a salad for a light meal.

2 tablespoons butter or mild-flavoured oil
1 shallot or small onion, chopped
1 cup arborio rice, washed and drained
2 1/2 cups good quality stock (if using a commercial product,
use 1 1/2 cups of stock with 1 cup water)
1/2 cup dry white wine
1 1/2 cups fresh shelled peas or small frozen peas (not minted)
4 small thin slices ham (about 100 g), cut into strips
2 tablespoons chopped parsley
1 tablespoon chopped summer savory or 1 teaspoon finely
chopped winter savory
1/3 cup finely grated Parmesan cheese
freshly ground black pepper

Sauté the shallot or onion in the butter or oil in a heavy-based saucepan. When softened but not browned, add the rice and cook with constant stirring for 1 minute until the grains are well coated with the butter or oil. Pour in the stock and wine. Bring to boiling point. Cover, lower the heat and simmer very gently for 15–20 minutes, until the rice is tender but firm to bite and most of the liquid has been absorbed. While the rice is cooking, simmer the peas until just tender. Drain and add to the cooked rice. Add all the remaining ingredients. Stir gently to combine. Serve in bowls and provide spoons and forks.

As a variation, 1 small stick of celery, finely sliced, may be sautéed with the onion and garlic.

SAVORY & ORANGE BAKED CHICKEN
Serves 4

Savory and chicken are natural partners in this well-flavoured dish.

1 tablespoon grated fresh ginger root
1/4 teaspoon ground cloves
1/4 teaspoon salt
black pepper
1/2 teaspoon coriander seeds, dry roasted
8 sprigs savory (2 sprigs chopped and 6 left whole)
1 tablespoon mild-flavoured honey
1 teaspoon olive oil
4 whole chicken legs, skinned
2 oranges (1 used for garnishing)
150 ml white wine
2 teaspoons cornflour
2 tablespoons water
extra savory sprigs for garnishing (use flowering
sprigs if available)

Preheat the oven to 190°C. Grind the ginger root, cloves, salt, pepper, coriander seeds and 2 chopped savory sprigs together in a mortar. Add the honey and oil and mix to a paste. Brush over the chicken pieces. Place the chicken on a bed of the remaining savory sprigs in a heavy baking dish. Grate the rind from one orange and set aside. Squeeze out the juice from this orange and pour over the chicken. Bake until tender, about 40–50 minutes, basting twice.

To make the gravy, boil the grated orange rind with the wine in a small saucepan for 3 minutes. Remove from the heat. When the chicken is cooked, place it on a serving platter. Add the pan juices to the wine mixture and bring back to boiling point. Mix the cornflour with the water and pour into the saucepan. Stir until thickened. Spoon over the chicken. Remove the skin from the remaining orange and cut the flesh into neat slices. Garnish with the orange slices and small decorative sprigs of savory.

French tarragon (*Artemisia dracunculus* var. 'sativa') is variously described as 'the royal herb', 'the most aristocratic', 'the Rolls Royce of herbs', 'one of the most famous' and 'the king of all culinary herbs'. It is certainly one of our most prized herbs. Apart from its well-known presence in several classic French dishes, why is it so little used in other ways? Helen's herb 'biography' provides one of the answers: it is not prolific like most other herbs. Also, it succeeds only when fresh—it smells like hay when dried, making it unsatisfactory as a packaged herb. Fresh tarragon is seldom seen in supermarkets. Tarragon vinegar is the only way its flavour can be made available out of season.

With such high praise from the cook's point of view, and the knowledge that French tarragon is saved from extinction only by garden cultivation, all serious cooks should include, and look after, at least two plants in their gardens.

VARIETIES
It is important to ensure that your tarragon plants are indeed French tarragon and not its close cousin, Russian tarragon (*A. dracunculus* subsp. *dracunculoides*). Russian tarragon is a much more robust plant, growing to 1.5 m tall, with a coarse texture and inferior flavour. The leaves are longer, lighter coloured and matt, owing to the presence of tiny hairs (visible with a magnifying glass). French tarragon is shorter (60–90 cm) and has shiny, darker green, hairless leaves. When you nibble a leaf by itself, it produces a strange, almost numbing effect on part of the tongue, which does not occur with Russian tarragon.

As French tarragon doesn't set seed, it must be propagated vegetatively, so purchase plants or obtain root cuttings from friends. Any seed labelled as tarragon is likely to be Russian tarragon.

CULTIVATION
Tarragon is an almost hardy herbaceous perennial—in other words, it dies back to the ground in winter. In areas

Tarragon

TARRAGON
(*Artemisia dracunculus*)

Of all the herbs we have investigated, tarragon has the most intriguing past. The chief mystery is why such an appealing plant, an icon of French cuisine, didn't make its appearance in Western Europe until the 16th century.

A late introduction might be understandable if the wild *Artemisia dracunculus* had to be transported across the Atlantic from the Americas. But, though it occurs there as the silky wormwood (also known as the false tarragon sagewort), it was the wild tarragon of Russia or Siberia that seems to have been the parent of the improved garden form often referred to as French or German tarragon. Botanists used to label the Russian/Siberian tarragons as a separate species, *A. dracunculoides*, but it is now believed that only one species is involved and the difference between the culinary herb and its wild relatives is expressed at subspecies or variety level. Thus the garden tarragon is sometimes known as *A. dracunculus* var. 'Sativa' and the Russian form as *A. dracunculus* subsp. *dracunculoides*.

The fact that garden tarragon does not produce viable seed, is short-lived and has to be cloned through root-stock division suggests that it was a mutation or 'sport' of the wild tarragon. The critical change was in the composition of its essential oils: garden tarragon produces estragol, the wild tarragon does not. The sterility of the garden tarragon makes it a true domesticate, totally dependent on humans to keep it alive. The famous botanist Edgar Anderson pointed out in 1936 that 'when we take a plant of the true tarragon into our gardens and grow it, and at length divide the root, we are the last link in a long chain of such people'.

Tarragon seems to have arrived in Western Europe about 1530, possibly via Spain and North Africa. In 1580 Thomas Tusser included it in his list of herbs 'for sallets and sauce', while his contemporary Thomas Hill noted that it had similar properties to rocket and should be eaten with the 'cold' herbs lettuce and purslane. In 1597 John Gerard introduced it as 'Tarragon the sallade herbe', commenting picturesquely on its mode of reproduction: 'The root is long and fibrous, creeping farre abroad under the earth, as doe the rootes of Couch-grasse, by which sprouting forth it increaseth, yeelding no seede at all, but as it were a certaine chaffie or dustie matter that flieth away with the winde'.

Significantly, neither Gerard nor John Parkinson in 1629 was aware of any uses for tarragon other than in tempering the coldness of lettuce in salads. It seems that they too could offer no explanation for its dragon-related names. Both *dracunculus* and 'tarragon' are derived from the same classical Greek term for 'little dragon'. Contrary to the impression given by some 20th-century herb writers, they did not describe its roots as snake-like, nor did they argue that it could cure reptile bites.

While the salad remained an important part of English diet, tarragon was mentioned in recipe and gardening books. However, it was not to everyone's taste and in the 18th century underwent a decline. Philip Miller wrote in 1731 that tarragon 'was formerly in great Esteem for Sallads and Soops, but at present it is not so much us'd'. This situation continued in England until the late 19th century. Meanwhile, across the Channel, tarragon use was increasing: it was infused in vinegar which was then added to dressings and to mustard mixes, it was an ingredient of the 18th-century sauces that evolved into the French classics such as béarnaise and tartare, and it was added to stuffings. When the English spoke of it, they increasingly called it 'French tarragon'.

The revival of interest in herbs in the 20th century saw the wild (Russian) tarragon introduced into herb gardens, probably mistakenly through the purchase of seed by ill-informed gardeners. Disappointment with its qualities led to increasing criticism in print, culminating in the 1980s when it was described as a 'great usurper', a 'six-foot-tall imposter', 'virtually useless' and 'virtually tasteless'. It seems to have got caught up in a Cold War of its own—Alan Paterson recommended getting rid of it 'lest it overwhelms its more delicate cousin from the West'. The problem is that garden tarragon is not only more refined in taste but more delicate in constitution. Clones often lose their vigour and can have relatively short life spans. We may one day be urging genetic engineers to insert the genes for estragol into this same useless imposter to save the incomparable flavour of tarragon for future cooks.

Tarragon in early spring—the right stage to lift the clump and divide.

Identify true French tarragon by its glossy, darker green leaves and excellent flavour.

with extremely low winter temperatures, the roots should be thickly mulched to provide insulation. Late frosts can sometimes damage new shoots. It also does not do well in hot humid climates.

Tarragon growing well in a raised bed in the vegetable garden.

Tarragon prefers a rich, slightly sandy soil, though it copes well in heavier soils providing they have been lightened with plenty of organic mater. Good drainage is vital, particularly during winter months, as roots tend to rot while they are dormant. Tarragon thrives in raised beds.

Full sun is preferred, though a little shade in the afternoon may be beneficial in hotter climates.

Tarragon is not an easy plant to propagate. We have found that the most successful method is to dig up the whole or part of an established plant in early spring, just as the new growth is seen. Gently tease the short, white, brittle rhizomes or underground stems apart. Separate into small pieces, each with part of last year's stem and obvious growing nodules and roots. Choose vigorous rhizomes from the outside of the old plant. Replant immediately into a different location, or pot up to plant out later. Wilting is a common reaction of newly planted cuttings— it may last several days. Keep moist and provide some temporary shade. If growing on in pots to give away, trim the roots to 8–10 cm, each with a growing nodule, and place in 10 cm pots with a coarse potting mix containing extra horticultural grit (see page 13). Once over the initial transplanting shock, keep watering to a minimum and plant out when vigorous growth has begun and plants have been hardened off.

Position tarragon plants 45–60 cm apart in their permanent positions. They resent disturbance once they are in full leaf production. We recommend a minimum of 2 plants so that, while one is being divided and replanted, the other ensures continuity of supply. As tarragon gradually crowds itself with a vigorous and tangled root system and loses vitality, it is best to divide and relocate it every 3–4 years.

Keep newly planted tarragon moist but, once established, tarragon plants are reasonably tolerant of drought conditions. However, better leaf production is ensured with regular watering and an occasional boost with half-strength liquid fertiliser, especially after pruning.

As young, tender shoots are best for culinary uses, it pays to prune tarragon regularly if harvesting for the kitchen is not keeping up with the plant's vigorous growth. Trim about a third off each shoot, cutting just above where an obvious side shoot is beginning to grow. Trim back any flower spires in the same manner. This encourages each stem to branch and to produce new tender growing tips. In areas experiencing only mild winter frosts, tarragon can be cut right back in autumn. Where frosts are harder, leave the dead stems as they will help to protect the roots. They should then be cut back in spring after the new growth starts.

GROWING IN CONTAINERS

Tarragon needs to be planted in large enough pots to accommodate its vigorous root runners. It quickly loses vigour and flavour if potbound.

Fill your containers, of at least 25 cm diameter, with a coarse potting mix plus some additional horticultural grit (see page 15). Keep young plants or cuttings well watered until established. After that, water only when required to keep moist but not saturated. A twice-monthly feed of half-strength liquid fertiliser will keep plants growing well. Don't water at all in winter when plants are dormant. Pots should be placed in a protected position during cold winter months. Once new growth starts in spring, position the pots on a sunny patio. As the flavour of tarragon deteriorates with age, and this happens more quickly if the plant is rootbound, it is wise to keep several potted plants at different stages of growth. This will ensure an ongoing harvest for the kitchen during summer.

HARVESTING

Start picking as soon as sprigs are long enough to be worthwhile—they don't have much smell at this stage but, when chopped, release a desirable and delicate flavour. Don't be greedy, though, as the plant is just recovering from dormancy and needs leaves to build up energy reserves. This is another reason why we recommend having at least 2 tarragon plants.

As the season progresses, harvest frequently. The tender growing tips or sprigs (5–10 cm long) are the best in cooking, and frequent harvesting will encourage plenty of new growth. If your plants need to be pruned further, cut each long stem back to where an obvious new side shoot appears.

As a very soft herb, tarragon wilts rapidly, so pick it at the last moment and handle gently to avoid bruising.

IN THE KITCHEN

The flavour of tarragon is elusive. How much to use can worry cooks new to this herb. The leaves have very little odour until cut, so the general rule is to scissor or slice finely. Heat increases the flavour, though too long a cooking will bring out its bitter side. Use less tarragon in hot dishes and add near the end of cooking, reserving a little to sprinkle over at serving time. As tarragon is often used to flavour delicate dishes, it must be added with restraint. Larger quantities of new season's tarragon can be used fresh in mixed green salads.

We find the easiest way to cut tender sprigs of tarragon is with scissors, though slicing on a wooden board with a sharp knife is also efficient. If the stems have become woody, then strip the leaves from the stems, which are discarded, and chop the leaves only.

Tarragon is called the summer herb because it is most abundant at this time. As it dies down completely in winter, cooks often attempt to preserve it for year-round use. Unfortunately, apart from tarragon vinegar, there are no really satisfactory ways of doing this. Dried tarragon tastes like hay and the frozen version like grass. We make tarragon vinegar, the best of all herb vinegars, during the height of the tarragon season in early summer, and enjoy its flavour in dressings during winter months (see page 17 for general instructions on making herb vinegar). As a herb that is not always available, it is greeted each spring with great joy.

HOW TO USE TARRAGON

- The classic French sauces—béarnaise, tartare, ravigote, verte, messine and gribiche—can be made only if tarragon is available.
- Tarragon complements many vegetables, particularly beans, asparagus, broccoli, courgettes, Florence fennel, potatoes, avocado and mushrooms. Add 3 or 4 sprigs, finely sliced, just prior to serving or make tarragon butter as an accompaniment.
- Tarragon is best on its own or combined with parsley, chervil and chives in the classic fines herbes (see page 180). Never use it with strongly aromatic herbs such as rosemary, sage or thyme.
- Make tarragon butter, the most delicious of all herb butters, to serve with asparagus, new or jacket potatoes, grilled salmon and chicken. Follow the general herb butter recipe on page 19. Use 1–2 tablespoons of finely sliced tarragon and omit the other herbs and garlic.
- Tarragon is the classic herb to serve with chicken and fish. Use it lightly, to enhance the flavours rather than dominate.
- As a refreshing variation on tomato salad, use tarragon instead of the ubiquitous basil.
- The refreshing, mild aniseed flavour of tarragon is delicious in green leafy salads. We almost always include a sprig or two in most bunches of herbs we gather for the salad bowl.
- Use tarragon in your favourite chicken liver pâté.
- Tarragon is the time-honoured herb for egg dishes. Use on its own or in fines herbes, adding near the end of the cooking time for omelettes (see pages 46–47), scrambled and baked eggs. It is delightful in stuffed eggs and in mashed eggs for sandwiches.
- Tarragon adds a refreshing flavour to oranges. Add several sprigs to a jug of pure orange juice and leave to infuse until well chilled. Finely chopped tarragon imparts an intriguing flavour to orange salads, whether savoury or sweet.
- Make tarragon-flavoured marinated mushrooms as an antipasta (see recipe on page 39), adding 1 tablespoon of finely sliced tarragon after the mushrooms are cooked.
- We enjoy a brew of Earl Grey tea flavoured with fresh tarragon (see page 20 for recipe).

TARRAGON-FLAVOURED VODKA
Makes sufficient to fill six 30 ml liqueur glasses

According to two American food writers, Rosalind Creasy and Carole Saville in their book *Herbs: a Country Garden Cookbook*, herb-flavoured vodkas are 'Old World favorites called little rays of sunshine'. They suggest serving their tarragon-flavoured vodka with smoked salmon or other smoked fish. Mary made it recently for a group of neighbours, who declared it a great success and requested the recipe. Here is our adaptation.

Mary uses a small old crystal sauce bottle with a glass stopper as the serving container. Placed on a large silver tray with the glasses and accompanied by rye bread canapés topped with smoked salmon and garnished with tarragon, this sets a festive atmosphere.

3/4 cup vodka (37.2% alc/vol)
2 tender sprigs of tarragon, each about 10 cm long

Measure the vodka into a small glass jar with a lid, add the tarragon sprigs and gently push them down until immersed. Cover and leave at room temperature for 12–24 hours or until the vodka has a definite tarragon flavour. Discard the tarragon and pour the flavoured vodka into your serving bottle. Place in a freezer (the high alcohol content of the vodka prevents it from freezing—it just becomes syrupy). Allow a minimum of 8 hours' chilling time. Pour into glasses (which should also be chilled in the freezer) and serve immediately.

TARRAGON AIOLI

Aioli is a garlic-flavoured mayonnaise made in France, and eaten with a variety of vegetables, fish or meats. It can be served simply as the sauce for a steamed vegetable such as new potatoes, carrots, beans or asparagus. Alternatively, making it the focus of a platter, place the aioli in a small bowl surrounded by steamed hot or cold vegetables, or raw ones such as tomatoes, cucumber, celery, etc. More elaborate versions may include hot or cold meats or fish, making a complete meal.

Our non-traditional tarragon version is a wonderful sauce, easy to make ahead, to serve with the first new potatoes of the season or asparagus or globe artichokes. We use our basic mayonnaise recipe from *The Cook's Salad Garden*, which is quickly made in a food processor or blender and tastes far better than any commercial brand.

Mayonnaise
1 egg
2 tablespoons white wine vinegar
1 teaspoon sugar
1/4 teaspoon mustard powder
1/4 teaspoon salt
freshly ground white pepper, or black pepper if you don't mind dark specks in your mayonnaise
1 cup mild-flavoured salad oil

Place all the ingredients (except the oil) in a food processor or blender. Blend for a few seconds and then, with the machine still running, add the oil in a thin, steady stream. Store in a glass jar in a refrigerator or leave in the processor and go on to make the aioli. Makes 1 1/4 cups.

Tarragon aioli
1 1/4 cups mayonnaise (freshly home-made is best)
2 cloves garlic, finely chopped
2 tablespoons finely sliced tarragon
grated rind and juice (about 2–3 tablespoons) 1 lemon
1 teaspoon Dijon-style mustard
extra salt to taste (optional)

Add all the ingredients (except the salt) to the mayonnaise in a food processor or blender. Blend until well mixed. Taste for salt. Spoon into a small bowl and store in a refrigerator for up to 2 days.

KUMARA (SWEET POTATO) & ORANGE SALAD WITH TARRAGON
Serves 4

We have been making the original version of this popular salad since we tested it for our book *The Cook's Garden*, first published in 1980. Recently, Mary adapted it slightly to take advantage of the first spring harvest of tender tarragon shoots. The salad can be made several hours ahead of serving time, if stored in a refrigerator.

500 g kumara (sweet potatoes), peeled
2 large oranges
3–4 large chive stalks, finely scissored
1 tablespoon finely scissored tarragon
4 tablespoons salad oil
1 tablespoon white wine vinegar
1/4 teaspoon salt
black pepper

Cook the kumara in boiling water until just tender. Drain. Cut into 5 mm slices as soon as they are cool enough to handle. Using a sharp knife, cut the rind and all the white pith from the oranges. Cut horizontally into thin rings. Combine the salad oil, wine vinegar and seasoning with a whisk or fork.

Layer the kumara, oranges, herbs and dressing in a shallow serving dish. Allow to cool. Store in a refrigerator until required.

JOAN'S FAST-TRACK TOMATO SOUP WITH TARRAGON
Serves 3–4

Our friend Joan Bishop, a well-known Dunedin food writer, presented this fast and fabulous soup in her regular column for the *Otago Daily Times* in 1993. Since then we have made it often, adding tarragon in season for a fresh summer taste.

400 g can peeled tomatoes in juice
2 cloves garlic
1 shallot or half a small onion
1/4 cup tomato paste
1 1/2 cups chicken stock
1 tablespoon lemon juice
1 teaspoon sugar
black pepper
6 sprigs 4–5 cm long tarragon (keep 2 aside for garnishing)
3–4 tablespoons cream or sour cream (optional)

Place all the ingredients, except the 2 sprigs of tarragon and the cream, in a food processor or blender and process until smooth. Tip into a saucepan and simmer for 3 minutes. Ladle into soup bowls and garnish with the cream and finely scissored tarragon.

ASPARAGUS & TARRAGON FRITTATA
Serves 2–3

Mary's first flush of tender tarragon leaves appears at the same time as the local asparagus-grower puts up his sign out at the roadside.

250 g trimmed asparagus spears (cut or snap off any tough woody ends)
1 tablespoon butter or cooking oil
1 shallot or 1/2 small onion, finely chopped
4 eggs
4 tablespoons cream or milk
1/4 teaspoon salt
black pepper
1 tablespoon finely scissored tarragon
3 tablespoons finely grated Parmesan cheese

Peel the lower half of each asparagus spear with a vegetable peeler or special asparagus peeler. Slice the spears into 2 cm lengths. Heat the butter or oil in a large, heavy-based, ovenproof frying pan. With moderate heat, stir-fry the asparagus and onion until tender-crisp. Meanwhile, beat the eggs lightly with the cream and seasonings. Stir in the tarragon.

Lower the cooking temperature under the pan and preheat the oven grill. Pour the egg mixture over the asparagus and cover the pan with a lid. Once the egg is almost set, sprinkle the surface with the Parmesan cheese and place under the hot grill until the cheese has melted and begins to colour. Cut into wedges and serve immediately.

The frittata can be cooked completely in an electric frying pan, though the top will not be golden brown.

TARRAGON & ORANGE FISH FILLETS
Serves 4

Tarragon complements both fish and oranges, giving a gourmet touch to this very simple microwave fish dish.

2 tablespoons cooking oil
4 fish fillets (about 100–150 g each)
1/2 teaspoon garlic salt
grated rind and juice 1 orange
black pepper
1 tablespoon finely sliced tarragon

Measure the oil into a large, shallow, microwave-proof dish. Tip gently to spread evenly over the base. Place the fish fillets in the dish and turn them over to coat with the oil. Arrange them with their thickest ends towards the outside of the dish. Sprinkle evenly with the garlic salt, orange rind and juice, pepper and the tarragon. Cover with plastic food film and microwave on high for 4–5 minutes or until the fish is opaque (this may take less or more time depending on the wattage of your microwave). Leave to stand for 3 minutes before serving.

TARRAGON CHICKEN
Serves 2 very hungry people, or 4 as a lighter meal

The idea of replacing the cream and butter in the classic French dish *poulet à l'estragon* (chicken with tarragon) with coconut milk comes from Sally Anne Scott in her beautiful book, *Aromatic Herbs*.

4 chicken breasts, skins removed
3 tablespoons flour
1/4 teaspoon salt
black pepper
2 tablespoons cooking oil
1 shallot or 1/2 small onion, finely chopped
1/2 cup thick coconut milk
6 sprigs (about 6 cm long) freshly picked tarragon, finely scissored

Combine the flour, salt and pepper on a large plate and coat the chicken breasts evenly. Shake off and retain any excess flour. Heat the oil in a large, heavy-based frying pan with a lid, or electric frying pan. With moderate heat cook the chicken and shallot or onion in the oil for about 5 minutes with the lid in place. Check twice to ensure that browning is not excessive. When golden, turn the chicken over, cover again and cook a further 5 minutes or until the chicken breasts are cooked. Tip the reserved flour into a small bowl and gradually stir in the coconut milk until smooth. Pour over the chicken and reheat gently, with stirring, until thickened. Sprinkle with the tarragon and serve immediately.

GOOSEBERRY SAUCE WITH TARRAGON

We first made gooseberry sauce when holidaying in an isolated valley in Central Otago, New Zealand, 40 km from the nearest shop. Faced with the prospect of eating freshly caught trout without lemon, we had to think of a substitute food to provide a tart flavour. Self-sown gooseberries abound in Central Otago, and gooseberry sauce has been a traditional accompaniment to fish in England since mediaeval days, so what better ingredient could we use? The addition of tarragon from our kitchen gardens is more recent. It is now our most popular sauce with grilled salmon steaks.

250 g green gooseberries (fresh or frozen)
1/4 cup of water for fresh gooseberries, or 2 tablespoons for frozen ones
1–2 tablespoons white sugar
2 tablespoons butter
1 tablespoon finely sliced tarragon

Combine the gooseberries, appropriate quantity of water, 1 tablespoon of the sugar and the butter in a small saucepan. Cook gently, stirring occasionally, until a sauce-like consistency is obtained. Taste and add extra sugar if necessary (the sauce should be a good balance between sweet and sour). Add the tarragon and stir through. Remove from the heat. Serve warm or at room temperature with any simple fish dish.

ORANGES WITH VODKA & TARRAGON SYRUP
Serves 2–3

An unusual and refreshing dessert to follow a rich main course.

3 tablespoons sugar
1/3 cup water
4 sprigs tarragon
1 tablespoon vodka
3 oranges
blue borage flowers (optional)

Make the syrup by simmering the sugar and water in a small saucepan for 2 minutes. Remove from the heat, add 3 of the tarragon sprigs, cover the saucepan and leave to infuse until cooled to room temperature. Remove the tarragon and stir in the vodka. Meanwhile, cut the rind and pith from the oranges with a sharp knife. Slice into thin circles and arrange in a shallow serving dish. Pour the syrup over the oranges. Scissor the remaining sprig of tarragon over the surface of the oranges and garnish with blue borage flowers if available.

thYme

Our introduction to thyme (*Thymus* species) came during family holidays in Central Otago, New Zealand. By the 1950s thyme had become naturalised and well established over thousands of hectares of dry, sunny land along the Clutha and Kawarau rivers. A yearly tradition was to pick fresh supplies of this 'wild' thyme for kitchen use back in Dunedin, and always a flowering branch was attached behind the rear-vision mirror to provide the perfume we all associated with those happy days.

Even during the first half of last century, when culinary herbs were all but forgotten, thyme continued to hold its place, along with parsley, chives and sage. As one of the few herbs that retains its fresh flavour when dried, thyme was more often than not contained in a packet in the pantry rather than having a place with parsley and chives in the vegetable garden.

Nowadays, serious gardening cooks grow several kinds of thyme and harvest supplies throughout the year. However, the current fashion for collecting garden thymes has been inspired not by culinary interests alone but by the desire to achieve a so-called 'cottage garden' look. Many decorative, often creeping, thymes lack flavour and, although pretty to look at, are no substitute for the few kitchen varieties. In the kitchen, when a recipe calls for thyme, it usually refers to *T. vulgaris* and specifically to the variety called English thyme or common thyme.

VARIETIES

According to the Royal Horticultural Society in Britain, there are about 350 species of *Thymus*. They admit that thymes are notoriously difficult to classify and identify.

Many cultivars are also surprisingly variable.

Fortunately for cooks, there are only 3 or 4 main species of culinary thyme, with the others being merely decorative or collector's plants. That is not to say that they have no place in the kitchen but that the culinary species have a superior flavour. We grow many of these decorative forms and occasionally snip sprigs to add flavour and colour to particular dishes. But we are serious about growing the culinary thymes and harvest from them almost daily.

The first group consists of *T. vulgaris*, also called common thyme and garden thyme. The variety called English thyme has broader and darker green leaves than the variety known as French thyme, which has narrower and softer grey leaves. A cultivar of *T. vulgaris*, 'Silver Posie', has pretty white-edged leaves but tastes similar to the species form. *T. vulgaris* varieties have a full, rich and wonderful flavour which is not lost with long, slow cooking. They are the favoured choice for casseroles, roasts, soups and marinades.

For a delightful citrus flavour, grow thymes from the second group: *T.* x *citriodorus*, commonly called lemon thyme. It forms a mound rather than a bush and its branches tend to be softer. Two cultivars of this species we have grown are the golden-leaved *T.* x *citriodorus* 'Aureus' and *T.* x *citriodorus* 'Fragrantissimus', the so-called orange thyme, which has a citrus scent but not an obvious orange taste. Lemon thymes are our favourites for kitchen use. Their softer leaves and stalks and less powerful but slightly sweet, lemon flavour make them suitable for salads, or added at the last minute to cooked dishes.

Common thyme with fresh spring growth.

Lemon-scented variegated thyme

Thyme 'Silver Posie'

Pizza thyme

The third culinary thyme, *T. herba-barona*, is known as the caraway thyme. It is a dwarf, mat-forming plant with strongly flavoured, caraway-scented dark green leaves. We prefer to use it in small quantities in meat dishes which require long, slow cooking.

The fourth type we grow is known in New Zealand as the 'pizza thyme'. So far we have been unable to ascertain its correct botanical name, though we have seen it referred to as *T. ? nummularius*. It is very vigorous and easy to grow, spreading to 1 m wide and 15 cm tall, making it an excel-lent edible groundcover. Its flavour is robust with a hint of oregano.

Gardening cooks should rely on their own sense of taste and smell when selecting varieties to grow primarily for kitchen use. If you also grow the creeping, decorative thymes, don't be afraid to sample them as well. Several unnamed ones in our own gardens have a delightful thyme fragrance and taste.

CULTIVATION

The key to successful thyme growing is excellent drainage. In the wild, thyme grows on dry, rocky ground on exposed hillsides. In a home garden with heavy and/or wet soil, you need to replicate these natural conditions by incorporating horticultural grit, pumice or other free-draining material. It is also beneficial to add a handful of dolomite lime per square metre before planting. Raised beds or rockeries are good homes, as thymes have fine root structures which are very prone to rot in wet, heavy soils.

Choose as sunny a position as possible. If thyme is grown in a shady, sheltered place it tends to become lanky and may be deficient in flavour. Although thyme appears to thrive in arid places, we have found that our vegetable garden examples do even better when receiving the same amounts of water, whether provided by nature or the garden hose, as our vegetable crops. Thyme is very hardy but in frosty areas a winter mulch is beneficial.

Thyme is best propagated by cutting, layering or division, depending on species type. Seed sowing is slow, as it takes 2 years for plants to be large enough for harvesting. Also, seedlings tend to be very variable and not necessarily as good as the parent thymes.

Well-grown small plants of many thyme varieties are available from specialist nurseries and better garden centres, though these are not always correctly labelled as to species and particular cultivar.

To raise your own plants from the upright, woody main trunk forms (*T. vulgaris*), take softwood cuttings from good specimens, preferably when not in flower. These should be 5–8 cm long. Plant in containers filled with a good free-draining cutting mix (see page 13). These can be taken at any time, though most writers recommend spring to early summer. Grow on in a glasshouse, frame or sheltered position outside. They probably won't be ready to plant out into final positions until the following spring.

The lower-growing, spreading thymes are more easily propagated from small rooted pieces found near the parent plant or by dividing an older plant. These can be potted up for a few weeks or planted straight into the garden. You can encourage the formation of rooted branches by partially burying any side shoots showing a running tendency (see page 13).

The planting depth of thyme when setting out is important, especially the creeping forms. Each plant must be deep enough to ensure that the fine roots are not exposed. They are easily uprooted and tend to burn in hot weather. Lucinda Hutson suggests placing flat rocks around the base of each plant to hold its roots in place. We often use a good layer of grit as a mulch.

Most writers recommend a no-feeding policy for thyme. Commercial growers producing thyme for drying or oil are advised to add a balanced base fertiliser at planting and additional applications of nitrogen during the growing season, after each harvest. We add a handful of home-made compost to each planting hole, and later feed established plants with a little blood and bone or bone meal sprinkled around each plant in spring.

Regular trimming is important to keep plants attractively shaped and to delay them from becoming woody prematurely. Common thyme does become woody and unsightly after about 2–3 years and then needs re-placing. Some writers recommend cutting back by a half to three-quarters in spring or after flowering. We find lighter regular trims, every 2 months during the growing season, works better for us. Trimming can be done while harvesting with scissors. It is a pleasant job, though watch out for bees if your thyme is flowering.

GROWING IN CONTAINERS

All varieties of thyme grow well in containers, providing they receive at least 5 hours' sun a day and the potting mix is very free-draining. Choose medium-sized terracotta pots and place a good layer of irregular rocks or broken clay pots or tiles in the bases. Use a coarse potting mix combined with a similar amount of horticultural grit (see page 15).

Pot up young thyme plants, avoiding any that are rootbound. Water well initially and mulch the surface of each pot with grit or shells.

Keep the containers bordering on dry, especially through winter. Feed occasionally throughout the growing season with a liquid fertiliser. Keep the growing tips well pruned to encourage bushy growth.

HARVESTING

Use scissors to snip individual stems or hold a small handful and cut them together about half-way down the stems. Pick evenly around each bush to keep them shapely. Leaves, stems and flowers can all be harvested for kitchen use.

Thyme plants are at their most aromatic just before flowering, so this is the best time to harvest for drying. Thyme is one of the easiest and most rewarding herbs to use when dried. In a hot, dry summer the stems and leaves are partially dried while still on the plant. Most of the flavour is retained, with none of the hay-like taste common with many other dried herbs. The exception is lemon thyme, which loses its flavour. Tie the stems in bunches and hang them in a dry, airy place, away from sunlight. Once dry, strip the leaves and flowers from woody stems and store in dark containers. If the stems were soft when picked, they can be crumbled once dry and not discarded. Use within 6 months and substitute 1 teaspoon of dried thyme for 1 tablespoon of chopped fresh thyme.

IN THE KITCHEN

Stems of thyme picked in spring or early summer, or from a new flush of growth from previously trimmed bushes, can be chopped or scissored. When the bushes are older and woody, the leaves should be stripped off and the stalks discarded.

Sprigs can be added whole to food, as the leaves will fall off during cooking and stalks can then be removed before serving. A whole branch of thyme is a basic ingredient of a bouquet garni (see page 180), tied in with other herbs and removed at the end of cooking.

Common thyme is usually cooked with food, as its flavour survives long simmering in casseroles. Lemon thyme, on the other hand, should be added at the end of cooking as its flavour fades when cooked with moist heat.

Only soft-stemmed thyme or lemon thyme should be used for garnishing or in salads. Chop lemon thyme just prior to using as it loses flavour rapidly and blackens.

The quantity of thyme depends on the food it is to accompany, and whether you are using it to make a statement or to provide a subtle hint. Start with about 1 teaspoon of chopped thyme and be prepared to increase the amount up to 2–3 tablespoons. Remember that it is not a delicate herb so use it to flavour more robust foods and add cautiously.

HOW TO USE COMMON THYME

- Common thyme enhances most meats: beef, veal, lamb or hogget, poultry, fish and shellfish. Add common thyme to casseroles, roasts, stuffings, sausages, fish stews and chowder, meat loaves and meat balls, pâtés, terrines and pies.
- The taste of many vegetables is enhanced by thyme, particularly tomatoes, onions, carrots, aubergine, parsnip, leeks, mushrooms, peppers, potatoes, corn, pumpkin and kumara (sweet potato).
- Use in home-made soft cheeses, either mixed in or as a coating.
- Cook sliced carrots in 2 tablespoons of oil, 4 tablespoons of water, 1 tablespoon of honey, 1 tablespoon of chopped thyme and seasoning to taste. Most of the liquid will evaporate and the carrots will be nicely glazed. Serve garnished with a sprinkling of freshly chopped lemon thyme.
- Thyme is a vital ingredient in traditional chicken stuffing. Use garden-fresh thyme and lots of parsley for a flavour far superior to the ubiquitous mixed herbs.
- Scalloped potatoes with thyme are mouth watering, both the cooking smell and the savoury taste. Sprinkle chopped thyme over each layer of sliced potato and onion. A basic recipe for scalloped potatoes appears in our first book, *The Cook's Garden*.
- Add a sprig or two to an oil marinade for olives. Store in a refrigerator and use within a couple of weeks.
- Thyme is often used in Creole and Cajun cuisine— try our jambalaya recipe on page 112.
- Thyme is indispensable in French cooking—it flavours everything from the simplest stew to the elaborate cassoulet.
- Add thyme to hearty soups based on vegetables, meat, lentils or beans.
- Thyme combines well with other Mediterranean

THYME
(*Thymus* spp.)

Two thousand years ago the ancient Greeks thought so highly of the wild thyme that grew on Mt Hymettus that they frequently transplanted it to Athens. Thyme plants were moved from the mountains of Thrace and Sicyon to other settlements. What qualities of thyme made it so valuable? The Greek playwright Antiphanes remarked that 'Nobody eats thyme when meat is to be had, not even they who profess to be . . . vegetarians'. In fact, thyme was considered food of the poor. We know that the wild thyme was used in wreaths for the head and as a source of perfume, but it was a less direct use that inspired their efforts. As a bee plant, this thyme was the source of what both the Greeks and Romans thought was the best honey in the world. Pliny described Attic honey as 'of a gold colour' with 'an extremely agreeable taste'. If only they could taste the thyme honey from Central Otago!

To reproduce this honey, the Romans imported thyme flowerheads from Attica and managed to grow the plants with some difficulty. Their problem, as Pliny explained, was that the 'seed of thyme is imperceptible to sight', so they had to sow the dried flowers. We may smile at their persistence in an age before magnifying lenses were invented; however, in the case of *Thymus vulgaris*, evolutionary biologists have discovered that the composition of the essential oils is genetically controlled. Slight seasonal variation occurs but transplanting to a different environment does not change the plant's chemotype. So a particularly aromatic thyme, wild or cultivated, is well worth moving.

The Greeks used two words for their thymes: *herpyllus* (which became *serpyllum* in Latin) and *thymon* (*thymum* in Latin). These words supplied both the genus name and the name of one of the important species, the creeping thyme (*T. serpyllum*). The Greek word *thymon* can be traced back to an Indo-European root, *dheu*, to cause to smoke. It seems that in the Bronze Age, and possibly even earlier, dried thyme was burnt during sacrifices, producing an aromatic smoke. As for *herpyllus*, it refers to the creeping character of the plant, shared with the English word 'serpent'.

It is not easy picking which species or subspecies of thyme supplied the forms used in the ancient world. Some references have turned out not to be of *Thymus* species at all. A sprig of 'wild thyme' recorded from Tutankhamun's tomb is actually from the related taxon *Thymbra spicata*, sometimes called spike thyme. The Egyptians are said to have used *Thymus acinos* in wreaths, medicine and food, but that plant has been reclassified as *Acinos arvensis*, also known as basil thyme. The problem is made worse by the sheer number of thyme species, about 350, which occur in Europe and Asia. A few species occur in the wild in North Africa, while one spread through the Mongolian deserts and reached Japan. The majority evolved in a band from Southern Russia west to Spain and Portugal. The Greeks may have known more than ten species. However, on the basis of plant distribution and their descriptions, it is likely that the famous Attic honey came from *T. capitatus* (cone-head thyme), which has a head like a stoechas lavender. In the western Mediterranean, other thymes occurred, including *T. herba-barona*, the caraway thyme from Corsica and Sardinia, and the most important culinary thyme, *T. vulgaris*. It was the hybridisation, possibly in Italy, of *T. vulgaris* with the widespread European species *T. pulegioides* which produced the other significant edible thyme, the lemon-scented *T. x citriodorus*.

There is no evidence that this hybrid was known to the Romans. The thyme that was an ingredient of their numerous sauces and dressings may well have come from wild sources, for Columella commented that thyme and wild thyme 'are sown carefully rather by those who look after bees than by gardeners'. For those who wanted them in their gardens, he advised 'a spot which is neither rich nor manured but sunny since they grow of their own accord in very thin soil'. His advice is equally applicable today. By Roman times the stony plains of southern France were covered in common thyme and thousands of sheep were brought there from distant regions to browse on the plant, perhaps as a form of pre-seasoning.

The many medicinal uses of thymes relate to the properties of their essential oils, especially thymol, which is antibacterial and thereby a preservative. Mediaeval herbals were more concerned with these roles than with any culinary uses. However we know that thyme was one of the pot-herbs boiled with meat in 13th-century London, and it was ingredient of the stuffing for capons in the 15th century.

In Elizabethan England, thyme was one of the semi-woody, low-growing plants utilised in knot patterns along with hyssop or winter savory. This was before dwarf box became the preferred knot plant. John Gerard tried to sort out the various types of thyme under two headings, 'wild' and 'garden'. He mentioned lemon thyme as one of the wild thymes introduced into gardens. John Parkinson organised his thymes according to whether they were ornamental additions to the flower garden or more suited to the kitchen garden. He listed the culinary uses of thyme as follows: in broths with rosemary, with stuffing herbs as in roast goose, in sauces for both 'fish and flesh', and as a powder (with breadcrumbs) to sprinkle on roasted meat or fried fish. With the exception of the seasoning, these roles continued into the 19th century, though culinary thyme was seldom singled out for special mention by either food or garden writers. In the 17th century the latter became preoccupied with ornamental gold and silver variegated thymes, not unlike the 20th-century collectors of colourful mat-forming thymes. Only lemon thyme acquired more distinctive uses in the kitchen, in particular for flavouring delicate fish and veal dishes, and even custards.

Thyme has been an ingredient in Western cuisines for over two millennia, never as the subject of strong praise or fashion hype, but consistently providing its savoury undertone to many favourite traditional dishes. Christmas dinner would not be the same without it. But we should not always equate thymes with old-fashioned food ways. New forms have been introduced, such as the pizza thyme (*T. ? nummularius*), which contrib-ute interesting flavours to contemporary cuisine.

herbs—oregano, marjoram and sage—as well as bay and parsley.

- Place thyme branches on the barbecue coals to heighten appetites.
- Make thyme bread: use your favourite basic white bread recipe, either handmade or using a breadmaker, substi-tuting honey for the sugar and adding 2–4 tablespoons of wholegrain rolled oats, 2 tablespoons of chopped sunflower seeds and 2 tablespoons of chopped thyme.
- Add several thyme sprigs, tied together, to winter fruit compotes.

HOW TO USE LEMON THYME
- Lemon thyme and common thyme are not inter-changeable, though they may be used together in some dishes.
- Use lemon thyme with any vegetable you would add lemon to: beetroot, carrots, asparagus, green beans, fennel bulbs, salad greens, new potatoes, courgettes, globe artichokes.
- Make lemon thyme butter (see pages 18–19).
- Make lemon thyme vinegar (see page 17).
- Lemon thyme is delightful in fish and poultry dishes.
- Prepare a gourmet version of the traditional mashed

Creeping thymes in a rockery.

potato-topped fish pie by adding chopped lemon thyme to the cooked white sauce.

- Add to a fines herbes mixture for scrambled eggs or omelettes (see pages 46–47).
- For a subtle lemon flavour, add sprigs of lemon thyme to poaching syrups for fruits, especially pears and quinces (add for the last few minutes of cooking).
- We make treacle tart in memory of our maternal grandmother, who prepared it often for us as teenagers. A little lemon thyme added to the golden syrup and breadcrumb filling is delectable.

MUSHROOMS WITH THYME ON TOAST
Serves 2–3

Thyme and mushrooms are a great combination in this simple breakfast, lunch or appetiser dish.

250 g cultivated flat brown mushrooms or, if you are lucky enough, wild mushrooms
2 tablespoons oil or butter
2 cloves garlic, very finely chopped
6 soft sprigs thyme, chopped
1 tablespoon dry sherry
salt and black pepper to taste
1 teaspoon cornflour
1 tablespoon water
chopped parsley as garnish

Slice the cleaned mushrooms. Heat the oil in a sauté pan, add the garlic and cook over a moderate heat for a minute of two, until just changing colour to gold. Add the mushrooms and cook, stirring occasionally, until soft. Lower the heat and add the thyme, sherry and seasonings. Thicken, if necessary, with the cornflour mixed with the water. Stir until boiling. Remove from the heat and serve on triangles of fresh toast. Garnish each serving with a sprinkling of parsley.

SPINACH SALAD WITH FETA CHEESE & THYME VINAIGRETTE
Serves 4

A simple salad with a Mediterranean influence. Make the thyme vinaigrette ahead to allow the flavour to develop.

Thyme vinaigrette
6 tablespoons salad oil
2 tablespoons red wine vinegar
1 teaspoon finely chopped soft thyme sprigs
black pepper

Salad
sufficient spinach leaves to fill a suitable bowl, stalks and midribs removed
1/2 small red-skinned onion, sliced thinly into half rings
12–16 black olives, drained, rinsed and pitted
100 g feta cheese, cut into 1 cm cubes
8–12 cherry tomatoes or the equivalent of larger tomatoes cut into pieces

Make the vinaigrette by whisking all the ingredients together in a small bowl. Leave at room temperature for at least 1 hour before dressing the salad.

Fill the salad bowl with the spinach leaves, torn into bite-sized pieces. Add the remaining ingredients. Just prior to serving, add the vinaigrette and toss gently.

RAY MCVINNIE'S BRAISED RATATOUILLE
Serves 6

This is by far our favourite ratatouille! Since it appeared in *Cuisine* (May 1997), we have made it many times. It is the ideal recipe when entertaining, as it looks after itself in the oven and when cooked is best served at room temperature. The liberal use of fresh thyme is vital to its success. Our version has developed only slightly from the original.

1/4 cup good quality olive oil
3 cloves garlic, very finely chopped
2 tablespoons chopped thyme
1 tablespoon sugar
1 onion, chopped
3 courgettes, chopped
1 red or yellow pepper, deseeded and flesh chopped
1 aubergine, diced
400 g peeled and deseeded pumpkin, cut into 1 cm chunks
1 cup black olives, drained and stoned
salt to taste
black pepper

400 g can tomatoes in juice, roughly broken up
3 tablespoons tomato paste
100 ml water

Preheat the oven to 200°C. Heat the oil in a heavy, metal casserole. Add all the ingredients from the first group and stir-fry until the vegetables are hot and coated with oil.

Add the ingredients from the second group and mix well.

Cover tightly with aluminium foil and the lid and bake for 1 hour. Serve warm or at room temperature.

COURGETTES WITH LEMON THYME & TOMATOES
Serves 3–4

Lemon thyme adds a fresh lemon flavour to our preferred way of cooking courgettes. The cooking time can vary according to the desired texture of the courgettes—still slightly crunchy or tender and soft.

500 g courgettes (or the larger zucchini), cut into 5 mm slices
3 cloves garlic, very finely chopped
2 tablespoons olive oil
4 medium-sized tomatoes (peeled if time permits), roughly chopped
salt to taste
black pepper
1 tablespoon white wine vinegar
1 teaspoon chopped lemon thyme

Sauté the courgettes and garlic in the oil over a medium heat until beginning to soften. Add the tomatoes, salt and pepper. Cook for a few minutes until the tomatoes start to soften. Remove from the heat and add the wine vinegar and lemon thyme. Serve immediately.

LEMON THYME ROAST CHICKEN WITH LEMON HALVES
Serves 4–5

Lemon halves combine with lemon thyme to produce a tender, succulent and visually attractive roast chicken. Roasting time is shortened by cutting the bird through the breast bone, flattening it in a dish and marinating it for several hours.

1 chicken (approximately 1.5kg)
4 large juicy lemons
2 cloves garlic, finely chopped
12 sprigs lemon thyme, chopped
small handful of parsley, chopped
plenty of black pepper
1/2 teaspoon salt

Remove any extra fat from the chicken cavity. Cut lengthwise through the breast bone and spread the chicken flat. Place in a large, non-metal dish. Squeeze the juice from the lemons and pour over the chicken. Combine the garlic, herbs and seasoning and sprinkle over the flattened chicken. Add the 8 lemon shells. Cover with plastic food film and place in a refrigerator for 2–6 hours, turning the chicken over once or twice during this time.

Lift the chicken into a roasting dish and spread flat again with the skin side up. Pour the marinade over and place the lemon shells, skin side up, around the chicken. Roast at 200°C for 45 minutes to 1 hour or until the chicken and lemon halves are golden brown and the chicken is cooked. Check by piercing the thickest part with a sharp knife: the juices should run clear. Carve the chicken into the appropriate number of pieces and serve hot with the lemon halves, which can be eaten—they are delicious.

VEGETARIAN CHRISTMAS NUTMEAT LOAF WITH THYME STUFFING
Serves 4–6

Mary first made this festive savoury loaf from Rose Elliot's *Gourmet Vegetarian Cooking* (1983) when faced with the need to provide an alternative to roast turkey for a then-vegetarian daughter and a family friend. The result was so popular that the non-vegetarians partook as well! We serve it with redcurrant jelly or Cumberland, apple or gooseberry sauce (see page 165).

Loaf
200 g mixed nuts (whole unskinned almonds plus cashews and, if fresh, a few pinenuts)
1 tablespoon cooking oil
1 small onion, finely chopped
130 g soft white breadcrumbs
2 eggs
4 tablespoons milk
black pepper
1/4 teaspoon salt
1/4–1/3 whole nutmeg, grated

Stuffing
180 g soft white breadcrumbs
grated rind and juice 1/2 lemon
10 sprigs pizza thyme, finely chopped (common thyme can be substituted)
10 sprigs lemon thyme, finely chopped
small handful parsley, finely chopped
black pepper
80 ml cooking oil or melted butter

Garnish
extra nuts, roasted (see page 21) and roughly chopped
extra sprigs lemon thyme

For the loaf mixture, chop the nuts finely in a food processor and tip into a large bowl. In a small pan, sauté the onion in the oil until soft. Add to the nuts, along with the breadcrumbs. In a small bowl beat the eggs and milk until combined. Pour into the nut mixture and add the seasonings. Stir with a fork to combine. Line the base and sides of a loaf tin (1.3–1.5 litres) with baking paper. Carefully spoon half of the nut mixture into the tin and press evenly into the corners.

Combine all the stuffing ingredients in a bowl with a fork. Spoon onto the nut layer in the tin and spread evenly.

Cover with the remaining nut mixture and smooth the top. Cover with greased aluminium foil. Bake at 180°C for about 1 hour. Uncover, and if necessary bake for a further 5–10 minutes or until the top is golden brown. Turn out onto a platter and garnish with toasted nuts and tiny sprigs of lemon thyme.

LEMON THYME PESTO

The idea for this pesto comes from Renee Shepherd, a gardening chef from California. We make it each year in late spring when our lemon thyme bushes are due for a good trimming. Use the pesto as a topping on baked jacket potatoes, steamed new potatoes or cooked carrots, or stir into hot pasta or rice.

1/2 cup whole, unskinned almonds, lightly roasted
(see page 21)
1/2 cup roughly chopped lemon thyme sprigs
1/3 cup finely grated Parmesan cheese
black pepper
1/4 teaspoon salt
1 clove garlic, chopped
1 tablespoon lemon juice
4–5 tablespoons mild-flavoured oil

Combine all the ingredients, except the oil, in a food processor or blender and process until very finely chopped. Add 4 tablespoons of the oil and process again to form a moist paste, adding the extra tablespoon if necessary. Spoon into a small bowl or jar, cover, and store in a refrigerator for up to a week.

THYME MARINADE
Sufficient to marinate meat to serve 4

This marinade is particularly good with lean lamb cuts—rump, tenderloin or rack.

1/3 cup cooking oil
grated rind and juice 1 large juicy lemon
2 tablespoons dry white wine
lots of black pepper
2 tablespoons chopped thyme
1 teaspoon chopped rosemary
2 cloves garlic, finely chopped
1 bay leaf

Mix all the ingredients together and pour over the meat in a ceramic or glass dish. Cover and refrigerate for at least 3 hours or overnight. Turn the meat occasionally. Grill or barbecue the meat, basting frequently with the marinade.

STRAWBERRIES WITH A LEMON THYME MARINADE
Serves 6–8 with other foods as part of an antipasto platter, or 3–4 with a soft cheese such as a brie or camembert and fresh crusty bread.

The idea for this recipe comes from Jackie French in her delightful *Book of Thyme* (1993).

Marinade
1/3 cup mild–flavoured olive oil or other oil
grated rind 1/2 orange
3 tablespoons orange juice
black pepper
1/4 teaspoon salt (optional)
1/4 teaspoon sugar
1 teaspoon finely chopped lemon thyme

300 g ripe strawberries, hulled (cut any extra-large fruit in half)

Whisk the marinade ingredients together in a bowl. Add the strawberries and stir gently to coat. Cover and leave in cool place for at least 30 minutes and up to 2 hours. Serve with the marinade and plenty of fresh bread to use as mops.

MORE HERBS

Inevitably, some herbs are harvested less frequently than others. There are many reasons. Some are so new that we have not fully integrated them into our cooking style, while others are mainly used as floral garnishes, contributing little in the way of flavour. Still others are specialised, suiting just a few dishes we make. Though they did not, at this stage, deserve their own sections, we couldn't bring ourselves to omit them altogether.

The table on pages 178, 179 provides the basic information on cultivation and some notes on use.

RECIPES
ROSE GERANIUM

ROSE-FLAVOURED RHUBARB CRUMBLE
Serves 6

A subtle rose flavour from the geranium leaves permeates this simple rhubarb crumble, elevating it to gourmet status. Serve with thick yoghurt, vanilla ice-cream or whipped cream.

juice 2 oranges (about 1/4–1/3 cup)
4 rose geranium leaves, roughly chopped
800 g rhubarb, trimmed and cut into 1 cm slices
finely grated rind 1 orange
3/4 cup sugar
2 tablespoons cornflour

In a small saucepan, heat the orange juice with the rose geranium leaves until hot but not boiling. Put the lid on the saucepan, remove from the heat and allow the mixture to infuse for 1 hour. Strain to remove the leaves.

Place the rhubarb in a large bowl, pour in the flavoured orange juice and add the grated orange rind. Stir to mix. In a small bowl, combine the sugar and cornflour until well mixed. Stir into the rhubarb. Tip into a greased baking dish (approximately 30 x 20 cm).

Crumble
1/2 cup white flour
1/2 cup packed brown sugar
1 cup rolled oats
60 g butter, cut into pieces
1/2 cup whole, unskinned almonds, lightly roasted (see page 21)

Combine all the crumble ingredients in a food processor and chop until the mixture resembles fine breadcrumbs.

Spoon evenly over the rhubarb and bake at 180°C for 50–60 minutes or until golden brown and bubbly, and the rhubarb in the centre is soft when pierced with a sharp knife.

ROSE CREAM
Serves 4–6

This recipe was included in our book *More from the Cook's Garden*. It is so simple and impressive that we have included it here too. Spoon the delicately flavoured and tinted cream over fresh, well-ripened summer berries. Garnish with pink rose petals ('Cécile Brunner' are delightful) or rose geranium flowers.

1 carton (250 ml) UHT long-life whipping cream
4 tablespoons caster sugar
4 rose geranium leaves
250 g cream cheese
1–2 drops red food colouring (optional)

Combine the cream, caster sugar and whole rose geranium leaves in a small saucepan. Heat gently, stirring occasionally, until just below boiling point. Allow to cool.

In a small bowl, soften the cream cheese and beat until very smooth. Gradually stir in the flavoured cream. The geranium leaves will not break with gentle stirring. If desired, tint to the palest of pinks with food colouring. Cover and leave in a refrigerator for several hours or overnight to thicken. Remove the geranium leaves. Spoon over the fresh berries and garnish with the flowers.

LAVENDER

LAVENDER LEMONADE
Serves 6 in tall glasses

The idea for this recipe comes from Lynda Dowling's lavender lemonade in the magazine *Sunset* (June 1998). Lynda grows lavender on her farm outside Victoria, British Columbia.

The sweetly perfumed drink turns the prettiest shade of pink when the lemon juice is added. Serve in tall glasses, a third filled with ice, and garnish each with a sprig of lavender.

1 cup sugar
2 1/2 cups water
1/4 cup fresh English lavender flowers, stripped from the stalks

1 cup freshly squeezed lemon juice
2 1/2 cups chilled water or mineral water
extra lavender sprigs for garnishing

Heat the sugar and water in a small saucepan until the sugar has dissolved and boiling point is reached. Remove from the heat and immediately add the lavender flowers. Stir. Cover the saucepan and leave to infuse for 1 hour. Strain through a fine sieve and discard the flowers. Chill.

When ready to serve, pour the lavender syrup into a glass jug. Stir in the lemon juice and second quantity of water. Pour onto ice in tall glasses and garnish with lavender sprigs.

BORAGE LEAVES
Frankfurt green sauce (page 183)

EPAZOTE
Black bean soup (page 110)

LEMON GRASS
Laksa (page 134), Chicken and noodle salad with perilla and rau răm (page 127)

SALAD BURNET
Frankfurt green sauce (page 183)

MITSUBA
Japanese-style soup (page 128)

SORREL

MEDIAEVAL GREEN SAUCE
Serves 3–4

Green sauces have been made for a millennium or more in Western European and Mediterranean cuisines. They had an acidic base (vinegar, verjuice, sour orange or lemon juice) to which green herbs such as sorrel, parsley or mint were added. Sometimes garlic or aromatic herbs were included. They were considered essential accompaniments to fried fish and certain roast meats.

Green sauce is the perfect accompaniment to grilled salmon, providing a foil for its oiliness and a wonderful colour contrast. It makes a great sauce to serve with any pan-fried, grilled or oven-baked fish. Green sauce, made with vinegar instead of lemon juice, was also a traditional accompaniment to roast lamb—try it as a delicious change from mint sauce.

9 medium-sized sorrel leaves (more if using the small-leaved
R. scutatus)
1 tablespoon lemon juice
1 tablespoon sugar

Pound all the ingredients together with a mortar and pestle, or combine in a food processor or blender, to make a thick, bright green purée. Serve within an hour.

Common names	Botanical names	Preferred location	Soil	Moisture	Size	Perennial/biennial/annual	Cultivation	Harvesting	How to use
Borage (blue flowered and white flowered)	*Borago officinalis*	Sun to half shade.	Well-drained, loamy to sandy soil.	Average.	40–90 cm high, 60 cm spacing.	Annual/biennial. Short-lived so sow successive crops.	Sow direct in spring. Does not transplant well. Will readily self-sow.	Pick open flowers. Pick young leaves for mild cucumber flavour.	Just before serving, remove the hairy sepals from behind the petals. Decorate salads, desserts, cold drinks. Use leaves in moderation, sliced in salads or in Frankfurt green sauce (see 183).
Epazote	*Chenopodium ambrosioides*	Sun to half shade.	Moisture retentive.	Damp.	1–1.5 m high, 60 cm spacing.	Annual or short-lived perennial in warm climates.	Sow seed in spring or autumn (mild climates). Requires light for germination. Cuttings will grow roots when placed in water.	Pick mild-flavoured sprigs in spring and stronger but not overpowering ones in summer.	Flavour Mexican-style bean stews (4 sprigs in spring, 2 in summer, add during last 15 minutes of cooking). Add to refried beans. Add to quesadillas (cheese-filled tortillas with chilli and fresh epazote).
Scented geraniums Rose geranium (most popular)	*Pelargonium* spp. *Pelargonium graveolens*	Warm climates: in garden with full sun or half shade. Frosty climates: in containers, outdoors in summer (full sun), under cover in winter (full sun).	Well-drained, rich, loamy soil. Pot mix: commercial rub mix with added horticultural grit (5:1).	Drought resistant but responds well to occasional deep watering.	Up to 1 m high, 50 cm spacing.	Tender perennials.	Start in summer/autumn from softwood cuttings. Purchase plants in spring.	Pick leaves as required. Pick flowers for garnishing.	For desserts, infuse leaves in syrup, milk, cream. Layer leaves in sugar. Cover bottom of cake tin to flavour cakes. Add leaves for the last few minutes of cooking when making jelly or jams. Recipes on page 176.
Lemon grass	*Cymbopogon citratus*	Cool climates: in garden in warm, sunny and sheltered site. Frosty areas: in pots (indoors during winter).	Well-drained, moisture-retentive, rich soil. Apply liquid fertiliser monthly.	Provide adequate water in summer. Mulch soil surface to retain moisture	60–90 cm tall, leaves bend over.	Tropical perennial, clump-forming grass.	Carefully divide established clump into small sections with roots attached. Plant with 2.5 cm of swollen stem base in soil. Purchase plants.	Cut stem close to the ground. Trim off top grassy section. Use the bulbous lower stem.	Peel away tough outer layers. Bruise a whole stem section to add to stocks, soups, marinades. Discard before serving. Slice finely before grinding to paste with spices for curry pastes. Finely slice tender sections for stir-fries.
Lovage	*Levisticum officinale*	Sun to half-shade. Roots survive hard winter frosts. Attractive back of the border plant.	Most well-drained, deeply dug soil types. Mulch with compost in spring.	Water in dry weather.	Full height of up to 2 metres by 3–5 years.	Hardy, long-lived perennial. Dies down in winter and requires dormant period. Grow as annual in hot climates.	Sow fresh seed in late summer/early autumn. Divide roots in autumn or spring—each piece with bud or 'eye'. Purchase plants.	Cut outer leaves off at base. Harvest seedheads and dry in paper bag in warm, airy place.	Use tender leaves cautiously when celery flavour is required—stews, soups, stock, with green vegetables, smoked fish, potato dishes and rich tomato sauce.
Mexican tarragon, Mexican mint, Mexican marigold	*Tagetes lucida*	Full sun. Frost tender: bring indoors in winter.	Loose, well-drained soil.	Average	50–75 cm tall, 40 cm spacing.	Tender perennial. Grow as annual in cold climates.	Sow seed in containers 6 weeks before planting out after frosts. Cuttings will root in water. Pinch out growing tips to make bushy.	Harvest individual leaves or sprigs. Pick flowers for pretty edible garnish.	Use as you would tarragon (is a popular substitute in climates too hot to grow French tarragon); has a stronger flavour, best with spicy foods.

Common name	Botanical name	Position/Climate	Soil	Water	Size	Type	Propagation/Growing	Harvesting	Uses
Pineapple sage	*Salvia rutilans*	Warm, frost-free climates: grow outdoors in full sun. Frosty climates: grow in containers; outside in summer, indoors in winter or outside in sheltered position against wall.	Well-drained, light soil, enriched with compost.	Requires more water than other culinary sages.	2 m tall, 1 m spread.	Tender evergreen perennial. Grow as annual in very cold climates.	Grow from softwood cuttings. Will root in water. Produces suckers, can be separated from parent plant. Prune after flowering to prevent plant becoming too woody.	Pick young leaves as required. Pick flowers for garnishing.	Leaves smell of pineapple sweets, taste not as nice as smell. Use leaves in cream cheese, fruit salads, pork & chicken dishes, jellies and jams, tea, butter. Use flowers to garnish flans, sorbets, cakes, desserts, fruit punch.
Salad burnet	*Sanguisorba minor*	Sun or half-shade. Tolerates hard frosts. Makes attractive edging.	Average. Fertilise once a year in spring.	Prefers moist soil but will tolerate drought due to deep-rooting habit. Water in hot, dry weather but don't overwater in winter.	Forms a neat, light green mound, 30–60 cm tall and 45–60 cm across.	Hardy, evergreen perennial. Grows best in cooler weather.	Sow seed *in situ* or in containers in spring. Division of established clumps possible but difficult. Self-sows easily. Keep cutting back to encourage fresh young leaves.	Pick youngest leaves for salads (older leaves taste bitter). Available all year	Pick individual leaves off wiry stalks and add whole to salads and coleslaw. Chop leaves and add to soups and sauces—can be added before or after cooking. Leaves have mild cucumber flavour.
Tree onions, Egyptian onions	*Allium cepa* var. *viviparum*	Full sun.	Well-drained, light soil containing plenty of humus. Topdress with compost each spring.	Keep well watered. Provide less water in late summer.	90–150 cm high, forms 30 cm clumps.	Very hardy perennial. Dies down in late summer, resprouts in winter/early spring.	In spring or autumn plant either large bulbs divided from established clump or individual bulbils. Plant 2.5 cm deep. Divide established plants every 3 years and shift to new location.	Snip young leaves as they emerge. Remove a few outer bulbs from clump. Pick fresh bulbils in summer. Bulbils may be stored in dry place for winter use.	Use young leaves like chives. Use bulbs like shallots. Finely chop peeled bulbils to add to salads, dressings or use like shallots. They have a very mild, sweet, onion flavour.
English lavender	*Lavandula angustifolia* Recommended culinary cultivars: *L. a.* 'Avice Hill', 'Munstead', 'Hidcote'.	Full sun. Late frosts may damage flower spikes.	Very well drained—raise beds if necessary. Apply well-balanced compost and lime in spring.	Water regularly until established. Mature plants more tolerant of dry conditions.	30–80 cm tall, 70 cm spacing from other plants, 30–40 cm spacing for hedges.	Hardy, evergreen, compact, bushy shrub.	Grow from soft or semi-hardwood cuttings. Prune back 1/3 after flowering. Prune hedges twice a year: trim sides in spring, and top and sides after flowering.	Pick just as first flowers on spike open. Dries well.	Infuse whole spikes or stripped buds and flowers in hot milk or cream, or sugar syrups—strain before using. Chop stripped buds and flowers and add to biscuits, cakes, and fruit desserts—use 2–3 teaspoons. Make lavender lemonade (see page 177).
Mitsuba	*Cryptotaenia japonica*	Temperate climate. Light shade	Add plenty of well-rotted compost. Well-drained	Moist	30 cm tall 30 cm spacing	Perennial. Usually grown as an annual.	In spring sow seed *in situ* or in containers. Transplant while still small. Mulch.	Harvest as seedlings. Harvest stems and leaves from older plants.	Leaves and stems may chopped or left whole as a garnish. Blanch older leaves. Use in Japanese-style dishes. Add seedling leaves to salads. Recipe on page 128.
Sorrel Garden or common sorrel True French sorrel	*Rumex* species *Rumex acetosa* *Rumex scutatus*	Full sun or part shade. Cooler climates	Well-drained Humus rich	Moist	Common sorrel has long leaves (15–25 cm). True French sorrel leaves are 3–6 cm long and a similar width.	Hardy perennials	Divide established plants in spring or autumn. Remove flower stalks to maintain leaf production.	Pick individual leaves from outside of the clump.	Discard stalks and midribs. Slice finely and add to salads or add to hot dishes just before serving. Has a high oxalic acid content so should be eaten in moderation. Recipe on page 177.

MIXED HERB RECIPES

The following recipes are for dishes where no one herb dominates. Instead, all the herbs contribute in a subtle way to an overall flavour which can best be described as both mellow and rich. The recipes we have allocated to particular herb sections have been selected according to classical associations or as our personal choice. Many of these recipes also contain more than one herb, used in a complementary way. The featured herb is not necessarily the only one which would work in each dish. Be prepared to make substitutions if necessary, or try others, thus creating your own individual style.

Two famous traditional herb mixes are fines herbes and bouquet garni. Both come originally from French cuisine but are now widely used in most Western countries.

FINES HERBES—the classical blend of fresh, mild-flavoured herbs used to sprinkle on simple egg, fish and poultry dishes, and fresh cheeses, just prior to serving. The usual mix consists of 3 tablespoons of finely chopped parsley with 1 tablespoon each of finely scissored or chopped chives, tarragon and chervil.

BOUQUET GARNI—a bundle of herbs used to flavour slowly cooked dishes. It is traditionally made up of 2–3 sprigs of parsley, 1 sprig of thyme and 1 bay leaf, but other herbs and flavourings can be included. We add tarragon and lemon thyme for fish, summer savory and marjoram for poultry, and winter savory, rosemary and oregano for rich beef or game stews. Make up your own variations.

Tie the bunch with a piece of string, having one end long enough to hang over the side of the saucepan or casserole. Remove the bouquet before taking the dish to the table.

HERBES DE PROVENCE—mixtures of dried herbs called herbes de Provence are sold in markets in Provence. They include a variety of locally grown herbs, such as basil, fennel, marjoram, mint, oregano, rosemary, sage, thyme and sometimes even lavender. The dried mix is used to flavour braised meat, game, roasted root vegetables, soups, breads (see recipe for herb focaccia on page 184) and pissaladière. At the height of summer, when supplies of herbs are bountiful, Mary gathers bunches of the ones listed above, ties them by the stems and suspends each bunch separately from the rafters in an airy loft. It is a very pleasant winter job to strip the dried leaves from the stems and to blend and crumble them into storage jars.

A favourite winter picnic treat is a pissaladière, or the French equivalent of a pizza. These are often made without tomatoes and instead use plenty of onions sautéed slowly in olive oil to bring out their sweetness. We prefer these bread bases to the rich pastry ones found in quiches. Pissaladières can be eaten warm or cold and they travel well.

PISSALADIERE
Serves 4–6

Bread dough
2 teaspoons Surebake yeast (or other brand instant dried yeast: check packet for quantity to use)
320 g white bread flour
2 teaspoons milk powder
1 teaspoon sugar
1/4 teaspoon salt
1 tablespoon olive oil
220 ml warm water

Breadmaker method: following the manufacturer's instructions, make the dough. After the first 10 minutes of kneading, lift the lid and check on consistency. The dough should be soft and still a little sticky. Adjust if necessary by adding a little extra water or flour.

Handmade method: in a large bowl, combine the yeast, flour, milk powder, salt and sugar. Add the oil and warm water. Stir to mix and then knead on a floured board, adding just enough extra flour to prevent the dough from sticking. Knead for 10 minutes. Place the dough in a greased bowl and leave to rest for 15 minutes.

While waiting for the dough, prepare the onion topping.

Topping

600 g (2 large) red-skinned onions, thinly sliced
2 cloves garlic, finely chopped
3 tablespoons olive oil
50 g can anchovy fillets, soaked in milk for 15 minutes to
remove excess salt, then drained
stoned black olives, cut in half
1 tablespoon herbes de Provence
black pepper
salt to taste (be cautious as anchovies and olives tend
to be salty)

In a large, lidded pan, sauté the onions and garlic in the oil for about 30 minutes or until soft and mushy. Keep covered while cooking but stir at intervals to check progress. Allow to cool a little.

Lightly grease a Swiss roll pan (20 by 30 cm). Knead the prepared dough briefly by hand for 1–2 minutes, then roll it out to fit the pan. Use your fingers to push the dough well into the corners. Spread the onion mix evenly over the dough. Arrange the anchovies and olives to create a pattern, if desired, and then sprinkle with the herbs, pepper and salt. Leave in a warm place for about 30 minutes or until the dough has started to rise.

Preheat the oven to 220°C. Bake in the hot oven for 20–30 minutes or until the underside of the bread base is golden (lift the edge with a spatula or fish slice). Slide onto a board for immediate serving, or a rack if it is to be eaten cold later.

LENTIL SOUP WITH HERBES DE PROVENCE
Serves 2 as a substantial main-dish soup

In winter, the fragrance of dried herbs cooking in this soup reminds one of hot summer days. We enjoy it both as a chunky soup and a puréed one. Chop the vegetables finely if they are not to be puréed. Though it is not essential, we prefer to soak the lentils for 2 hours prior to cooking.

150 g green or brown lentils (we use the small dark green
French lentils from Le Puy)

2 tablespoons oil
1 large onion, chopped
1 clove garlic, chopped
1 tablespoon herbes de Provence
1/2 teaspoon salt
black pepper
250 g tomatoes, chopped
1 tablespoon tomato paste
1 tablespoon red wine vinegar or lemon juice
2 cups water
2 tablespoons chopped flat-leaved or curly parsley, plus extra
small sprigs for garnishing

Wash the lentils, and if time permits soak them in cold water for 2 hours. Drain and rinse again.

In a medium-sized saucepan, heat the oil and sauté the onion and garlic until softened. Add the herbes de Provence and seasoning. Sauté for a few minutes. Add the tomatoes, tomato paste, vinegar, drained lentils and water. Simmer for 20–30 minutes for Puy lentils or longer for larger varieties. They should be soft to bite.

If desired, purée the soup in a blender or food processor, or put through a sieve. Return to the saucepan and reheat. Stir in the parsley and ladle into large bowls. Garnish with several small parsley leaves.

HERB DUMPLINGS WITH HUNGARIAN-STYLE VEGETABLE STEW
Serves 4

The cheese and herb dumplings cook on top of a rich, paprika-seasoned vegetable stew for the last 30 minutes of cooking, rising to become light and moist and absorbing the rich flavours. Use the dumplings on meat-based casseroles too. Other vegetables may be substituted for the ones listed.

Stew
1 tablespoon oil
1 clove garlic, finely chopped
1 large onion, chopped
1 tablespoon paprika
250 g carrots, peeled
300 g potatoes, peeled or scrubbed
300 g pumpkin, peeled
1 green capsicum, sliced
1 stalk celery, sliced
100 g button mushrooms, sliced
1/2 cup vegetable or beef stock
400 g can tomatoes in juice, chopped
1/4 cup red wine
1 tablespoon tomato paste
bouquet garni (see page 180)
1/4 teaspoon caraway seeds
salt to taste
black pepper

sour cream or yoghurt for serving

Heat the oil in a metal casserole or, if this is not available, use a frying pan and transfer the ingredients later to a pottery or pyrex casserole for oven cooking. Sauté the onion and garlic until soft. Add the paprika and cook gently for a minute. Cut the carrots, potatoes and pumpkin into 2 cm chunks and add to the casserole. Add the remaining raw vegetables and cook gently for a few minutes before adding the stock, tomatoes and their juice, wine, tomato paste, bouquet garni, caraway seeds and seasoning. Cover tightly with aluminium foil and the lid and cook in a moderate oven (180°C) for 1 1/2 hours.

Herb dumplings
1 cup self-raising white flour
1/2 cup grated tasty Cheddar cheese
3 tablespoons finely chopped fresh herbs (e.g. parsley, winter savory, oregano, chives, lemon thyme)
milk to mix

In a bowl combine the flour, cheese and herbs. Add sufficient milk to make a damp scone-type dough. On a floured board, pat the dough out to about 1.5 cm thick. Cut into 4 large dumplings.

Increase the oven temperature to 200°C. Have some boiling water available in case the stew has insufficent liquid remaining, as the dumplings will absorb some while cooking. Remove the stew from the oven and uncover. Discard the bouquet garni and add extra water if needed. Place the dumplings on top of the vegetables. Cover with the lid and return to the oven for 25–30 minutes or until the dumplings are well risen and cooked.

Serve with a small bowl of sour cream or yoghurt to spoon onto individual servings.

BASIC VEGETABLE & HERB QUICHE
Serves 4–6

Fill a crisp wholemeal pastry case with a combination of available vegetables, enhanced by their special herbs, and a creamy, cheese-topped custard. A food processor speeds the preparation by mixing the pastry, grating the cheese and combining the custard ingredients. Make your own selection of herbs to complement the vegetables or choose any one or a mixture from the following vegetable/herb combinations:

courgettes or zucchini *with* parsley, tarragon, lemon thyme *or* parsley, fennel, lemon balm
spinach or silverbeet *with* rosemary (1 teaspoon, chopped), sorrel, oregano, parsley
broccoli *with* parsley, basil or tarragon, marjoram
asparagus *with* tarragon, lemon thyme, parsley
leeks *with* thyme, sage (1 teaspoon, chopped), parsley
tomatoes *with* basil, oregano, thyme
mushrooms *with* fennel or tarragon, parsley
carrots *with* marjoram *or* oregano, parsley, lemon thyme

or lemon basil, savory, parsley

Wholemeal pastry
1 cup wholemeal flour
1/4 teaspoon salt
50 g cold butter, cut into cubes
water to mix

With the metal blade in position, combine the flour, salt and butter in the processor bowl. Chop until the mixture resembles fine breadcrumbs. With the motor running, pour in water slowly, adding just sufficient for the dry ingredients to start clumping together. Process for a few seconds longer until the dough forms a ball. On a floured board, briefly knead the dough until it shows no tendency to crumble. Roll out thinly to fit a 20–25 cm diameter quiche dish.

Filling
100 g tasty Cheddar cheese, grated

1 tablespoon oil
4 cups sliced or chopped raw vegetables
1 chopped shallot or small onion.

3–4 tablespoons finely chopped herbs (make parsley the bulk herb when using stronger-flavoured herbs) plus extra herbs for garnishing

Custard
3 eggs
1 cup milk or cream, or half milk and half cream (for a creamy taste with less fat, use canned evaporated low-fat milk)
1/4 teaspoon salt
black pepper

Preheat the oven to 190°C. Sprinkle half of the cheese over the quiche pastry base.

Stir-fry vegetables in oil until tender-crisp, drain well and place on the cheese-lined base. Sprinkle with the herbs.

Mix the custard ingredients in the food processor and pour over the vegetables. Sprinkle with the remaining cheese. Bake for 30–40 minutes or until the custard has set. Serve warm or at room temperature, garnished with a sprinkling of freshly chopped herbs.

FRANKFURT GREEN SAUCE
Serves 4

The traditional recipe for this beautiful sauce requires 7 herbs: borage leaves, parsley, chervil, chives, sorrel, salad burnet and cress (water or garden variety). In the modern versions, the herbs are finely chopped in a food processor with hard-boiled egg yolks, seasonings and crème fraîche, yoghurt or sour cream. In Germany the sauce is served with boiled meats, new potatoes, vegetables and fish. We enjoy it with a simple dish of hot, steamed, freshly dug new potatoes, garnished generously with slices or pieces of smoked salmon. The sauce is served in a small bowl, passed around separately.

Note: don't use watercress from the wild, as this needs to be cooked to destroy small snails which may be present in the hollow stems, and which are the intermediate host of the liver fluke.

30 g (about) of the herbs, weighed after coarse stalks have been trimmed and discarded
2 yolks from hard-boiled eggs
1/2 teaspoon German- or French-style mustard
freshly ground white pepper
1/4–1/2 teaspoon salt
1 teaspoon white wine vinegar
1/2 cup crème fraîche or yoghurt or sour cream

Roughly chop the herbs and place in the bowl of a food processor. Add the remaining ingredients and process until a smooth sauce is obtained. You may need to stop and scrape the sides of the bowl from time to time. Spoon into a small bowl and store in a refrigerator until required. Use within 24 hours.

HERB FOCACCIA
Makes 1 loaf the size of a Swiss roll pan (a shallow rectangular pan about 30 x 20 cm)

This focaccia is made easily with the assistance of a breadmaker. Use individual herbs or a combination of 2–3. We enjoy the taste of the herbs alone and prefer to serve olives and dried tomatoes in small bowls as an accompaniment.

Herb oil
1–2 tablespoons finely chopped fresh herbs (basil, oregano, thyme, sage, rosemary, savory: use a smaller quantity of stronger-flavoured herbs, such as sage and rosemary), or 1–2 teaspoons dried herbs (such as basil or herbes de Provence: see page 180)
2 tablespoons olive oil

In a small bowl, combine the chopped fresh herbs or crumbled dried herbs and the olive oil. Put aside to allow the oil to absorb the herb flavours.

Bread
3 teaspoons Surebake yeast or 1 1/2 teaspoons instant yeast
2 cups white bread flour (280 g)
1/2 cup wholemeal flour (70 g)
1 teaspoon sugar
1/2 teaspoon salt
1 tablespoon olive oil
1 cup water (250 ml)

Place all the ingredients in the breadmaker pan in the order recommended by the manufacturer. Select the white dough setting and start the machine. After a few minutes into the first kneading cycle, lift the lid and check the consistency. The dough should be smooth, soft and slightly sticky. If not, add a little extra flour or water.

As soon as the dough is ready, brush a warm Swiss roll pan with a little of the herb oil. Place the prepared dough in the pan. With floury fingers, keep patting and pushing the dough firmly into the corners until it fits the pan. Spoon the oil and herbs over the surface. Brush to spread evenly. Cover loosely with plastic food film. Leave to rise in a warm place until the dough is just below the rim of the pan. Use a finger to make holes well down into the risen dough, giving the surface a dimpled appearance.

Bake in a hot oven (220°C) for 15–20 minutes or until the bread is golden on top and underneath (lift one corner with a metal spatula to check). Remove from the pan onto a wire rack and allow to cool a little before cutting into chunks on a board

POTTED CHEESE WITH SEVEN HERBS

The addition of fresh herbs adds colour and interest to this version of the traditional potted cheese. We have used the same 7 herbs as specified in a recipe from Eleanour Sinclair Rohde's book *Culinary and Salad Herbs*. Her source was an old Cumberland recipe, claiming to be at least 200 years old. This 21st-century version takes advantage of a food processor.

150 g mature Cheddar cheese
50 g melted butter
1/4 teaspoon freshly grated nutmeg
black pepper
2 tablespoons port wine or tawny sherry
1 tablespoon each of finely chopped parsley and chervil
1 teaspoon each of finely chopped tarragon, summer or winter savory, sage and thyme
1 teaspoon finely sliced chives

With the grating disc in place, grate the cheese and tip out into a small bowl. Change to the chopping blade and return the cheese. Add the remaining ingredients and process until evenly blended. Spoon into a small bowl or jar. Cover and store in a refrigerator until required.

GREEN HERB SQUARES
Makes about 36 bite-sized squares

This is our adaptation of a recipe contributed to *Sunset* Magazine (December 1998) by Chatom Vineyards of California, where these tasty green herb squares were served at wine tastings. They can be made up to a day ahead and stored in a refrigerator.

4 tablespoons whole, unskinned almonds, lightly roasted (see page 21)
1 1/2 cups coarsely chopped silverbeet leaves minus their stalks and midribs
1 medium-sized onion, roughly chopped
4 large, trimmed spring onions, sliced
1/4 cup coarsely chopped sorrel leaves minus stalks and midribs
1/4 cup coarsely chopped mint
2 tablespoons chopped parsley
1 tablespoon chopped coriander leaves
1 tablespoon chopped dill or young fennel leaves
1 tablespoon chopped tarragon
4 large eggs
2 tablespoons white flour
1/2 teaspoon salt
black pepper

Process the almonds in a blender or food processor until finely chopped. Add the remaining ingredients and process to a fine purée. Pour into a well-greased 20 cm square baking pan. Bake at 155°C for about 30 minutes or until the centre is firm to touch. Allow to cool and then cut into 3 cm squares and lift out with a spatula. The green herb squares look attractive served on a white or glass platter and garnished with sprigs of the contributing herbs.

BOOKS WE HAVE FOUND USEFUL

Alexander, Stephanie, 1996, *Stephanie Alexander: The Cook's Companion*. Viking, Ringwood, Victoria, Australia.

Anon., 1744, *Adam's Luxury, and Eve's Cookery; or, the Kitchen-Garden display'd*. Prospect Books, London, 1983.

Beeton, Isabella, 1899, *The Book of Household Management*. Ward, Lock & Co., London.

Bond, Robert E., 1988, 'Southeast Asian Herbs and Spices in California', in *Petits Propos Culinaires* 30: 11–33.

Bown, Deni, 1995, *The Herb Society of America Encyclopedia of Herbs and Their Uses*. Dorling Kindersley, New York.

Bradley, Richard, 1736, *The Country Housewife and Lady's Director*. Prospect Books, London, 1980.

Burnie, Geoffrey and John Fenton-Smith, 1996, *Better Homes and Gardens: A Grower's Guide to Herbs*. Murdoch Books, Sydney.

Browne, Mary, Helen Leach and Nancy Tichborne, 1997, *The Cook's Salad Garden*. Godwit, Auckland.

Browne, Mary, Helen Leach and Nancy Tichborne, 1987, *More from the Cook's Garden*. Reed Methuen, Auckland.

Browne, Mary, Helen Leach and Nancy Tichborne, 1980, *The Cook's Garden*. Reed, Auckland.

Columella, *On Agriculture and Trees*. Loeb Classical Library, Heinemann, London, 1955.

Cook, Alan D. (ed.), 1983, 'Oriental Herbs and Vegetables. A Handbook', in *Plants and Gardens. Brooklyn Botanic Garden Record*, 39(2), special issue.

Creasy, Rosalind, 1998, *Cooking from the Garden*. Sierra Club Books, San Francisco.

Crockett, James Underwood and Ogden Tanner, 1979, *The Time–Life Encyclopaedia of Gardening: Herbs*. Time–Life Books, Amsterdam.

Dalby, Andrew, 1996, *Siren Feasts: A History of Food and Gastronomy in Greece*. Routledge, London.

Darby, William J., Paul Ghalioungui and Louis Grivetti, 1977, *Food: The Gift of Osiris*, Vol. 2. Academic Press, London.

David, Elizabeth, 1954, *Italian Food*. Revised ed., Barrie & Jenkins, London, 1996.

David, Elizabeth, 1979, *Spices, Salt and Aromatics in the English Kitchen*. Penguin Books, Harmondsworth, Middlesex.

Davidson, Alan, 1999, *The Oxford Companion to Food*. Oxford University Press, Oxford.

Dille, Carolyn and Susan Belsinger, 1992, *Herbs in the Kitchen: A Celebration of Flavor*. Interweave Press, Loveland, Colorado.

Dunn, Dawn, 1997, *Growing Herbs in New Zealand*. David Bateman, Auckland.

Earle, Mrs C. W., 1897, *Pot-pourri from a Surrey Garden*. Century Publishing, London, 1984.

Evelyn, John, 1699, *Acetaria. A Discourse of Sallets*. Prospect Books, London, 1982.

Facciola, Stephen, 1998, *Cornucopia II: A Source Book of Edible Plants*. Kampong Publications, Vista, California.

Flower, Barbara and Elisabeth Rosenbaum, 1958, *The Roman Cookery Book: A Critical Translation of* The Art of Cooking *by Apicius for Use in the Study and the Kitchen*. Harrap, London.

Foley, Daniel J. (ed.), 1974, *Herbs for Use and for Delight*. Dover Publications, New York.

Freeman, Meera and Lê Văn Nhân, 1995, *The Vietnamese Cookbook*. Viking, Ringwood, Victoria.

French, Jackie, 1993, *Book of Thyme*. Angus & Robertson, Pymble, NSW.

Garland, Sarah, 1993, *The Complete Book of Herbs and Spices*. Frances Lincoln, London.

Gerard, John, 1633, *The Herbal or General History of Plants*. Dover Publications, New York, 1975.

Gray, Patience, 1986, *Honey from a Weed: Fasting and Feasting in Tuscany, Catalonia, the Cyclades and Apulia*. Prospect Books, London.

Harrington, Geri, 1978, *Grow Your Own Chinese Vegetables*. Collier Books, New York.

Harvey, John, 1981, *Mediaeval Gardens*. B. T. Batsford, London.

Hedrick, U. P., 1919, *Sturtevant's Edible Plants of the World*. Dover Publications, New York, 1972.

Hemphill, Rosemary, 1966, *The Penguin Book of Herbs and Spices*. Penguin Books, Harmondsworth, Middlesex.

Hieatt, Constance B., Brenda Hosington and Sharon Butler, 1996, *Pleyn Delit: Medieval cookery for modern cooks*, 2nd ed. University of Toronto Press, Toronto.

Hill, Thomas, 1652, *The Gardener's Labyrinth*. Oxford University Press, Oxford, 1987.

Hutson, Lucinda, 1987, *The Herb Garden Cookbook*. Texas Monthly Press, Austin, Texas.

Klein, E., 1966, *A Comprehensive Etymological Dictionary of the English Language*. Elsevier, Amsterdam.

Kowalchik, Claire and William H. Hylton (eds), 1998, *Rodale's Illustrated Encyclopedia of Herbs*. Rodale Press, Emmaus, Pennsylvania.

Larkcom, Joy, 1991, *Oriental Vegetables: The Complete Guide for Garden and Kitchen*. John Murray, London.

Leach, Helen, 2000, *Cultivating Myths: Fiction, Fact and Fashion in Garden History*. Godwit, Auckland.

Loewenfeld, Claire, 1964, *Herb Gardening*. Faber & Faber, London.

Marcin, Marietta Marshall, 1984, *The Complete Book of Herbal Teas*. William Collins, London.

McClure, Susan, 1996, *The Herb Gardener: A Guide for All Seasons*. Gardenway Publishing, Vermont.

McNaughton, Virginia, 2000, *Lavender, the New Zealand Gardener's Guide*. Penguin Books, Auckland.

McVicar, Jekka, 1994, *Jekka's Complete Herb Book*. Kyle Cathie, London.

Norman, Jill, 1997, *The Classic Herb Cookbook*. Dorling Kindersley, London.

Ortiz, Elisabeth Lambert, 1979, 'Coriander', in *Petits Propos Culinaires* 1: 18–22.

Page, Mary and William T. Stearn, 1979, *Culinary Herbs*. Wisley Handbook 16. Royal Horticultural Society, London.

Painter, Gilian E., 1983, *Cooking with Unusual Herbs*. Published by the author, Oratia, Auckland.

Painter, Gilian E., 1983, *A Herb Cookbook*. Hodder & Stoughton, London.

Painter, Gilian and Elaine Power, 1982, *The Herb Garden Displayed*. Hodder & Stoughton, Auckland.

Parkinson, John, 1629, *A Garden of Pleasant Flowers* (*Paradisi in Sole: Paradisus Terrestris*). Dover Publications, New York, 1976.

Paterson, Allen, 1990, *Herbs in the Garden*. J. M. Dent, London.

Phillips, Roger and Nicky Foy, 1990, *Herbs*. Pan Books, London.

Pliny the Elder, *Natural History*. 10 vols. Loeb Classical Library. Heinemann, London, 1938–1963.

Proulx, E. Annie, 1985, *The Fine Art of Salad Gardening*. Rodale Press, Emmaus, Pennsylvania.

Proulx, E. Annie, 1987, *The Gourmet Gardener*. Fawcett Columbine, New York.

Ranson, Florence, 1949, *British Herbs*. Penguin Books, Harmondsworth, Middlesex.

Rohde, Eleanour Sinclair, 1940, *Culinary and Salad Herbs. Their Cultivation and Food Values with Recipes*. Dover Publications, New York, 1972.

Root, Waverley, 1980, *Food*. Simon & Schuster, New York.

Rozin, Elisabeth, 1983, *Ethnic Cuisine: the Flavor Principle Cookbook*. Stephen Greene Press, Battleboro, Vermont.

Rutherford, Meg, 1975, *A Pattern of Herbs*. George Allen & Unwin, London.

Santich, Barbara, 1995, *The Original Mediterranean Cuisine: Medieval Recipes for Today*. Wakefield Press, Kent Town, South Australia.

Scott, Sally Anne, 1992, *Aromatic Herbs*. Conran Octopus, London.

Shipley, J. T., 1984, *The Origins of English Words: A Discursive Dictionary of Indo-European Roots*. Johns Hopkins University Press, Baltimore.

Solomon, Charmaine and Nina Solomon, 1996, *Charmaine Solomon's Encyclopedia of Asian Food*. William Heinemann Australia, Port Melbourne.

Stobart, Tom, 1997, *Herbs, Spices and Flavourings*. Penguin Books, Harmondsworth, Middlesex.

Stobart, Tom, 1980, *The Cook's Encyclopaedia: Ingredients and Processes*. B.T. Batsford, London.

Theophrastus, *Enquiry into Plants*. 2 vols. Loeb Classical Library, Heinemann, London, 1916.

Traunfeld, Jerry, 2000, *The Herbfarm Cookbook*. Scribner, New York.

Tutin, T. G. (ed.), 1964–1980, *Flora Europaea*. 5 vols. Cambridge University Press, Cambridge.

Vaughan, J. G. and C. Geissler, 1997, *The New Oxford Book of Food Plants*. Oxford University Press, Oxford.

Vilmorin-Andrieux, MM., 1885, *The Vegetable Garden*. Jeavons-Leler Press, Palo Alto, California, 1976.

Visser, Margaret, 1993, 'Moretum: ancient Roman pesto', pp. 263–74 in Walker, H. (ed.), *Spicing Up the Palate: Studies of Flavourings—Ancient and Modern*. Proceedings of the Oxford Symposium on Food and Cookery 1992. Prospect Books, London.

Wilder, Louise Beebe, 1932, *The Fragrant Garden: A Book about Sweet Scented Flowers and Leaves*. Dover Publications, New York, 1974.

USEFUL ADDRESSES

NEW ZEALAND

Kings Seeds (NZ) Ltd
(seed catalogue)
P.O. Box 283
Katikati
BAY OF PLENTY
Phone 7 549 3409
Fax 7 549 3408
e-mail: kings.seeds@xtra.co.nz

Somerfields
(plant catalogue)
22 Somerset Drive
Glen Tui R.D., Oxford
CANTERBURY
Phone 3 312 4321
Fax 3 312 4213

Yates New Zealand Ltd
P.O. Box 1109
AUCKLAND 1

Cottage Plants
(plant catalogue)
Petit Carenage Bay
R.D. 2
AKAROA HARBOUR
Phone/fax 3 304 5882

The Superb Herb Company
(growers of living herbs for supermarket sales)
AUCKLAND
Phone 9 837 0500
Fax 9 837 0514

AUSTRALIA

Kings Herb Seeds
(seed catalogue)
Australian Distributor
P.O. Box 975
Penrith
N.S.W. 2751
Phone 2 4776 1493
Fax 2 4776 2090

Yates Vegetable Seeds Ltd
Private Bag 118
Wetherill Park
N.S.W. 2164

New Gippsland Seeds and Bulbs
(catalogue)
P.O. Box 1, Silvan
VICTORIA 3795
Phone 3 9737 9560
Fax 3 9737 9292

Royston Petrie Seeds Ltd
(seed calaogue)
P.O. Box 77
Kenthurst
N.S.W. 2156
Phone 2 9654 1186
Fax 2 9654 2658

Phoenix seeds
(seed catalogue)
P.O. Box 207
Snug
TASMANIA 7054
Phone 3 6267 9663
Fax 3 6267 9592

BRITAIN

Jekka's Herb Farm
(plant and seed catalogue)
Rose Cottage, Shellards Lane,
Alveston
Bristol BS35 3SY
Web site for on-line catalogue:
www.jekkasherbfarm.com

The Royal Horticultural Society
Web site: www.rhs.org.uk

INDEX OF RECIPES & PLANT NAMES

(The recipes are listed under the name of their dominant herb and also according to recipe categories, such as soups, breads, main dishes etc. Where a recipe name fails to indicate the main herb, this has been added in brackets.)

Allium schoenoprasum see CHIVES
Allium cepa var. *viviparum* see tree onions
Allium tuberosum see GARLIC CHIVES
Aloysia triphylla see LEMON VERBENA
Anethum graveolens see DILL
Anthriscus cerefolium see CHERVIL
appetisers and snacks
    A true Italian pizza (rosemary) 139
    Aunt Maude's meat paste (bay) 39
    Fresh spring rolls with salad (rau ram, perilla) 134
    Green herb squares (sorrel, mint, parsley, coriander, dill or fennel, tarragon) 185
    Guacamole (coriander) 61
    Hummus with parsley 120
    Marinated mushrooms Italian-style (bay and/or tarragon) 39, 162
    Mushrooms with thyme on toast 172
    Nancy's carrot spread (dill, mint, parsley) 66
    Pissaladière (*herbes de Provence*) 180
    Poor man's aubergine caviar (chervil) 46
    Potted cheese with seven herbs 184
    Purple basil cheese ball 29
    Rosemary and garlic flavoured bean pâté 140
    Salmon pâté with chives 53
    Strawberries with a lemon thyme marinade 175
    Tabbouleh (parsley) 120
    Tarragon aioli 163
apple mint 92
Artemisia dracunculus see TARRAGON
Asian chives see GARLIC CHIVES

Basic vegetable and herb quiche 182
BASIL
    Basil bread 33
    butter 28
    Fresh tomato and basil pasta sauce 32
    hints for use 28
    Lemon basil fruit sauce 33
    Mushroom and corn chowder with basil 31
    Pesto (handmade) 29
    Pesto for freezing 30
    Pesto made in a blender or food processor 30
    Polenta with a basil, capsicum and tomato sauce 32
    Purple basil cheese ball 29

Rich tomato and vegetable pasta sauce 32
Soupe au pistou 30
Vietnamese-style chicken and cabbage salad with purple basil 31
vinegar 28
BAY
    Aunt Maude's meat paste 39
    Bay leaf junket 41
    Chicken and potato curry with three bay leaves 40
    hints for use 38
    Honey bay custards with a touch of rum 41
    Lentil and vegetable soup 40
    Marinated mushrooms Italian-style 39
bay laurel see BAY
beverages
    Iced lemon balm and Assam tea 85
    iced tea 20
    Lavender lemonade 177
    Lemon balm rum fruit punch 83
    Mint green sparkler 102
    Mint julep 99
    Moroccan mint tea 102
    Sangria (lemon verbena) 89
    Tarragon-flavoured vodka 162
    tisanes 19
borage 178
Borago officinalis see borage
bouquet garni 180
breads, muffins, scones
    A true Italian pizza (rosemary) 139
    Basil bread 33
    Dill and Cheddar muffins 69
    Fennel and cheese scones 74
    Herb focaccia 184
    Minted treble chocolate muffins 101
    Parsley, corn and cheese bread 121
    Pissaladière (herbes de Provence) 180
    Rosemary Hemphill's rosemary scones 141
    Swedish limpé (fennel seeds) 74
    Thyme bread 171
broad-leaf parsley 115
bronze fennel 70
bush basil 23

cakes see desserts
caraway thyme 167
Chenopodium ambrosioides see epazote
CHERVIL
    Cream of mushroom soup with chervil 47
    Fish with chervil 47
    French omelette 46
    hints for use 45
    Poor man's aubergine caviar (chervil) 46

Puffy omelette 46
Salad of carrots and courgettes with a chervil dressing 45
Sauce ravigote 45
vinegar 45
CHIVES
    Beetroot with chives and lemon 52
    butter 53
    Chicken scaloppine with herbs 53
    hints for use 52
    Perfect scrambled eggs with chives 54
    Salmon pâté with chives 53
cilantro see CORIANDER
common basil 23
common sage 142
common sorrel 179
common thyme 166
CORIANDER
    Bevy's sautéed chicken and coriander 60
    Coriander fruit salad 61
    Fresh coriander and mint relish 59
    Garam masala 59
    Green masala 58
    Green salsa 60
    Guacamole 61
    hints for use 58
    Red salsa 60
Coriandrum sativum see CORIANDER
Cryptotaenia japonica see MITSUBA
curly-leaf parsley 114
Cymbopogon citratus see lemon grass

dark opal basil see purple basil
desserts and cakes
    Bay leaf junket 41
    Creamy lemon verbena spread or dip 90
    Honey bay custards with a touch of rum 41
    Lemon balm flavoured yoghurt 85
    Lemon basil fruit sauce 33
    Lemon verbena fruit salad 91
    Lemon verbena syrup cake 91
    Oranges with vodka and tarragon syrup 165
    Rhubarb and lemon balm 85
    Rose cream (rose geranium) 176
    Rose-flavoured rhubarb crumble (rose geranium) 176
    Rosemary icecream 141
    Upside-down apple and sage cake 149
DILL
    Beef stroganoff 69
    Borscht 67
    Cucumber salad with dill 66
    Dill and Cheddar muffins 69
    Gravlax 65

hints for use 65
Lemon, butter and dill sauce for fish 65
Nancy's carrot spread 66
Roast lamb with dill 68
Russian-style vegetable salad 67
Smoked salmon and dill pasta sauce 68
dressings see sauces
drying herbs 16, 17

eau-de Cologne mint 95
Egyptian onions 179
English lavender 179
　　Lavender lemonade 177
epazote 178

FENNEL
　　Fennel and salmon pasta sauce 75
　　Fennel dressing 75
　　hints for use 74
　　Spanish-style bean and potato soup 74
　　Swedish limpé (dark rye bread with fennel
　　　seeds) 74
fines herbes 180
flat-leaf parsley 115
Florence fennel 70
Foeniculum vulgare see FENNEL
Frankfurt green sauce 183
freezing herbs 17
French marjoram 104
French sorrel 179

garden sage 142
garden sorrel 179
garden thyme 166
GARLIC CHIVES
　　Garlic chive rice salad 79
　　hints for use 78
　　Pumpkin soup with an Asian flavour 79
Genovese basil 23
golden marjoram 104
golden oregano 104
gold-leafed lemon balm 80
Greek oregano 104
Green herb squares 185
green perilla 124
green-leafed sage 142

herb butters 18, 19
Herb dumplings with Hungarian-style
　　vegetable stew 182
Herb focaccia 184
herb teas 19
herb vinegars 17
　　tarragon 18
　　lemon-flavoured 18
　　marinade 18
　　rice vinegar with flavours of Asia 18
herbes de Provence 180
herb-flavoured oils 18

herb-flavoured teas 20

iced tisanes and teas 20

knotted marjoram 104

Laurus nobilis see BAY
Lavandula angustifolia 179
lavender see English lavender
LEMON BALM
　　Baked fish with lemon balm 84
　　butter 83
　　hints for use 83
　　Iced lemon balm and Assam tea 85
　　lemon balm flavoured yoghurt 85
　　Lemon balm rum fruit punch 83
　　Lemon balm salsa 85
　　Lemon balm vinaigrette 84
　　Rhubarb and lemon balm 85
　　Stirfried courgettes with lemon balm 84
　　tisane 83
lemon basil 24
lemon grass 178
lemon thyme 166
LEMON VERBENA
　　Chicken breasts with lemon verbena 90
　　Creamy lemon verbena spread or dip 90
　　hints for use 89
　　Lemon verbena fruit salad 91
　　Lemon verbena syrup cake 91
　　Sangria 89
　　tisane 89
Lentil soup with *herbes de Provence* 181
Levisticum officinale see lovage
lovage 178

main dishes (see also pasta, salads and soups)
　　Asparagus and tarragon frittata 164
　　Baked beans with savory and sage 156
　　Baked fish with lemon balm 84
　　Barley and mushroom risotto (oregano or
　　　marjoram) 110
　　Basic vegetable and herb quiche 182
　　Beef stroganoff (dill) 69
　　Bevy's sautéed chicken and coriander 60
　　Chicken and potato curry with three bay
　　　leaves 40
　　Chicken breasts with lemon verbena 90
　　Chicken scaloppine with herbs (chives) 53
　　Fajitas (oregano) 113
　　Fish with chervil 47
　　French omelette (chervil) 46
　　Fried rice and rau răm 133
　　Herb dumplings with a Hungarian-style
　　　vegetable stew 182
　　Home-made crumbed sage and port
　　　sausages 148
　　Jambalaya (oregano, parsley, sage, bay,
　　　thyme) 112

Lemon thyme roast chicken with lemon
　　halves 174
Mediterranean-style beef stew with
　　rosemary and juniper berries 140
Mediterranean-style fish with mint 100
Middle Eastern-style meat patties in pitta
　　bread (parsley, oregano, lemon thyme)
　　112
Perfect scrambled eggs with chives 54
Polenta with a basil, capsicum and tomato
　　sauce 32
Puffy omelette (chervil) 46
Risi e bisi (savory, parsley) 157
Roast chicken with bay 38
Roast lamb with dill 68
Savory and orange baked chicken 157
Tarragon and orange fish fillets 164
Tarragon chicken 165
Tuscan-style liver with sage 148
Vegetable chilli (oregano) 111
Vegetarian Christmas nutmeat loaf with
　　thyme stuffing 174
Vietnamese-style beef stirfry with mint
　　100
Vietnamese-style chicken with pineapple
　　and cashews (rau ram) 133
marjoram see OREGANO AND
MARJORAM
Melissa officinalis see LEMON BALM
Mentha x *piperita* 95
Mentha x *piperita citrata* 95
Mentha species see MINT
Mentha spicata 92
Mentha suaveolens 92
Mexican marigold 178
Mexican mint 178
Mexican tarragon 178
MINT
　　Cabbage, tomato and mint sauté 99
　　Fresh mint chutney 99
　　hints for use 98
　　Mandy's beetroot sauce on pasta with
　　　mint 101
　　Mediteranean-style fish with mint 100
　　Mint and cucumber raita 99
　　Mint green sparkler 102
　　Mint jelly 98
　　Mint julep 99
　　Mint marinade for lamb 98
　　Mint sauce 98
　　Minted potato salad 100
　　Minted treble chocolate muffins 101
　　Moroccan mint tea 102
　　Red currant mint sauce 98
　　tea 98
　　tisane 98
　　Vietnamese-style beef stirfry with mint
　　　100
Mitsuba 179

Japanese-style soup 128
muffins see breads

Ocimum basilicum 22, 23
Ocimum minimum 23
Ocimum sanctum 24
Ocimum species see BASIL
Ocimum tenuiflorum 24
orange thyme 166
OREGANO AND MARJORAM
    Barley and mushroom risotto 110
    Black bean soup 110
    Carrot and marjoram soup 109
    Fajitas 113
    Greek-style salad 111
    hints for use 108
    Jambalaya 112
    Middle-Eastern-style meat patties in pitta
      bread 112
    Stuffing for roast chicken 109
    Vegetable chilli 111
    vinegar 108
Oriental chives see GARLIC CHIVES
Origanum onites 104
Origanum species see OREGANO AND
MARJORAM
Origanum vulgare subsp. *vulgare* 104
Origanum vulgare subsp. *hirtum* 104

PARSLEY
    butter 119
    Green sauce 121
    hints for use 119
    Hummus with parsley 120
    Parsley soup 122
    Parsley, corn and cheese bread 121
    Pumpkin soup with green sauce 121
    Tabbouleh 120
    Tuna, red capsicum and parsley pasta
      sauce 122
pasta dishes
    Fennel and salmon pasta sauce 75
    Mandy's beetroot sauce on pasta with
      mint 101
    Rainbow capsicums with sage pasta sauce
      148
    Smoked salmon and dill pasta sauce 68
    Tuna, red capsicum and parsley pasta
      sauce 122
Pelargonium graveolens 178
Pelargonium species 178
peppermint 95
PERILLA
    Asian-style mixed vegetable pickle 128
    Chicken and noodle salad with perilla and
      rau răm 127
    Cucumber, tomato, avocado and perilla
      salad 127
    hints for use 126

Japanese-style soup 128
    Kiwifruit, cucumber, radish and perilla
      salad 126
    vinegar 126
Perilla frutescens see PERILLA
Petroselinum crispum see PARSLEY
pineapple mint 92, 95
pineapple sage 179
Pissaladière 180
pizza thyme 167
Polygonum odoratum see RAU RAM
pot marjoram 104
Potted cheese with seven herbs 184
preserving herbs 16–19
purple basil 24
purple sage 142

RAU RAM
    Fresh spring rolls with salad 134
    Fried rice and rau răm 133
    hints for use 132
    Laksa 134
    Vietnamese-style chicken with pineapple
      and cashews 133
    Warm green bean, mushroom and rau răm
      salad 132
red perilla 124
rigani 104
rose geranium 178
    Rose cream 176
    Rose-flavoured rhubarb crumble 176
ROSEMARY
    A true Italian pizza 139
    bruschetta 140
    hints for use 138
    honey 138
    Mediterranean-style beef stew with
      rosemary and juniper berries 140
    Rosemary and garlic flavoured bean pâté
      140
    Rosemary Hemphill's rosemary scones 141
    Rosemary icecream 141
    sugar 138
    tea 139
    Thick pea soup with rosemary 140
    vinegar 139
Rosmarinus officinalis see ROSEMARY
Rumex acetosa 179
Rumex scutatus 179
Rumex species see SORREL
Russian tarragon 158

SAGE
    hints for use 146
    Home-made crumbed sage and port
      sausages 148
    Pumpkin and potato chowder with sage
      and bay 147
    Rainbow capsicums with sage pasta sauce

148
    Sage and orange wedge potatoes 147
    tisane 147
    Tuscan-style liver with sage 148
    Upside-down apple and sage cake 149
salad burnet 179
salads (main dish and side salads)
    Cabbage, tomato and mint sauté 99
    Chicken and noodle salad with perilla and
      rau răm 127
    Cucumber salad with dill 66
    Cucumber, tomato, avocado and perilla
      salad 127
    Fresh spring rolls with salad (rau răm,
      perilla) 134
    Garlic chive rice salad 79
    Greek-style salad (oregano or marjoram)
      111
    Kiwifruit, cucumber, radish and perilla
      salad 126
    Kumara (sweet potato) and orange salad
      with tarragon 163
    Marinated mushrooms Italian-style (bay
      and/or tarragon) 39, 162
    Mint and cucumber raita 99
    Russian-style vegetable salad (dill) 67
    Salad of carrots and courgettes with a
      chervil dressing 45
    Salad of savory with dried beans 155
    Spinach salad with fetta cheese and thyme
      vinaigrette 172
    Summer savory and green bean salad 155
    Vietnamese-style chicken and cabbage
      salad with purple basil 31
    Warm green bean, mushroom and rau răm
      salad 132
salsas see sauces
Salvia officinalis see SAGE
Salvia rutilans see pineapple sage
Sanguisorba minor see salad burnet
Satureja biflora 150
Satureja hortensis see SAVORY
Satureja montana see SAVORY
Satureja spicigera 150
sauces, salsas, dressings, spreads, marinades,
    chutneys
    Bread sauce (bay) 38
    Creamy lemon verbena spread or dip 90
    Fennel and salmon pasta sauce 75
    Fennel dressing 75
    Frankfurt green sauce 183
    Fresh coriander and mint relish 59
    Fresh mint chutney 99
    Fresh tomato and basil pasta sauce 32
    Gooseberry sauce with tarragon 165
    Green salsa (coriander) 60
    Green sauce (parsley) 121
    Indian-style green masala (coriander) 58
    Lemon balm salsa 85

Lemon balm vinaigrette 84
Lemon basil fruit sauce 33
Lemon thyme pesto 175
Lemon, butter and dill sauce for fish 65
Mandy's beetroot sauce on pasta with
     mint 101
Mediaeval green sauce (sorrel) 177
Mint jelly 98
Mint marinade 98
Mint sauce 98
Pesto (basil) 29–30
Rainbow capsicums with sage pasta sauce
     148
Red currant mint sauce 98
Red salsa (coriander) 60
Rich tomato and vegetable pasta sauce
     (basil) 32
Sauce ravigote (chervil, parsley, tarragon,
     chives) 45
Smoked salmon and dill pasta sauce 68
Tarragon aioli 163
Thyme marinade 175
Tuna, red capsicum and parsley pasta
     sauce 122
SAVORY
     Baked beans with savory and sage 156
     German-style green beans with summer
          savory 156
     hints for use 154
     Risi e bisi 157
     Salad of savory with dried beans 155
     Savory and orange baked chicken 157
     Summer savory and green bean salad 155
     vinegar 154
scented geraniums 178
scones see breads
shiso see PERILLA
side dishes
     Beetroot with chives and lemon 52
     Cabbage, tomato and mint sauté 99
     Courgettes with lemon thyme and
          tomatoes 173
     German-style green beans with summer
          savory 156
     Ray McVinnie's braised ratatouille
          (thyme) 173
     Sage and orange wedge potatoes 147
     Sautéed courgettes and tomatoes with
          basil 29
     Stirfried courgettes with lemon balm 84
Sorrel
     Mediaeval green sauce 177
soups
     Black bean soup (oregano) 110
     Borscht (dill) 67
     Carrot and marjoram soup 109
     Cream of mushroom soup with chervil 47
     Japanese-style soup (mitsuba, Perilla) 128
     Joan's fast-track tomato soup with
          tarragon 164

Laksa (rau răm) 134
Lentil and vegetable soup (bay) 40
Lentil soup with herbes de Provence 181
Mushroom and corn chowder with basil
     31
Parsley soup 122
Pumpkin and potato chowder with sage
     and bay 147
Pumpkin soup with an Asian flavour
     (garlic chives) 79
Pumpkin soup with green sauce (parsley)
     121
Soupe au pistou (basil) 30
Spanish-style bean and potato soup
     (fennel seeds) 74
Thick pea soup with rosemary 140
spearmint 92
storing fresh herbs in the kitchen 20
summer savory see SAVORY
sweet basil see common basil
sweet bay see BAY
sweet fennel 70
sweet laurel see BAY
sweet marjoram 104

Tagetes lucida see Mexican tarragon
TARRAGON
     Asparagus and tarragon frittata 164
     butter 162
     Gooseberry sauce with tarragon 165
     hints for use 162
     Joan's fast-track tomato sauce with
          tarragon 164
     Kumara (sweet potato) and orange salad
          with tarragon 163
     Oranges with vodka and tarragon syrup
          165
     Tarragon aioli 163
     Tarragon and orange fish fillets 164
     Tarragon chicken 165
     Tarragon-flavoured vodka 162
     tea 162
     vinegar 161–162
Thai basil 24
THYME
     Courgettes with lemon thyme and
          tomatoes 173
     hints for use 169, 171–172
     lemon thyme butter 171
     Lemon thyme pesto 175
     Lemon thyme roast chicken with lemon
          halves 174
     lemon thyme vinegar 171
     Mushrooms with thyme on toast 172
     Ray McVinnie's braised ratatouille 173
     Spinach salad with fetta cheese and thyme
          vinaigrette 172
     Strawberries with lemon thyme marinade
          175

Thyme marinade 175
Vegetarian Christmas nutmeat loaf with
     thyme stuffing 174
Thymus herba-barona see caraway thyme
Thymus nummularius see pizza thyme
Thymus species see THYME
Thymus vulgaris see common thyme
Thymus x citriodorus see lemon thyme
tisanes 19–20
tree onions 179
true French sorrel 179
Turkish oregano 104

variegated lemon balm 80
variegated sages 142
Vietnamese mint see RAU RAM

wild fennel 70
wild marjoram 104
winter mint 92
winter savory see SAVORY